UTMEG

"The intention of every other piece of prose may be discussed and even mistrusted; but the purpose of a cookery book is one and unmistakable. Its object can conceivably be no other than to increase the happiness of mankind."

—Joseph Conrad

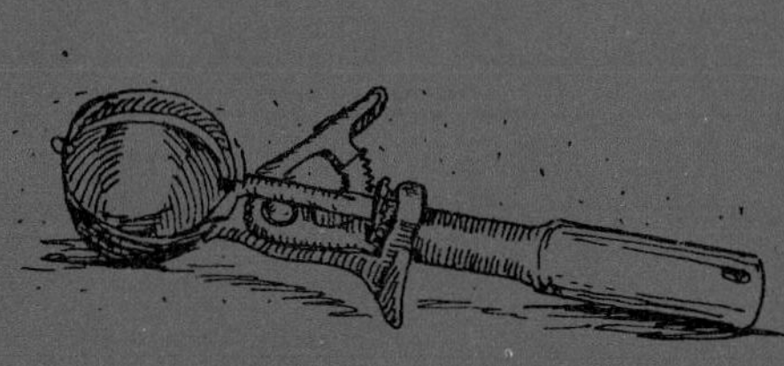

Martha Dixon's
Copper Kettle Cook Book

Martha Dixon's Copper

Book design and calligraphy by Cornelius Lambregtse

Kettle Cook Book

by

MARTHA DIXON

with drawings by

Ilse Eerdmans Weidenaar

WM. B. EERDMANS PUBLISHING CO., GRAND RAPIDS, MICH.

Printed in the United States of America. Library of Congress Catalog Card No. 63-17791.

First printing, June, 1963
Second printing, December, 1963

PHOTOLITHOPRINTED BY GRAND RAPIDS BOOK MANUFACTURERS, INC., GRAND RAPIDS, MICHIGAN, 1963

With fond appreciation dedicated to

HAROLD F. GROSS

whose recognized leadership in the broadcasting industry is marked by vision, courage, and initiative;
who is equally renowned at home and abroad as the perfect host and great connoisseur of fine foods;
and whose inspiration, guidance, and assistance have provided the necessary impetus to compile this cookbook and have made its publication possible.

Foreword

by Win Schuler

The excitement brought about by good food has given me a lifetime of pleasant experiences. Each day brings new friends, new dishes; and the wonderful memories of yesterdays almost as exciting.

People who are dedicated to the art of good eating and know the intricacies and refinements that lead to distinctive dining are in a fraternity all their own. They are motivated by a desire to serve and to please, and their gastronomic accomplishments delight their families and friends. Martha Dixon is a person so dedicated.

A lifetime of interesting and exciting work with food is presented by Martha in this her Copper Kettle Cook Book. Guided by the genial gourmet,

Hal Gross, and with a wealth of encouragement from her many friends, Martha has produced a masterpiece of culinary literature.

Here is a book on food that stirs the imagination and whets the appetite. May your adventures in the following pages be as pleasant as mine.

Win Schuler

Preface

It has been my wonderful privilege to work with foods for many years. I have always had a great love and flair for preparing good food. This love was greatly fortified by an expression I shall never forget. I was still in high school when the late John Gilbert, of the Gilbert Chocolate Co., Jackson, Mich., said one day to me: "Serving quality food is a rewarding experience."

I have found this to be very true throughout my entire career, first as dietitian at the Homestead Hotel Resort and private school on Lake Michigan, then as dietitian at that fabulous spot in the Bahamas, the Cat Key Club on Cat Cay Island, and afterwards as food and service supervisor in hotel and restaurant management with the Kellogg Center at Michigan State University, under the direction of Mrs. Evelyn Drake.

The highlight in my career came when I was asked to become the hostess on the Copper Kettle Show at WJIM-TV, Channel 6, Lansing, Mich., in 1954. I shall always remember the great patience and kindness shown to me by the entire crew working on the Copper Kettle Show at the time, and especially the assistance of Mr. Phillip Sherck and Mr. Howard Finch.

Serving as hostess on the Copper Kettle Show gave me the opportunity to share the recipes I had compiled and collected over a period of many years with thousands of women. In this book I have included some of these treasured recipes, but also many sent in by loyal and faithful viewers of my program, as well as some which the various well-known chefs in the Channel 6 area graciously supplied.

I believe culinary artists are made — not born; therefore anyone can aspire to be an artist in his own right. All it takes is determination, self-confidence, and a sense of well-being. The thought that our efforts will be greatly appreciated gives the necessary inspiration, and the reward is always immediate — the gratitude of those for whom we prepared the food. Cooking can be fun!

Although at first I was hesitant about coming out with a new cookbook, at last I gave in to the constant and persistent urging on the part of the Channel 6 viewers and my many friends and the encouragement of Mr. Harold F. Gross, President of Gross Telecasting, Inc. I most sincerely hope and trust that the following pages will bring fun, joy, laughter, love, and, especially, good eating into every home where the *Copper Kettle Cook Book* will occupy an important and prominent place on the kitchen bookshelf.

This preface would not be complete without expressing my great appreciation to the many people who in one way or another have had a hand in the compilation of this book. Special thanks go first to all loyal, dedicated Copper Kettle viewers, to the outstanding chefs in the Channel 6 area, and to the host of other friends for sharing their recipes. Next I wish to thank the entire staff at WJIM-TV for their splendid co-operation without which the publication of this book would have been impossible.

I further owe many thanks to Mr. Win Schuler for his moral support and general helpfulness and to Miss Annette Thrasher and Mrs. Wayne (Dixie Lee) Premer, who helped prepare the manuscript and did the proofreading. Mention should also be made of Mr. Gary Aube who took care of the lovely flower arrangements in the setting reproduced on the jacket.

Last, but not least, I especially want to thank the publishers, Wm. B. Eerdman's, Sr., and Jr., for their untiring patience, enthusiasm, and encouragement; Mrs. Ilse Eerdmans Weidenaar for embellishing the book with her delightful artwork, and Cornelius Lambregtse for his book design and calligraphy.

My sincere wish to everyone who uses my *Copper Kettle Cook Book* is: *"Bon appétit!"*

Martha Dixon

Lansing, Michigan

Contents

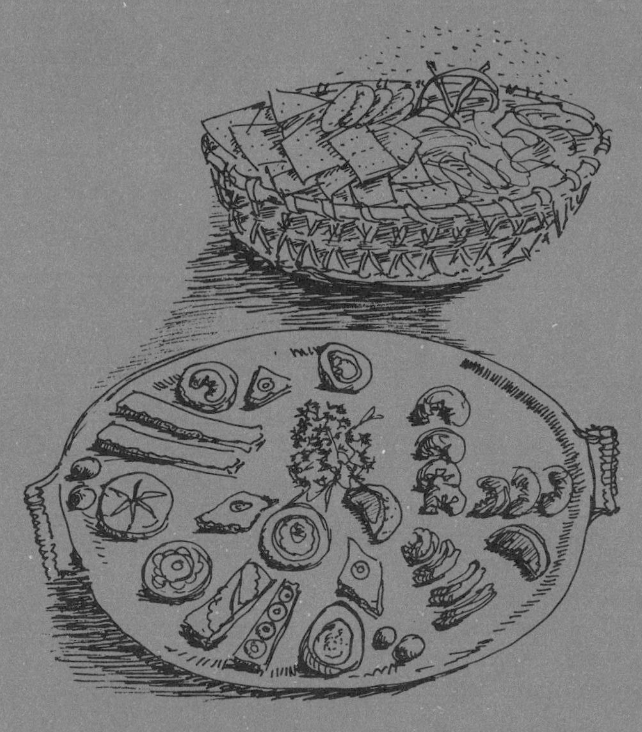

Cultivate enthusiasm. People will like you better for it; you will escape the dull routine of a mechanical existence; and you will make headway wherever you are — Jonathan Ogden Armour

Appetizers

That little something before dinner is commonly known as the hors d'oeuvre, appetizer, or canapé. These delightful little morsels can either be served hot or cold. The cocktail hour has grown tremendously in popularity and has become a definite part of the entertainment schedule for every household. Don't limit yourself to making the old stand-bys. Be creative; allow your imagination to transform your next party into a true gourmet's delight. Cooking can be a creative pleasure. Keep in mind that the object of serving hors d'oeuvres is to stimulate the appetite rather than dull it. Keep everything small in size. Hors d'oeuvres must be well seasoned. Allow your own taste buds to do the job for you.

MYSTERIOUS CHEESE BALL

1 (4-ounce) wedge blue cheese
1 (6-ounce) package sharp aged Cheddar cheese
1 (3-ounce) package cream cheese
1 tablespoon minced parsley
1 tablespoon grated onion
½ teaspoon Worcestershire sauce
½ cup very finely chopped nutmeats
¼ cup finely chopped nutmeats

Allow cheese to stand at room temperature to soften. Combine cheese, parsley, onion, Worcestershire sauce and the ½ cup very finely chopped nutmeats. Mix well. Place mixture on waxed paper and shape into ball. Refrigerate for 1 or 2 hours and then roll ball in the ¼ cup nutmeats. Refrigerate until about 1 hour before serving time. Use as a spread on crackers.

Water chestnuts can be used a million ways; for example:

COUNTRY HOUSE TRADER HORNS

Thinly sliced bacon, at room temperature
Chinese water chestnuts, well drained
Brown sugar

Roll a strip of bacon tightly around each water chestnut. Sprinkle on brown sugar. Broil until bacon is crisp. Put on wooden skewer. Serve.

BLACK SNOWBALLS

Elegant hors d'oeuvres that pack a real surprise are made by forming a ball of cream cheese around a whole pitted ripe olive and coating it with toasted instant minced onion. Simply toast onion in a pie pan in a slow oven.

HOT CHEESE TARTLETS

Muffin pans, very small
Preheated 425° oven
½ pound sharp Cheddar cheese, cubed
1 tablespoon cream or milk
½ teaspoon dry mustard
¼ teaspoon paprika
¼ teaspoon Worcestershire sauce
Pie crust (½ box pie crust mix)
Grated Parmesan cheese

Melt Cheddar cheese in saucepan over very low heat. Add milk or cream, mustard, paprika, and Worcestershire sauce, and mix well.

Roll out pie-crust dough and cut into 2¾-3-inch rounds. Line very small muffin pans, forming small shells. Bake 10-12 minutes. Pour hot cheese mixture into shells and top with Parmesan cheese. Return to oven 3-5 minutes or until tops are bubbly.

Variations:

Place in bottom of baked tartlets any one of the following before pouring over the hot cheese mixture: cube of sweet pickle, stuffed olive slices, piece of salami, crumbled cooked bacon, slice of cocktail onion. *Makes 12-18 small tarts.*

CRABMEAT GRUYÈRE

1 *cup crab meat, canned or fresh*
¼ *cup shredded Swiss Gruyère cheese*
1 *tablespoon sauterne*
½ *teaspoon salt*
Mayonnaise to moisten

Mix and pile high on sautéed rounds of white bread and run into a 450° oven until hot.

STUFFED MUSHROOMS

Stuffed mushrooms are becoming a most popular cocktail item, also a luncheon entrée. For cocktails you use the small, one-bite size; for luncheon, the bigger the better. You may stuff them with all sorts of things—fish, fowl, or meat—but I do think that the crab-meat-stuffed ones are the best. Sauté the mushrooms in butter and fill the cavities (made when stem is pulled out) with this crab-meat mixture (for 24 small or 8 large mushroom caps):

2 *tablespoons fine white bread crumbs*
¼ *cup mayonnaise*
¼ *cup medium cream sauce*
1 *pound fresh or canned crab meat, flaked and cut in small pieces*
¼ *teaspoon Worcestershire sauce*

Mix and pile over the mushrooms, and sprinkle liberally with grated

Parmesan cheese. Bake at 350° for 15 minutes, then run under the broiler to brown. Serve hot. For cocktails, spear with plastic toothpicks.

Chicken-liver quiche is an ideal entrée for a bridal luncheon or party. The chopped livers acquire further piquancy from instant minced onion, Swiss cheese, and spices.

CHICKEN-LIVER QUICHE

Unbaked pastry for single-crust 9-inch pie
3 eggs
4 slices bacon
6 ounces chicken livers
Salt, pepper
1 cup light cream or milk
1 tablespoon instant minced onion
Dash nutmeg, dash cayenne
Pepper
½ teaspoon salt
1 cup shredded, aged Swiss cheese
1 tablespoon flour

Line pie plate with pastry and brush lightly with a little of one egg white. Dice bacon and fry crisp; drain. In 1 tablespoon of bacon drippings, fry livers until browned and cooked through. Sprinkle with salt and pepper.

Chop fine. Add cream to onion; season with nutmeg, cayenne, and ½ teaspoon salt. Add bacon and livers. Mix cheese and flour; sprinkle into pie shell. Beat eggs well; add cream mixture and pour over cheese. Bake in 400° (hot) oven 15 minutes. Reduce heat to 325° (moderately slow) and bake 30 minutes longer. Cut into wedges to serve.

MUSHROOM CAPS STUFFED WITH POULTRY DRESSING

Carefully select young button-mushroom caps which are about an inch or so in diameter. Wash and drain. Lightly sauté desired number in butter. Drain.

Blend ¼ cup prepared packaged poultry stuffing with 3 tablespoons pan butter and 1 tablespoon grated onion. (If this is not sufficiently moist, add more pan butter or water.) Fill sautéed mushroom caps with this mixture. Garnish each portion with paprika or chopped fresh parsley.
Makes 10 portions.

This is one of our favorite and delicious canapés served at the popular M.S.U. Football Parties at the Country House each fall.

CHICKEN LIVERS WITH WATER CHESTNUTS

Sauté chicken livers in melted butter, dash of majoram and thyme, in medium-sized frying pan. Add ¼ cup sherry. Cook gently for 5 or 10 minutes. Do not overcook. Slice water chestnuts in half, place between pieces of chicken livers and wrap in half a slice of partially fried bacon. Secure bacon with toothpick. These can be brushed with soy sauce or, if you prefer, marinate chicken livers in soy sauce before frying—either way is good. Place on cookie sheet, and just before ready to serve, run under the broiler until they are heated through thoroughly and bacon browns and sizzles. These are delicious. You'll find your guests will rave about them!

If you like the flavor of liver paste try this one.

LIVER-PASTE PUFFS

Mash 1 (4½-ounce) can liver paste. Blend with about 2 tablespoons thick commercial sour cream and ⅓ teaspoon grated nutmeg. Fill pre-baked tiny puff cases. *Makes approximately 15 portions.*
And for a change, try this:
Mash 1 (4½-ounce) can liver paste. Blend with ¼ cup crisp bacon broken into bits, and 3 tablespoons grated onion. Fill pre-baked tiny puff cases. *Makes approximately 20 portions.*

Celery served this way is always popular.

STUFFED CELERY, CLUB STYLE

Separate stalks of celery, wash, cut in small pieces. Cream cheese softened and mixed with ground shrimp, lobster, or Roquefort cheese makes a nice filling. Season the mixes with Worcestershire sauce, 1 teaspoon of finely chopped shallots and work to a smooth paste. Turn into a pastry bag with a small rose tube and fill celery stalk hollows with the mixture. Dust with paprika and serve chilled.

SWEET-'N'-SOUR COCKTAIL WIENERS

1 *6-ounce jar (¾ cup) prepared mustard*
1 *10-ounce jar (1 cup) currant jelly*
1 *pound (8 to 10) frankfurters, canned Vienna sausages, or cocktail wieners*

Mix mustard and jelly in chafing dish or double boiler. Diagonally slice frankfurters in bite-size pieces (cut Vienna sausages or cocktail wieners in half); add to sauce and heat. *Makes 8 servings.*

HOT CLAM DIP

1 *6½- or 7½-ounce can (about 1 cup) minced clams*
2 *tablespoons minced onion*
2 *tablespoons butter or margarine*
1 *tablespoon catsup*
A few drops Tabasco
1 *cup diced sharp process American cheese*
2 *tablespoons chopped pitted ripe olives*
1 *teaspoon Worcestershire sauce*

Drain clams, reserving 1 tablespoon of the liquid. Cook onion in butter till tender but not brown; add clams, reserved clam liquid, and remaining ingredients. Heat till cheese is melted and mixture is hot. Serve with crackers and chips.
Makes 1¼ cups.

Easy—but tasty and good.

CHILI-CHEESE SPREAD

1 *cup finely shredded sharp Cheddar cheese*
2 *tablespoons chili sauce*

Combine ingredients and mix until well blended. Spread on crackers and broil until cheese melts.
Yield: ¾ cup.

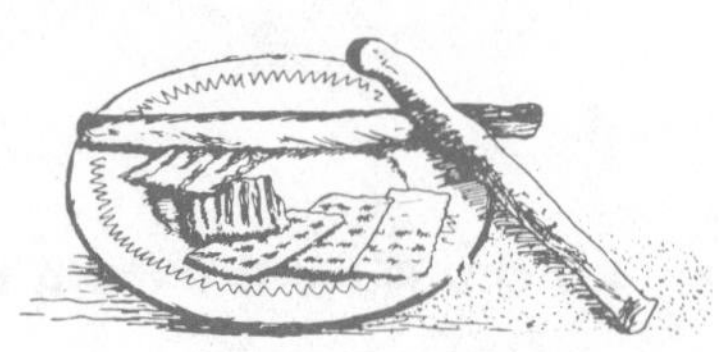

Thanks to Doris Wetters——a hot, taste-tempting appetizer!

SWEDISH MEAT BALLS

1 *pound ground beef*
3 *slices bread, crusts removed*
1 *egg*
1 *bouillon cube*
1 *cup boiling water*
Salt and pepper
2 *teaspoons nutmeg*
2 *teaspoons allspice*
2 *tablespoons grated onion*
½ *cup milk (approximately)*

Mix ground beef, salt and pepper, nutmeg, allspice, egg, and grated onion together. Add bread which has been soaked in milk until soft. Mix thoroughly and, if necessary, add a little more milk to make mixture fairly soft. Form into small balls and brown thoroughly in beef drippings or butter.

Remove from pan and stir flour into fat remaining in pan. Add hot water gradually, stirring constantly. Add bouillon cube and stir until mixture thickens. Return meat balls to gravy, cover, and simmer about half an hour.
Serves 6-8.

Wonderful for cocktail parties. Small plates and forks are needed. Worth the trouble, though.

BEEF MARIA

2 *pounds flank steak*
¼ *cup butter or margarine*
4 *cloves garlic*
¼ *cup chopped parsley*
½ *teaspoon salt*
½ *teaspoon rosemary*
½ *teaspoon orégano*
¼ *teaspoon thyme*
1 *basil leaf*
1 *small can tomato purée*
1 *cup dry red wine*
12 *fresh mushrooms, sliced*

Trim fat from meat. Cut, cross-grain, into ¼-inch-thick slices. Brown meat in butter in Dutch oven. Add remaining ingredients except mushrooms. Simmer, covered, until meat is tender. Add mushrooms. Continue cooking until mushrooms are tender.
Yield: 6 servings.

SAVORY CANAPÉS

If you like fresh mushrooms, you'll like this one!

Pan-fry finely chopped mushrooms with a little minced onion in butter. Season with garlic salt. Blend in 1 tablespoon flour and 1 tablespoon cream. Pile on crackers, Melba toast, etc., and keep warm in oven, if desired. Garnish with parsley, chive, or watercress sprigs.

One of the simplest and best tidbits I know of is made as follows: Cut baker's bread in 1-inch squares, spread mayonnaise on top and sides, cover with grated Parmesan cheese, and put in oven at 450° to brown.

For the aristocrat, artichokes are required. Everyone try them—they're good!

ARTICHOKE BOTTOMS STUFFED WITH DEVILED HAM

When cooked artichokes (or you can use canned ones) are thoroughly cold, take a sharp knife and cut off all the leaves close to the base. Scrape out the fuzzy interiors of each base and cut off the stem.

Blend 1 (2¼-ounce) can deviled ham spread with ⅓ cup finely grated store cheese. Fill artichoke bottoms with this mixture. If portions are too large, serve them in halves or quarters. Spear each portion with a toothpick. Chill thoroughly. (This is important as it brings out the flavor, especially if canned artichoke is used.)
Makes filling for 10 artichoke bottoms.

Place your punch bowl on a holly-trimmed tray; then dip this foamy, fresh drink into dainty glass cups.

FAMILY HOLIDAY EGGNOG

¼ *cup sugar*
¼ *teaspoon cinnamon*
¼ *teaspoon ginger*
¼ *teaspoon cloves*
Nutmeg
2 *quarts orange juice, chilled*
6 *well-beaten eggs*
1 *quart ginger ale, chilled*
½ *cup lemon juice, chilled*
1 *quart vanilla ice cream*

Beat sugar and spices into beaten eggs. Stir in chilled orange and lemon juices. Cut ice cream in chunks; put in punch bowl. Pour ginger ale over ice cream. Then stir in egg mixture. Sprinkle with nutmeg.
Makes about 20 servings.

Children love this.

EGGNOG PUNCH

1½ quarts dairy eggnog
1 quart lime sherbet

Blend well and serve.

No one is rich enough to do without a neighbor—Anonymous

FOR CHRISTMAS OPEN HOUSE

Prepare a large bowl of cut-up fruit—oranges, grapefruit, bananas, pineapple, pears, maraschino cherries. Sprinkle with the juice of a lemon and sugar to taste. Store in a covered dish in the refrigerator. Just before serving, place a quart of lime sherbet in your prettiest bowl, and pour the cut-up fruit over the sherbet, and sprinkle it all with two liqueur glasses of Cointreau. This addition of the Cointreau is optional and may be omitted. Place the bowl on a large tray surrounded with sherbet glasses and sprigs of Christmas greens.

DELICIOUS HOT CRAB-MEAT DIP

Combine an 8-ounce package cream cheese (be sure cream cheese is at room temperature and is very soft) with 1 small can flaked crab meat, 1 clove crushed garlic, ¼ cup mayonnaise, 1 teaspoon onion juice, 1 teaspoon prepared mustard, 1 teaspoon powdered sugar, and a dash of salt. Combine all the ingredients and heat in small chafing dish. 2 tablespoons white wine can be added just before serving time but this is optional, of course. Dip into the crab mixture with chips and crackers.

Pass them while they are hot!

FISH BALLS

2 cups cooked finely flaked fish
½ teaspoon salt
½ teaspoon dry mustard
1 tablespoon lemon juice
1 cup thick cream sauce
1 tablespoon chopped parsley
½ teaspoon onion juice

Mix and chill. Shape into balls. Fry at 375° in deep fat. Drain on paper. A dip is nice to dunk them in, but not necessary. Serve with cocktail sauce or sour cream and French-fried-onion mixture.
Servings for 10.

DATE PARTY PICK-UPS

Fill pitted fresh California dates with strips of Cheddar cheese. Wrap in slices of dried beef and pop into a moderate oven to heat. Spear with toothpicks; serve warm.

Peanut butter and bacon are delightful served as partners.

DATE AND BACON ROLLS

Stuff each pitted fresh date with curried peanut butter (¼ teaspoon curry powder to ¼ cup peanut butter). Wrap half a slice of partially broiled bacon around each stuffed date. Spear with a toothpick. Oven-broil on a rack until bacon is crisp and heated through.

These require a little more work but are worth it.

MINIATURE TURNOVERS

Use a reliable packaged pie crust mix or your own pie crust recipe. Follow directions on box for mixing dough. Roll out dough on a floured board to ⅛-inch thickness. Cut in 3-inch squares or circles for each turnover. Fill with any of the fillings below. Take one corner of a square and fold it over filling to the opposite corner to make a triangular covered tart. Wet edges to seal. Use the prongs of a fork for pressing edges together. Deep-fry or bake at 400°. Drain fried turnovers on brown paper.

Fillings:

1. Highly spice ½ pound fresh ground beef with 1 teaspoon salt, ⅛ teaspoon black pepper, scant pinch of cayenne pepper, 2 tablespoons grated onion, and ¼ cup chopped fresh parsley. Sauté in ⅛ pound butter and add 2 teaspoons sherry. Chill mixture. Fill pastry squares with 1 teaspoon for each turnover (follow above directions for making turnover cases). Prick top of turnover after sealing to let out steam while baking.

2. Blend grated very sharp cheese with mustard butter to a good consistency. Fill each turnover case with a small spoonful.

3. Mash 1 (8-ounce) can of breakfast sausages and fat with ½ cup grated store cheese and a few grains of cayenne pepper. Fill each turnover case with a small spoonful.
Makes 24 turnovers.

The Ford Motor Company entertained the Detroit Chapter of American Women in Radio and Television at one of their monthly meetings. This delicious dip was served. The women loved it and the chef very graciously surrendered the recipe. It has a most unusual tangy flavor.

FORD MOTOR COMPANY DIP

1½ pound cream cheese
2 cups mayonnaise
6 tablespoons chopped onions
4 tablespoons horseradish
Generous dash Tabasco, pinch of salt, and a generous amount of chopped parsley

Have cream cheese at room temperature. Add remaining ingredients and beat in mixer to a very smooth consistency. Delicious with potato chips or crackers.

SAUTERNE CLAM PUFFS

1 large (8-ounce) package cream cheese
¼ cup sauterne or other white dinner wine, or sherry
1 (7-ounce) can minced clams, well drained (½ cup)
Toast rounds
Bacon

Soften cheese; blend in wine; add clams. Heap on toast rounds; top with bits of bacon. Place on cooky sheet; broil about 5 minutes, or until bacon is crisp. Serve hot.
Makes 18 to 20 one-inch rounds.

CHEESE PUFFS

½ cup (1 stick) butter, softened
2 cups shredded sharp Cheddar cheese
½ teaspoon Worcestershire sauce
Dash of cayenne pepper
1 cup flour

Mix together butter, Cheddar cheese, and seasonings. Mix in flour. Shape into smooth ball, wrap in waxed paper, and chill. Taking from refrigerator about ¼ of mixture at a time, shape into balls about the size of large marbles, flouring the hands to make rolling easier. Place on ungreased cooky sheet about 2 inches apart. Bake 12-15 minutes at 350°. Balls will spread a little. Serve piping hot. The dough may be rolled in advance and kept refrigerated until baking, or stored in freezer to be brought out and baked as desired.

LOBSTER BALLS

Blend 1 cup cooked fresh lobster meat (or 6-ounce can) with 2 tablespoons mustard butter, ¾ teaspoon curry powder, and ⅛ teaspoon Worcestershire sauce. Shape mixture into small balls. Roll balls in chopped almonds. Chill.
Makes 28 balls.

Elegant and good.

QUICHE LORRAINE

Line an 8-inch pie tin with pastry and bake at 450° for 10 minutes.

- 4 *slices crisp bacon, chopped*
- 4 *thin slices onion, sautéed until soft*
- 8 *paper-thin slices ham, shredded*
- 8 *paper-thin slices imported Swiss cheese*
- 3 *eggs*
- ¼ *teaspoon dry mustard*
- 1 *cup light cream, heated*
- *Nutmeg*

Sprinkle the bacon and onion over bottom of pie crust. Make 4 alternate layers of the ham and cheese. Beat the eggs and mustard, add the hot cream, and continue beating. Pour over the ham and cheese; let stand 10 minutes. Sprinkle a tiny bit of nutmeg on top and bake at 350° until custard is set.
Makes 6 servings.

SHERRIED CHEESE DIP

- 1 *(3-ounce) package cream cheese*
- 1 *small can deviled ham*
- 3 to 4 *tablespoons dry sherry*
- 1 *cup country-style or small-curd cottage cheese*
- *Few drops Tabasco sauce*
- *Salt*
- *Chopped green onion or parsley*

Blend cream cheese and deviled ham until smooth. Beat in wine, cottage cheese, Tabasco sauce and salt to taste. Pile into bowl and sprinkle with green onion or parsley. Serve with crisp crackers or potato chips.
Makes about 2 cups.

These are tiny, broiler-hot canapés. Filling is onion spiked.

SWISS SANDWICH PUFFS

16 *slices tiny "ice box" rye bread*
½ *cup mayonnaise or salad dressing*
¼ *cup finely chopped onion*
2 *tablespoons snipped parsley*
8 *slices process Swiss cheese*

Toast bread on both sides. Combine mayonnaise, onion, and parsley; spread on toast. Cut out rounds of cheese to fit toast; place a cheese round atop each slice, covering mayonnaise mixture. Broil 3 to 4 inches from heat till cheese is puffy and golden, about 2 to 3 minutes. Trim tops with sliced ripe olives, if desired. Serve hot. *Makes 16.*

A south-of-the-border bean snack. Like flavor "fire"? Add more chili powder to taste.

SOMBRERO SPREAD

½ *pound ground beef*
¼ *cup chopped onion*
¼ *cup extra-hot catsup*
1½ *teaspoons chili powder*
½ *teaspoon salt*
1 *8-ounce can (1 cup) red kidney beans*
½ *cup shredded sharp process American cheese*
¼ *cup chopped onion*
¼ *cup chopped stuffed green olives*
Corn chips or 1 recipe Mexican tostadas

Brown meat and ¼ cup onion in skillet or chafing dish. Stir in catsup, chili powder, and salt. Mash in beans (with liquid). Heat; fold in the cheese, ¼ cup onion, and the olives.
Makes 1½ cups.

Serve hot as a spread for corn chips or Mexican tostadas: Start with fresh, frozen, or canned tortillas. (If tortillas are frozen, thaw.) Cut each tortilla in quarters. Fry in shallow hot fat, turning once, about 4 minutes. Drain on paper towels.

Just about everybody loves chicken livers and this *pâté* combination is sure to please.

CHICKEN-LIVER PÂTÉ

¼ cup butter
½ clove garlic, finely chopped
3 medium onions, finely chopped
1 pound chicken livers
2 sprigs parsley, finely chopped
½ teaspoon salt
½ teaspoon Tabasco sauce
¼ teaspoon cloves
2 tablespoons sherry
½ cup softened butter or chicken fat

Heat butter in saucepan or skillet; add garlic and onions and cook slowly until vegetables are soft. Add chicken livers and cook slowly until tender; turn mixture into bowl and mash thoroughly or mix in blender until smooth. Blend parsley, salt, Tabasco, and cloves. Cream butter or chicken fat; blend in liver mixture and pack into small bowl or crock; cover and chill thoroughly.
Makes about 3 cups.

We made these for a party recently. They were a great success. Hot sauce or chili sauce added to the deviled ham makes them even better. Wonderful snack!

DELICIOUS HOT SNACKS

¼ cup butter, melted
1 cup sour cream
1 egg
1 teaspoon baking powder
1 teaspoon salt
2¼ cups flour
1 (4½ ounces) can deviled ham
¼ cup chopped mushrooms
¼ cup chopped celery
Dash Tabasco sauce

Combine first six ingredients; blend well. Flour board well, roll dough, cut into 3-inch circles. Pinch three points at even intervals around circle to make a "tri-corn." Place tri-corns on cookie sheet—prick bottoms with fork and bake at 425° for about 15 minutes until golden brown. Fill each tri-corn with mixture of deviled ham, celery and mushrooms. Return to oven until filling is hot.

Pastry may be prepared and baked well in advance of serving time and refrigerated until time to be filled and reheated.
Makes about 2 dozen canapés.

There are many variations of the cheese ball. This is a good basic one. You can take it from here.

CHEESE BALL

Let stand at room temperature until softened, 2 3-ounce packages Roquefort cheese, 2 5-ounce jars process Cheddar cheese spread and 4 3-ounce packages cream cheese. Combine cheeses with 1 teaspoon Worcestershire sauce, 2 tablespoons grated onion, ½ cup finely ground pecans and ¼ cup chopped parsley. Beat with a fork or an electric mixer until well blended. Shape mixture into a ball. Place in a small bowl lined with waxed paper. Chill overnight. About 1 hour before serving, roll ball in mixture of ½ cup ground pecans and ½ cup chopped parsley. Top with a sprig of holly. Place ball on tray and surround it with crackers.

Hot and tasty from the broiler. Festive-looking, too.

TOASTY CHEESE CANAPÉS

Sliced white bread
2 tablespoons melted butter or margarine
2 stiffly beaten egg whites
1¼ cups coarsely grated Swiss cheese
⅔ cup finely chopped green pepper
1 teaspoon chopped parsley
½ teaspoon salt
Dash pepper
3 slices bacon, finely diced

With 2-inch cooky cutter, cut 20 bread rounds. Toast on one side; brush untoasted side with butter. Into egg whites fold the cheese, green pepper, parsley, salt, and pepper; spoon on buttered side of bread rounds. Sprinkle bacon over top of each. Place on broiler pan; broil 4 to 5 inches from heat 10 minutes or until bacon browns and cheese melts.
Makes 20.

These are always popular at the WJIM Country House parties.

MIDGET BURGERS

10 *slices enriched bread*
Softened butter or margarine
1 *pound ground beef*
2 *tablespoons grated onion*
1 *tablespoon Worcestershire sauce*
1 *teaspoon salt*
¼ *cup chili sauce*

Toast bread on one side; cut four 1½-inch rounds from each slice. Lightly butter rounds on untoasted side. Combine remaining ingredients except chili sauce. Shape mixture in 40 marble-sized balls (1 heaping teaspoon each) and place one on buttered side of each bread round, leaving border of bread showing. Make indentation in center of balls. Broil 4 inches from heat 5 to 6 minutes or till meat is done and edges of bread are toasted. Fill indentations with chili sauce. Serve hot.

These are delicious—you'll not be able to make them fast enough at your next party.

PARMESAN CHEESE BALLS

2 *slices white bread, crusts removed*
½ *cup milk, scalded*
⅔ *cup grated Parmesan cheese*
1 *teaspoon flour*
1 *egg*
Pinch of cayenne pepper

Place white bread in saucepan. Pour scalded milk over bread and set aside until lukewarm. Place pan over low heat and stir until pasty. Remove from heat. Mix in cheese and flour. Blend egg into mixture; add cayenne pepper. If consistency seems too moist, add 1 tablespoon bread crumbs or cracker meal. Allow mixture to cool. Make into ¾-inch balls, using a teaspoon, and deep-fry in 350° fat until golden brown.
Yields approximately 25.

MINIATURE BISCUITS WITH TURKEY, HAM, AND CUMBERLAND SAUCE

The little biscuits, hot from the oven, broken open, and spread with butter, topped with a *paper-thin* slice of ham or turkey make an elegant appetizer. Red shimmering Cumberland sauce is a must when you decide to serve this fare at your next party. Place the sauce nearby so guests can ladle the Cumberland sauce over turkey and ham. Here is the recipe for the biscuits—I use a very small cutter for cocktail biscuits. These can be made, rolled, cut and placed on greased cookie sheets, and stored in refrigerator until time to place in oven. For best results with biscuit making—very little handling and hot oven.

This is definitely a non-fail biscuit recipe.

Hot Biscuits:

2 *cups flour, sifted*
3 *teaspoons baking powder*
1 *teaspoon salt*
⅓ *cup shortening or butter*
¾ *cup milk*

Sift flour, baking powder, and salt together; cut in shortening until mixture resembles coarse cornmeal. Add all of milk and mix to smooth dough. Turn out on lightly floured board. Knead lightly. Roll or pat ½" thick. Cut with biscuit cutter. Place on ungreased cooky sheet. Bake in very hot oven (450°) for 12 to 15 minutes.

For rich biscuits, spread a generous amount of butter on biscuits before placing in oven.

Makes 2 dozen small biscuits.

Easy Cumberland Sauce:

Slowly heat 1 cup currant jelly, add 2 to 3 tablespoons horse-radish sauce and juice of ½ lemon. Add ½ teaspoon dry mustard and 2 tablespoons grated orange peel. Heat through and serve hot or cold on turkey or ham.

CAT CAY BLINTZES

There are many versions of the popular and well-known blinis, sometimes called "bleeny" or blintzes. I learned to make these delicious little morsels when I was dietitian at the fabulous Cat Key Club on Cat Cay Island in the Bahamas. Our native chefs were real "pros" when it came to making several hundred of these for the colorful cocktail parties held at the club and in the homes on the island. The fillings can be made of almost anything you wish—I prefer lobster to anything else, and, of course, a goodly amount of curry added to the lobster is a must. The little pancakes are easy to make once you have invested in the round 6- or 7-inch bottom frying pan. Practice makes perfect—if they don't turn out, try again. You'll finally master the art of making them, I know; then watch your reputation soar as an outstanding cook and hostess! Here's my recipe for the Cat Cay blintzes.

2 eggs
½ cup sifted flour
¾ cup milk and water mixed
1 tablespoon melted butter
Pinch salt

Make a thin batter. Beat the eggs and add the flour alternately with the liquid. Beat with mixer (I use an electric mixer) until smooth, then add the melted butter and salt. Beat again until smooth.

Heat a heavy round 6- or 7-inch skillet and butter well before pouring in a thin stream of batter, (about 1 tablespoon) starting at the center and tilting pan to spread, as thin as possible, the mixture evenly across the bottom. Reduce the heat immediately after pouring in the batter. When brown on the underside, turn over for just a few seconds. Use a knife-like spatula to loosen pancake around the edges. Remove from skillet and turn out on clean towel or wax paper. I make them several hours before the party. By placing them on a towel, they will not stick together. Make filling—cool, spread thin layer of mixture on pancake. Roll, with sharp knife remove ends, cut in two or three pieces. Stick with picks. Serve at once or place on lightly buttered cookie sheet and when ready to serve slip in hot oven (400°) for about 10 minutes or until hot.

Filling:

2 *tablespoons butter*
2 *tablespoons flour*
½ *cup milk (I use half cream and half milk)*
½ *cup chicken broth*
1 *egg yolk*
2 *cups diced cooked lobster or crawfish*
Salt, pepper, curry, and a dash of nutmeg

Melt butter in saucepan, add flour, stirring constantly. Slowly blend in milk, chicken broth, and egg yolk. Season to taste. Be sure you use a generous amount of curry. When your sauce is perfectly seasoned, add the lobster. Be sure the filling is not too thin. It must be a little on the thick side—remember it is to stay inside the little rolled pancake.

MINIATURE PUFF SHELLS

Ruth Aspgren, our Swedish cook at the Country House, loves to make the tiny miniature cream puffs. She uses a pastry tube since we like to make them small. Guests complain when an hors d'oeuvre is too large. These tiny puffs are fun to make and can be filled with many different fillings. If you use cream cheese with Roquefort, add a dash of food color—for fun. My favorite filling is lobster in a rich cream sauce with a generous amount of curry powder added to the chopped lobster.

There are many who are timid about attempting puff shells. Follow these directions which I feel are practically foolproof:

1. Put 1 cup water and ½ cup margarine in a double boiler.
2. When fat is melted, add 1 cup sifted flour.
3. Stir until well blended into a white pastry batter.
4. Remove from heat and let cool.
5. Beat 4 eggs until they are thick.
6. Stir beaten eggs into paste until they are thoroughly mixed.
7. Drop ½ teaspoon of batter on greased cookie sheet.
8. Preheat oven and bake at 400° for about 15 minutes.
9. Split puffs open and fill with one of the following fillings:

   A mixture of 1 small package (3 ounces) cream cheese with 1 (5-ounce) jar Roquefort cheese spread. Moisten mixture slightly with sherry, milk or cream.
   Chicken salad (chopped fine)
   Deviled ham mixed with mustard mayonnaise
   Liver paste mixed with anchovy butter and turkey
   Crab meat mixed with herb mayonnaise

Season fillings according to your own taste, but remember canapés are on the *high-flavor* preparation list. They must complement the dishes to follow.

ANCHOVIADE

4 cans anchovy fillets
3 tablespoons minced parsley
2 cloves garlic, minced
2 tablespoons olive oil
1 tablespoon lemon juice
6 slices white toast, trimmed and cut in triangles

Finely mash the drained anchovies. Blend in the parsley, garlic, olive oil, and lemon juice. Heap on the toast and arrange on a greased baking sheet. Bake in a 500° oven for 3 minutes. Serve hot. *Makes 18.*

The addition of the cooked tongue gives this *pâté* an unusually good flavor.

MEAT PÂTÉ

1 pound calf's liver
1 pound sausage meat
½ pound ham
½ pound cooked tongue
1 onion
2½ teaspoons salt
¾ teaspoon freshly ground black pepper
½ teaspoon thyme
⅛ teaspoon Tabasco
1 tablespoon minced parsley
6 slices bacon
2 bay leaves

Using the finest blade of a food chopper, grind the liver, sausage, ham, tongue, and onion. Add the salt, pepper, thyme, Tabasco, and parsley. Mix until well blended.

Line a greased 10-inch loaf pan with bacon. Pack the mixture into it. Place the bay leaves on top and cover the pan with aluminum foil. Set in a shallow pan of water and bake in a 350° oven 1½ hours.

Remove the foil and bay leaves. Place a weight on top of the *pâté* and chill. Carefully turn out and slice thin.

Never be in a hurry; do everything quietly and in a calm spirit. Do not lose your inward peace for anything whatsoever. — Francis de Sales

Soups

Nothing can take the place of a bowl of soup. Often we overlook the goodness of this long-time American tradition. A bowl of soup ladled from a gorgeous soup tureen, or from a gleaming kettle on the kitchen range—either way it is served—is great for the soul.

Season sour cream with a bit of curry powder, or salt and ginger, before adding as a garnish to cream soups.

A different one for guests. Soup adds much warmth and charm to any meal!

UNUSUAL CLAM SOUP WITH MUSHROOMS

Into saucepan, empty broth from 1 7-ounce can minced clams, saving the tender bits of minced clams in a dish with 1 4-ounce can sliced mushrooms well drained. Next, to the clam broth add a few celery leaves and small onion cut into chunks. Simmer five minutes. Strain. To this broth add 1 cup top milk or light cream and a generous chunk of butter with freshly ground black pepper and dash of salt. Now add the dish of minced clams and sliced mushrooms, keeping heat low. Never boil. Scald soup cups and spoons. After guests are seated at table, pour soup into hot cups, crumble buttery crackers into each cup and serve immediately. This soup loses its charm unless piping hot.

Different – Canadians love it!

CANADIAN CHEESE SOUP

3 *tablespoons minced onion*
3 *tablespoons grated carrot*
3 *tablespoons butter*
4 *cups chicken broth*
½ *teaspoon dry mustard*
½ *teaspoon paprika*
2 *tablespoons cornstarch*
¼ *cup milk*
¼ *pound (1 cup) grated Cheddar cheese*
1 *cup beer or ale*
2 *tablespoons minced parsley*

Cook the onion and carrot in the butter for 10 minutes, stirring occasionally. Add the broth, mustard, and paprika. Cook over low heat 15 minutes. Mix together the cornstarch and milk; stir into the soup. Cook 5 minutes. Add the cheese and beer or ale stirring over low heat until cheese melts. Taste for seasoning. Sprinkle with the parsley.
Serves 6.

Potato soup – delicious when served on a cold winter evening. Freshly grated nutmeg on top enhances the already good flavor.

POTATO SOUP

¼ *cup butter*
4 *cups potatoes, diced*
1 *cup finely cut celery*
1 *medium onion, chopped*
1 *pimiento, minced*
2 *tablespoons minced parsley*
4 *cups broth, stock, or bouillon*
½ *teaspoon paprika*
1½ *cups dairy sour cream*

Melt butter in a large saucepan and sauté the potatoes, celery, onion, and pimiento until the onion begins to brown. Add the parsley and the stock or bouillon and simmer until the vegetables are thoroughly cooked. Season to taste. Remove from the heat and blend in the sour cream. Serve at once.
Yield: 6-8 servings.

I dare you to try this one! Wonderful!

RUSSIAN BORSHCH

2 *cups chopped beets, canned*
2 *tablespoons butter*
½ *cup chopped onion*
1 *cup chopped celery*
Beet juice and water to make 4 cups
2 *cups canned consommé*
2 *teaspoons salt*
¼ *teaspoon pepper*
3 *tablespoons lemon juice*
Sour cream

Chop the beets very fine. Melt butter, add onion and celery, and cook until soft, but not brown. Add beets, juice and water, and consommé, and simmer uncovered for 30 minutes. Season with salt and pepper and lemon juice. Pour into hot cups and drop a tablespoon of sour cream on top. Serve at once. Or serve cold, in chilled cups, adding a dash of caviar to the sour cream.
Makes 6 servings.

King Neptune's bottomless larder is chock-full of edible material. Out of that bountiful monarch's salty realms or out of fresh-water lakes or streams, fishermen can, if it is necessary and remunerative, haul in enough provender to defy the worst meat shortage ever to exist and, believe me, this delectable chowder is no exception. It's great. Hope you can locate the conchs.

Conch Chowder is a specialty of the Jack Tar Hotel, Grand Bahama. Nothing can quite measure up to a steaming bowl of this delicious chowder. Since we are unable to obtain the conchs in this part of the country, the good chefs on the island, Joe Schaeffer, head chef, Alfred George, and Carl Pinder offer a substitute – lobster, crab, or clams.

However, for the real thing one must have the conchs. Thanks to our friend and native Islander, Joe Cartwright.

CONCH CHOWDER

Ingredients:

(1) 1 *medium onion, 1 medium green pepper, 1 medium white potato, 2 stalks celery, 1 large carrot, 1 ripe tomato, 2 strips bacon, 1 pinch thyme, 2 teaspoons salt, 1 pinch black pepper*

(2) 1 *8-ounce can tomato soup*
3 *8-ounce cans water*

(3) 4 *conches bruised and cooked until tender, cut into small pieces*

(4) 3 *tablespoons Worcestershire sauce, a few dashes apricot brandy, 2 tablespoons lemon, lime juice*

(5) 6 *soda crackers or saltines broken into bits*

Prepare:

1 is diced and cooked in water. Do not use too much water, just enough to cover ingredients. Add more if necessary.

Add #2 and #3 to #1, cook for ten minutes; add #4 and cook for 45 minutes over medium fire. Add #5 by spreading over top, let set for 10 to 15 minutes.

Stir well before serving.

So good it requires no garnishing!

SHRIMP BISQUE BRETONNE

Shell, devein, and chop 2 pounds raw shrimp as finely as possible, or put them through a food chopper, using the finest blade. Cook them over a very low flame for 3 minutes with 4 tablespoons shrimp butter, together with 1 generous tablespoon carrot and 4 tablespoons fresh mushrooms, both finely chopped.

Transfer the mixture to a soup kettle and add 2 cups strained, clear chicken stock, 2 tablespoons finely chopped celery leaves, salt and pepper to taste, and a few grains of cayenne and nutmeg. Cook for 15 to 20 minutes over a gentle flame and then press the mixture through a fine sieve into another saucepan. Bring to a boil for 2 minutes. Remove and add 1 cup each heated dry white wine and scalded cream. Taste for seasoning, reheat to the boiling point, and serve at once either in cups or in soup plates, without garnishing.

A different soup – you may like it!

SCOTCH BROTH

3 pounds center-cut beef shank
3 quarts water
6 carrots, diced
6 whole green onions, chopped fine
1½ cups pearl barley
1½ tablespoons salt
½ teaspoon pepper
1 cup canned or fresh tomatoes
2 tablespoons fine-chopped parsley

Place beef shank, barley, and salt in a 5- or 6-quart saucepan, pour in cold water; then bring to a boil. Add carrots, onions, tomatoes, and parsley. Cover, and simmer very slowly 3 hours. Remove shank from broth and when cool enough to handle, remove meat from bone. Return meat to broth. Reheat.
Serves 8 generously.

Of the honesty and the sincerity of our sentimental fondness for the pumpkin there is no doubt. It is impossible, indeed, that the aura of sanctity with which we have surrounded that gourd has limited our desire to find new culinary uses for it; for the French, who have no emotion one way or the other about the pumpkin, which they call "potiron," have gone far beyond pumpkin pie. On a cold winter night, serve your family a bowl of rich, creamy, pumpkin soup. It's divine!

CREAM OF PUMPKIN SOUP

Cook 3½ pounds of peeled and diced pumpkin in 1½ quarts of salted water until the pumpkin is tender. Empty the entire contents of kettle into a fine-meshed wire sieve and rub through into a saucepan. Stir in 1 quart of milk which has been boiled with 1 bay leaf, 4 thin slices of onion, and 3 sprigs of fresh parsley, then strained; return to the fire, stir in 1 tablespoon of sugar (more or less, according to taste), and a pinch of freshly grated nutmeg. Keep the mixture over hot water. Then cook until tender 3 tablespoons of quick-cooking tapioca in 2 cups of chicken stock and add to soup. Taste for seasoning and, when ready to serve, stir in 1 pint of scalded fresh sweet cream. Serve with croutons and a dash of freshly grated nutmeg on top.

Cold Senegalese and Cold Créme of Chicken were two of the most popular luncheon soups served around the pool at the Cat Key Club, Cat Cay, in the Bahamas.

COLD SENEGALESE

Bring 3½ cups chicken stock to a boil and add 1 cup finely chopped cooked chicken meat and ½ teaspoon curry powder, more or less to taste. Beat 4 egg yolks, stir in a little of the hot stock, and blend with 2 cups cream. Add this to the chicken stock, stirring constantly over low heat until the soup is just thickened, being careful not to allow the egg to curdle. Taste for seasoning, cool, and chill in the refrigerator.

COLD CRÈME OF CHICKEN

Bring 2 cups chicken consommé to a boil, remove the saucepan from the fire, and stir in 4 egg yolks, one at a time, beating briskly after each addition. Return the pan to the fire and cook but do not boil the soup over a gentle flame until the mixture begins to coat the spoon, stirring constantly to prevent scorching. Remove the pan from the fire and add ¾ cup cold purée of fresh peas. Rub through a fine sieve into a mixing bowl and add 2 cups chilled light cream. Season to taste with salt and white pepper and stir in 2 tablespoons chopped red pimiento. Serve at once in chilled bouillon cups.

Gaspacho is the characteristic dish of the Andalusian province. It is a very refreshing soup to serve on a hot day.

ANDALUSIAN COLD SOUP

2 cucumbers
6 tomatoes
3 pimientos
1 onion
3 tablespoons oil
3 tablespoons vinegar
2 cloves garlic, crushed
1 cup ice water
Salt
Black pepper
2 egg yolks (optional)

Chop cucumbers, tomatoes, pimientos, and onion as fine as possible. Reserve juice. Mix oil, vinegar, garlic; pour over vegetable mixture together with juice. Add water (and egg yolks). Mix well. Season to taste. Chill and serve with an ice cube as garnish in each individual platter.
4 servings.

CHICKEN VELVET SOUP

½ cup butter
½ cup flour
1 cup warm water
4 cups chicken stock, hot
1 cup warm cream
1 cup chopped, cooked chicken
¼ teaspoon salt
Dash pepper

Blend butter and flour in double boiler. Add warm milk and 2 cups of the chicken stock. Stir until smooth. Add cream and cook 15 minutes. Add remaining 2 cups chicken stock. Just before serving, stir in chicken and seasonings. Add more seasoning if desired. Serve hot with a sprinkle of chopped parsley.

Les Halles in Paris is a colorful wholesale food market. There French onion soup is a regular early-morning treat for truck drivers, salespeople, artists, and tourists ending up a gay night—it's really a national favorite.

FRENCH ONION SOUP

Brown and cook 4 cups sliced onions (very thin) in ½ stick butter (¼ cup) until done. Add 1 quart liquid (1 pint chicken consommé and 1 pint beef consommé), 2 tablespoons grated Parmesan cheese, 3 tablespoons sherry wine, 1 tablespoon Worcestershire sauce. Heat to boiling point.

Never, never throw the carcass away. If you do, be sure it's into the stewing kettle.

TURKEY SOUP

Break the carcass in pieces, add any leftover stuffing. Put in kettle with remnants of the meat; cover with cold water, bring slowly to boiling point, and let simmer about 4 hours; add 1 onion sliced, ¼ cup diced celery, and ¼ cup diced carrot, and let boil ½ hour longer. Strain, remove fat. Serve with noodles or dumplings.

LOBSTER STEW

¾ pound cooked lobster meat, cubed
½ cup butter
½ cup sherry
Pinch of paprika
Salt and freshly ground black pepper to taste
1 pint heavy cream
1 pint milk
1 tablespoon sweet butter

Melt butter in a pot and add lobster meat and sauté until golden brown. Add salt, pepper, paprika, and sherry and let cook slowly for 5 minutes. Add milk and cream and let come to boiling point. Remove from fire, add butter, and serve at once.
Serves 4.

Any time, any temperature, corn chowder is good—especially when it's howling cold out-of-doors. Don't overlook the popcorn.

CORN CHOWDER

6 slices bacon, diced
½ cup chopped onion
2 1-pound cans cream-style corn
1 12-ounce can whole-kernel corn
¼ teaspoon pepper
1 teaspoon salt
1 quart milk
2 cups light cream
Popcorn (garnish)

Sauté the bacon in a saucepan until crisp. Drain on paper toweling. Add onion to 3 tablespoons of the bacon drippings and sauté until the onion is tender; then add corn, pepper, salt, milk, and cream. Simmer (do not boil) for 15 minutes. Crumble bacon into soup. Serve very hot. Garnish with popcorn if you wish.
Yield: about 2½ quarts.

This is my favorite soup. Actually, it's old-fashioned potato soup dressed in high-fashion style and served cold. Try it. You'll love it!

VICHYSSOISE

4 leeks, white part only
1 medium onion
½ stick (2 ounces) butter or margarine
5 medium potatoes, sliced fine
4 cups chicken consommé
Salt to taste
2 cups milk
2 cups cream

Chop leeks and onion fine and brown very lightly in butter. Add potatoes, consommé, and salt and cook covered for 35 minutes. Put through a sieve and return to heat. Add the milk and heat, but do not boil, for 5 minutes. Cool. Add the cream and chill thoroughly before serving. Top with finely chopped chives.
Serves 8.

Great works are performed not by strength but by perseverance – Samuel Johnson

Salads and Their Dressings

It doesn't take a great deal of ingenuity to make a delectable, taste-tempting salad. Beautiful fruits, greens, and vegetables are so easily made available to us from our fast-moving supermarkets today. There is positively no excuse for not producing the epitome in salad-making, be it of fresh fruits or greens, molded fruit and vegetables, or the glorious sea-food salads so remarkably good. There are more opinions given on the subject of salad-making than on any other gastronomical feat; therefore, be creative, imaginative, and express your own individuality in salad-making.

We make this often, especially during the summer, for parties served around the beautiful pool here at the WJIM Country House.

I use Roquefort cheese and pile fresh Michigan blueberries in the center.

ROQUEFORT CHEESE RING

1 *package lime-flavored gelatin*
1 *cup boiling water*
1 *tablespoon vinegar*

1 3-ounce package cream cheese
1 cup whipping cream, whipped
3 ounces Roquefort cheese
Salt to taste

Dissolve gelatin in boiling water and add the vinegar. When partially cool, add the cheeses, mixing to form a smooth paste. When mixture begins to thicken, fold in whipped cream. Turn into a ring mold. When serving, fill center with fresh fruit or sea-food salad. Double the amount of cream cheese and omit Roquefort for a milder tasting salad, especially with fruit. Double recipe for large mold.

Wonderful for Thanksgiving and Christmas. Our good friend Uncle Howdy Finch used to ask for his favorite cranberry salad. I can see him now in the Copper Kettle Kitchen eating this salad and remarking how tasty it was. Howard is now with Station KTRK, Channel 13, Houston, Texas.

CRANBERRY MOLD

1 package cherry-flavored gelatin
1 cup hot water
¾ cup sugar
1 cup crushed pineapple, drained
1 tablespoon lemon juice
1 tablespoon plain gelatin dissolved in
1 cup pineapple juice, then melted over hot water
1 cup chopped celery
1 cup ground raw cranberries
1 orange and rind ground fine
½ cup chopped pecans
Lettuce

Dissolve cherry gelatin in hot water; add sugar, lemon juice, and pineapple-juice-gelatin mixture; stir until blended. Chill until partially set; add remaining ingredients; pour into ring mold. To serve, unmold on lettuce leaves, garnish with turkey or chicken salad, using grape halves in place of celery. *Serves 10.*

It's the dressing that's special – makes every leaf glisten.

TOSSED GREEN SALAD

½ head of lettuce
2 tablespoons chopped onion
¼ cup sliced radishes
1 cup sliced carrots
⅓ cup chopped celery
2 tomatoes, cut in wedges

Combine ingredients in salad bowl. Toss lightly with Crystal Salad Dressing: Combine ⅓ cup vinegar, 2 tablespoons sugar, 1 teaspoon salt, and ½ teaspoon dry mustard. Heat to boiling and cook 1 minute. Cool. Stir in ¼ cup salad oil and 1 teaspoon onion juice.

BEAN SALAD

¼ cup French dressing
1 can (16-17 ounces) kidney beans, drained
½ cup finely sliced celery
¼ cup chopped sweet pickle
2 tablespoons chopped onion
½ teaspoon salt
Dash cayenne pepper
Dash freshly ground pepper
Dash Accent

Heat dressing in saucepan, add remaining ingredients and heat thoroughly, stirring frequently. Remove from heat and chill until ready to serve. For variation, substitute cooked green beans, lima beans, or butter beans.
Serves 4-6.

TOMATO ROSE SALAD

Firm small tomatoes, peeled, cream cheese, milk, hard-cooked egg yolk, watercress, French dressing.

Chill the tomatoes. Slightly soften cream cheese with milk. Form two rows of petals on each tomato by pressing level teaspoons of the softened cheese against the side of the tomato, then drawing the teaspoon down with a curving motion. Sprinkle the center of each tomato with hard-cooked egg yolk pressed through a strainer. Serve on crisp water cress, with French dressing.

(One 3-ounce package cream cheese should be sufficient for 3 small tomatoes.)

BING CHERRY MOLD

- 1 *package cherry gelatin*
- 1 *cup cherry juice*
- 1 *cup grape juice or red port wine*
- 1 *No. 2 can Bing cherries, pitted*
- ½ *cup almonds, chopped*

Dissolve gelatin in hot cherry juice. Cool. Add grape juice or wine and chill until gelatin begins to congeal. Add cherries and almonds. Pour into a fluted mold and chill. Unmold on water cress and serve with whipped cream mixed with mayonnaise.
Serves 6 to 8.

PEACH AMBROSIA DESSERT OR SALAD

- 1 *No. 2 can (2½ cups) pineapple tidbits, drained*
- 1 *cup Tokay grape halves or seedless white grapes*
- 1 *cup orange sections (undrained)*
- 1 *cup tiny marshmallows*
- 1 *3½-ounce can (1¼ cups) flaked coconut*
- 1 *cup dairy sour cream*
- 1 *No. 2 can (2½ cups) peach halves chilled and drained*

Combine first 5 ingredients, stir in sour cream. Chill several hours or overnight. Serve in peach halves on endive.
Makes 6 or 7 servings.

Always a favorite.

TWENTY-FOUR-HOUR SALAD

3 *beaten egg yolks*
2 *tablespoons sugar*
2 *tablespoons vinegar*
2 *tablespoons pineapple syrup*
1 *tablespoon butter*
Dash salt
2 *cups drained canned pitted white cherries*
2 *cups drained canned pineapple tidbits*
2 *pared oranges, cut up, drained*
2 *cups tiny marshmallows or 16 large ones cut in eighths*
1 *cup whipping cream, whipped*

Combine first 6 ingredients in top of double boiler. Cook and stir over hot, not boiling, water till thick. Cool. Stir in fruits and marshmallows. Fold in whipped cream. Spoon gently into serving bowl. Chill 24 hours.

Trim with orange sections and white seedless grapes.
Makes 6 to 8 servings.

I begged for this recipe after eating it at Golly's House on Thanksgiving Day. Her real name, Mrs. Jack Miner, Chesterfield, Missouri. Thanks, dear!

GOLLY'S CUCUMBER SALAD

1 *package lime Jello*
¾ *cup boiling water*
1 *cup mayonnaise*
2 *3-ounce packages cream cheese (room temperature)*
1 *teaspoon horseradish*
2 *tablespoons lemon juice*
¾ *cup grated unpeeled cucumber (drained and squeezed)*
¼ *cup finely chopped green onions*

Pour boiling water over Jello and dissolve. Cool slightly. Stir in mayonnaise, cream cheese, horseradish, and lemon juice and beat until smooth with rotary beater or electric mixer. Let chill until slightly thickened, then stir in the cucumber and onion. Pour into mold.

(This amount takes about 2 medium-sized cucumbers or 1½ very large ones.)

My sincere thanks to our good friends Max R. and Stan Brauer of Brauer's 1861 House, Lansing, Michigan.

We take great pride in saluting them as an outstanding father-and-son team in the culinary arts. Try this delicious Red Cabbage, German Style.

RED CABBAGE, GERMAN STYLE

Take 8-pound head of red cabbage. Cut in quarters and cut out the core. Then shred the cabbage.

Grate 1 medium-sized onion. Add 2 cups of vinegar (strong), 2 cups of water, 1½ cups of sugar, 2 teaspoons salt, 1 teaspoon of white pepper.

Cook it all together. Then cut up ½ pound of bacon in small pieces. Sauté in frying pan until nearly crisp. When cabbage is done, add your bacon with fat into cabbage. Stir and let simmer. Then add 1 No. 303-can applesauce, about 1½ cups. Stir all together.

Good, good, good with steaks — be sure the vinegar is sharp!

WILTED-SPINACH SALAD

2 *pounds young, tender spinach*
5 *slices bacon*
6 *scallions cut into rounds*
3 *hard-cooked eggs*
½ *teaspoon finely ground pepper*
3 *tablespoons sugar*
½ *cup vinegar*
½ *cup water*

Wash spinach, remove stems. Drain. Store leaves in refrigerator. Use only the small leaves — the large ones are fine for cooking, but not for salad. Prepare the spinach the day before so it will be crisp. The dressing may be made in advance, but must be reheated to boiling point just before it is added to spinach. Fry bacon. Drain on

paper toweling and break into pieces. Add scallions, 1 chopped hard-cooked egg, pepper, sugar, vinegar, and water to drippings in the skillet. Pour boiling hot over spinach, add bacon and toss well. Garnish with 2 hard-cooked eggs cut into thin slices.
Six servings.

A winner for luncheon.

BAKED SEA-FOOD SALAD

1 *cup canned salmon*
1 *cup canned lobster*
1 *cup mayonnaise*
½ *chopped pimiento*
2 *tablespoons chopped onion*
½ *cup chopped green pepper*
½ *cup chopped celery*
½ *teaspoon salt*
⅛ *teaspoon cayenne pepper*
1 *teaspoon Worcestershire sauce*
3 *tablespoons butter, plus*
1 *cup fine cracker crumbs*

Combine salmon, lobster, and mayonnaise. Add pimiento, onion, green pepper, and celery. Stir gently to blend. Place in greased quart casserole. Melt butter. Add crumbs and stir to blend. Sprinkle crumbs over salad mixture. Bake at 350° for 40 minutes. Serve piping hot.

Good for the gang.

FIESTA HOT SLAW

½ *cup cider vinegar*
¼ *cup water*
½ *teaspoon salt*
¼ *cup sugar*
¼ *teaspoon paprika*
¼ *teaspoon dry mustard*
¼ *cup salad or olive oil*
2 *eggs, slightly beaten*
¾ *cup heavy cream*

1 *medium head cabbage, shredded fine*
1 *2-ounce can pimento, cut into thin strips*
½ *cup chopped sweet pickles*

Place vinegar, water, salt, sugar, paprika, mustard, and oil in pan and bring to boiling. Combine eggs and cream in bowl. Add boiling mixture slowly, stirring constantly. Return to pan and cook on low heat, stirring constantly for 5 minutes. Pour over cabbage, pimento, and pickles in large bowl and toss lightly. Serve immediately. *Makes 8 servings.*

A new view of the simple cabbage head. It's good—especially served with fried chicken.

CREAMED SLAW

1 *can (15-ounce) sweetened condensed milk*
1½ *teaspoons dry mustard*
2 *teaspoons salt*
1 *tablespoon Worcestershire sauce*
¾ *cup cider vinegar*
1 *medium head cabbage, shredded*
4 *carrots, coarsely grated*
3 *green peppers, seeded and chopped*
1 *Spanish onion, chopped (optional)*
1 *teaspoon caraway seed (optional)*

Make the dressing first. Heat the condensed milk in a double boiler for 10 minutes; cool and put into a salad bowl. Add mustard, salt, vinegar, and Worcestershire sauce. Add vegetables and caraway seed; add dressing, toss well. Serve chilled.

Mrs. Charlotte Gross gave this recipe for Mustard Ring some years ago. Mrs. Gross is a real gourmet, loves good food, beautiful parties, and has an infinitely fascinating detail of the art.

MUSTARD RING

4 *eggs*
¾ *cup sugar*
1 *tablespoon dry mustard*

1 tablespoon gelatin
½ teaspoon salt
½ cup white vinegar
½ cup water
½ pint whipping cream, whipped

Beat eggs and add dry ingredients and vinegar. Dissolve gelatin in one tablespoon of water and fold into eggs immediately. Cook in double boiler until thick as custard. Cool. Fold in whipped cream. Pour in mold. Shoestring beets or small whole beets make a wonderful garnish for this salad. Marinate beets in a mixture of vinegar, sugar, salad oil, salt and pepper. Sweeten to taste. Allow beets to stand in marinade overnight. Drain thoroughly before placing in center of mustard ring.

The loveliest thing you can make for open house or party-giving.

DELLA ROBBIA FRUIT SALAD WREATH

½ pound red grapes, frosted
½ pound green grapes, frosted
8 pear halves (No. 2½ can)
2 large oranges, sectioned
16 apricot halves (No. 2 can)
2 grapefruit, sectioned
1 pomegranate (1 cup seeds)
12 spiced crab apples
½ cup whipping cream, whipped
1½ teaspoons grated orange rind

⅔ cup chopped dates
¼ teaspoon almond extract
¼ cup salad dressing
8 green maraschino cherries
2 3-ounce packages cream cheese
2 tablespoons cream (about)
Curly endive
Salad dressing

Drain all fruit and chill. Dry pear and apricot halves on paper towels. Fill pear halves with mixture of whipped cream, orange rind, dates, almond extract, and salad dressing and top with a cherry. Soften cream cheese with cream. Fill apricot halves, then press together in pairs. To seal edges additional cream cheese may be piped through a pastry tube.

To assemble fruit wreath: Arrange a bed of curly endive on a large round plate. Place salad dressing in a dish in center of plate and around it arrange the following fruits: pear halves with one orange section tucked under each side; apricot halves on pineapple slices; bunches of frosted grapes; groups of 3 crab apples and groups of 3 grapefruit sections in lettuce cups sprinkled with pomegranate seeds.

Excellent salad to serve on holidays.

FROZEN FRUIT SALAD

1 3-ounce package cream cheese
1 tablespoon mayonnaise
1 cup canned sweet cherries
¼ cup cut green maraschino cherries
½ cup cut red maraschino cherries
¼ cup cut-up orange sections
1 cup crushed drained pineapple
1 cup chopped walnuts
1 cup cream, whipped

Soften cheese, cream with mayonnaise. Add cherries and other fruits and nuts. Fold cream into mixture, and spoon into loaf pan; cover, and freeze. To serve, unmold and slice in cubes.
Makes 10 to 12 servings.

A new way to use fresh cranberries.

CRANBERRY-TOKAY SALAD

2 cups fresh cranberries
1 cup sugar
1 cup Tokay grapes
¼ cup broken California walnuts
½ cup heavy cream, whipped

Put cranberries through food chopper, using coarse blade. Stir in sugar. Let drain overnight; stir, pressing lightly to remove excess juice. (Use juice in fruit punch.)

Cut grapes in half and remove seeds. Add grapes and nuts to well-drained cranberry mixture. Just before serving, fold in whipped cream. Mound in lettuce cups. Garnish with clusters of grapes. Serve immediately.

Makes 4 to 5 servings.

CRANBERRIES

Cook fresh cranberries in the usual way. After removing berries from the range, add ¾ teaspoon vanilla flavoring and a generous dash of ground cinnamon.

Cool without stirring. Serve cold in a pretty glass dish.

The name is misleading. It's simple but awfully good.

CONEY ISLAND SALAD

Dissolve one package lemon-flavored gelatin in 2 cups hot water. Add 16 marshmallows which have been cut in small pieces, and 2 packages cream cheese (3-ounce size).

Let the above ingredients dissolve until smooth and fold in 1½ cups drained crushed pineapple, 3 heaping tablespoons mayonnaise and ½ pint whipping cream (whipped stiff). Combine all ingredients and place in flat pan or fancy mold. This salad does not require dressing.

HEAVENLY FRUIT HASH

1½ cups canned fruit cocktail (use fresh fruit if you prefer)
½ cup whipping cream
2 tablespoons granulated sugar
2 teaspoons lemon juice
6 finely cut marshmallows
1 banana

Drain fruit cocktail well. Whip cream until stiff. Then stir in sugar and lemon juice. Fold in fruit cocktail, marshmallows, and sliced banana. Chill at least 1 hour.

This is a beauty. I have made it on the Copper Kettle Show for years. The basic ingredient for this recipe is patience. If you have it, try it!

CHRISTMAS SPECIAL

1 package raspberry gelatin dessert
2 cups hot water
1 cup chopped fresh cranberries
1 package orange gelatin dessert
1 cup hot water
1 cup orange juice
1 3-ounce package cream cheese
½ pint heavy cream, whipped
1 package lime gelatin dessert
2 cups hot water
½ cup halved seedless grapes
¼ cup chopped celery
Lettuce
Sherry mayonnaise

Dissolve the raspberry gelatin in the 2 cups of hot water. Chill until slightly thickened. Fold in the cranberries. Pour into a 2-quart mold. Chill until firm.

Dissolve the orange gelatin in the 1 cup of hot water. Add the orange juice. Gradually add to the cream cheese, blending until smooth. Chill until slightly thickened. Beat until light and fluffy. Fold in the whipped cream. Pour over the raspberry layer. Chill until firm.

Dissolve the lime gelatin in the 2 cups of hot water. Chill until slightly thickened. Fold in the grapes and celery. Pour onto the second layer in the mold. Chill until firm. Unmold on a large chop plate and garnish with lettuce. Serve with sherry mayonnaise.
Makes 10 to 12 servings.

You cannot pass melon time up without making this one. It's lovely.

FROSTED CANTALOUPE

Select ripe, firm melon. Cut one end off, remove seeds, and pare whole melon. Stand melon in bowl, cut side up. Make gelatin mixture to pour inside cantaloupe. (One package of gelatin will make enough gelatin for two cantaloupes.)

Gelatin Mixture: To one package strawberry-flavored gelatin (or your favorite flavor) add 1⅓ cups boiling water and any desired fruit. (Peaches and blueberries are very nice.) Fill cavity of melon with gelatin mixture and let chill until mixture is firm. Place 2 or 3 packages of cream cheese in bowl. Add enough cream or milk until cheese is of nice spreading consistency. Cover melon with cream cheese mixture. The cheese must be thick on the melon to look nice. When melon is completely covered with cheese, place it on a bed of greens and garnish with additional blueberries and green grapes. To serve on salad plates, slice and place on greens. The whole melon makes a lovely centerpiece for parties.

Port wine adds to the delightful flavor of this colorful Bing cherry salad.

JUBILEE CHERRY SALAD

2 packages cherry-flavored gelatin
1½ cups boiling water
½ cup orange juice
1 cup port wine
2 No. 2 cans Bing cherries, drained
1 cup cherry juice
1 3-ounce package cream cheese

Dissolve the gelatin in boiling water. Add orange juice. Cool. Add wine and cherry juice. Chill until mixture begins to thicken. Fold in well-drained pitted cherries and tiny balls or cubes of the cream cheese. Turn into a 6½-cup mold and chill until firm.

To serve, unmold on chilled plate, garnish with crisp greens and serve with sour-cream dressing. *Makes 6 to 9 servings.*

VEGETABLE SALAD ITALIENNE

3 tablespoons finely cut onion
½ cup salad oil
Garlic
1 pint cooked green string beans
1 cup sliced stuffed olives
3 stalks celery
½ teaspoon salt
½ teaspoon paprika
¼ teaspoon mustard
1 teaspoon catsup
2 tablespoons vinegar

Marinate onion in oil. Rub bowl with garlic. Mix beans, celery, and olives. Make dressing of salt, paprika, and mustard, rubbing to a paste with catsup. Add oil and vinegar. Add to vegetables, mixing lightly with a fork. *Serves 6.*

Delicious when made with garden-fresh cucumbers.

CUCUMBERS IN SOUR CREAM

2 cups thinly sliced cucumbers
½ cup sugar
¾ cup sour cream
¼ cup vinegar
Salt and pepper to taste

Mix together and serve as a salad. Less vinegar may be used. Onion rings may be added to the cucumbers. *Serves 4 to 6.*

COLESLAW

6 cups shredded cabbage
½ bell pepper
2 small white onions
2 stalks celery
Dressing:
3 eggs
½ cup vinegar
1 teaspoon mustard
½ teaspoon salt
¾ cup sugar
¼ teaspoon freshly ground black pepper
2 rounded tablespoons butter

In a large salad bowl, place cabbage. Chop fine the pepper, onions, and celery and add to cabbage and toss all together. Place in refrigerator to crisp until ready to use.

Beat eggs, add sugar, then add vinegar, butter, and seasonings. Cook in double boiler until thick. Cool and place in covered jar in refrigerator. When ready to use, thin amount desired with cream. What is left will keep a couple of weeks in the refrigerator.

PINEAPPLE GRAPE SLAW

2 cups shredded cabbage
1 cup crushed pineapple, drained
1 cup chopped celery
½ cup chopped green pepper
1 cup seedless grapes
1 tablespoon wine vinegar
½ cup mayonnaise or salad dressing
¼ teaspoon salt
⅛ teaspoon pepper
Lettuce

Combine the cabbage, pineapple, celery, green pepper, and grapes. Slowly add vinegar to the mayonnaise or salad dressing, with salt and pepper. Add to salad mixture, tossing lightly. Chill and serve in lettuce cups.

DELICIOUS COLESLAW

1 *medium head shredded cabbage*
1 *pepper, chopped fine*
1 *large onion, chopped fine*
2 *carrots, sliced fine*
1 *tablespoon mustard seed*
1 *cup vinegar*
1 *cup sugar*
1 *tablespoon salt*

Boil last 3 ingredients 5 minutes. Let stand until cool. Pour over above and let stand overnight or longer if desired.

CHICKEN SALAD IN ARTICHOKES

2 *cups diced cooked chicken*
½ *cup diced celery*
¼ *cup chopped green pepper*
1 *tablespoon chopped pimento*
1 *tablespoon capers*
1 *tablespoon lemon juice, fresh, frozen, or canned*
½ *teaspoon salt*
¼ *teaspoon pepper*
¼ *cup mayonnaise or salad dressing*
4 *chilled cooked artichokes*

Combine ingredients except artichokes; chill. Remove center leaves of each artichoke, leaving a cup. Carefully remove choke. Fill artichokes with chicken salad. Serve with French dressing for dipping the leaves.
Makes 4 servings.

ALMOND CHICKEN SALAD

3 *cups cubed, cooked chicken*
⅔ *cup chopped candied dill strips*
½ *cup blanched, quartered, toasted almonds*
⅓ *cup seedless white grapes*
½ *cup mayonnaise or salad dressing*
½ *teaspoon salt*
1½ *teaspoons vinegar*

Combine first 4 ingredients. Blend mayonnaise, salt, and vinegar. Mix lightly with chicken mixture. Chill. Spoon into lettuce cups; garnish with water cress.
Makes 4-6 servings.

CHICKEN SALAD EXOTIC

2 *cups diced cooked chicken*
1 *cup thinly sliced celery*
⅓ *cup sliced canned water chestnuts*
3 *tablespoons chopped preserved ginger*
½ *cup toasted coconut flakes*
½ *cup mayonnaise*
1 *tablespoon fresh juice of a lemon*
Salt and cayenne pepper
Boston or butter lettuce
2 *midsummer cantaloupes*
Fresh dark sweet cherries

Combine chicken, celery, water chestnuts, ginger, and half the coconut. Toss lightly with mayonnaise and lemon juice. Season gently with salt and a tiny flick of cayenne. Heap onto lettuce leaves on 4 luncheon plates. Top with rest of coconut. Halve and peel cantaloupes. Slice thin and arrange a fan of slices on each plate. Decorate with a handful of fresh cherries-on-the-stem. It is wonderful when served with a basket of scones and sparkling hot tea.

Yes, hot chicken salad. I'll wager you will make it often.

HOT CHICKEN SALAD

2 *cups cooked, cubed chicken*
1 *cup mayonnaise*
2 *cups celery, diced fine*
2 *heaping tablespoons grated onion*
2 *tablespoons lemon juice*
½ *cup chopped walnuts*
½ *cup mushrooms*
1 *teaspoon salt*

Mix well and put in casserole. Mix ½ cup grated cheese and 1¼ cups crumbled potato chips. Spread on top of mixture. Bake at 450° for about 20 minutes or until nicely brown. It is delicious!

Always popular with the men.

CATALINA SALAD

- 1 *clove garlic, cut*
- 6 *tablespoons olive or salad oil*
- 1 *large head lettuce*
- 1 *head romaine*
- 2 *cups cubed bread*
- 3 *tablespoons small pickled onions, quartered*
- ⅓ *cup sliced pitted black olives*
- ¼ *teaspoon salt*
- ⅛ *teaspoon pepper*
- ⅓ *cup grated Parmesan cheese*
- 1 *egg*
- 3 *tablespoons lemon juice*
- 2 *tomatoes (optional)*

Soak the garlic in the oil overnight. Make the croutons by browning the bread cubes in 2 tablespoons garlic salad oil. Wash, dry, and chill the greens. Tear into bite-size pieces and put into a large salad bowl. Add the onions, olives, ¼ cup of the garlic-flavored oil, salt and pepper, and the cheese. Drop a raw egg on top of the greens. Pour the lemon juice on the egg. Toss the salad over and over and adjust seasoning. Add croutons and toss once more. Garnish with tomato wedges if you wish.
Six servings.

The artichoke is an expensive vegetable. Its place of origin is Africa, where legend says that it was a favorite dish with Anthony and Cleopatra. It grows almost everywhere in the temperate regions and belongs to the thistle family.

However, artichokes are by no means new to the soil of the United States, for as far back as 1605, Champlain, the French explorer, tells of seeing them in Indian gardens at Cape Cod.

ARTICHOKE HEART SURPRISE SALAD

Arrange a bed of shredded lettuce in the center of a salad plate. Place a large slice of peeled tomato on the lettuce. On top of the tomato slice arrange about 4 to 6 marinated artichoke heart halves so it is completely covered. Gently press to form a firm salad base. Cover the marinated artichoke hearts generously with cooked diced chicken, shrimp, crab meat, or lobster. Pour Thousand Island dressing over the ingredients and sprinkle finely chopped hard-boiled eggs over the top. Add several dashes of paprika.

CAESAR SALAD

- 1 *pound romaine lettuce*
- 24 *small croutons*
- 2 *medium-sized cloves garlic (more or less)*
- 1 *teaspoon salt (for salad bowl)*
- 6 *tablespoons oil*
- 2 *tablespoons wine vinegar*
- 1 *tablespoon fresh lemon juice*
- 1 *tablespoon Parmesan cheese*
- 1 *raw egg*
- ½ *teaspoon Worcestershire sauce*
- 1 *teaspoon dry mustard*
- ½ *teaspoon salt*
- 1 *teaspoon black pepper*
- 4 *fillets of anchovies cut into small pieces, or 3 ounces of Blue cheese*

In a large wooden salad bowl place garlic cloves cut into halves and 1 teaspoon salt; crush with a fork and rub in bowl until bowl is well flavored with garlic. This takes about 2 minutes. Discard garlic and salt. (If preferred, garlic and salt may be left in bowl. In this case omit salt called for in recipe.)

Add oil, and beat with fork until thick, about 1 minute; then add vinegar and lemon juice, and beat until thoroughly blended with oil. Add Worcestershire sauce, dry mustard, salt, pepper, anchovies, and Parmesan cheese; beat until well blended. Add chilled romaine lettuce that has been broken into medium-sized pieces. Toss well with a salad fork and spoon until well marinated, but not so vigorously as to bruise lettuce. Add raw egg and mix well. Last, add sautéed croutons, mixing and tossing salad gently to prevent croutons from becoming soggy. Serve at once in individual salad bowls.

Croutons:

Cut six slices of French or Italian bread ½ inch thick; then cut each slice into bite-size pieces. Sauté in oil or butter with 2 or 3 slivers of garlic in an open skillet until crisp and golden brown on each side. Croutons may be sautéed hours in advance.
Serves 4-6.

Sea-food Salads

Crabs are one of our popular shellfish because of their tender meat and distinctive flavor. Excellent for Crab Louis.

CRAB LOUIS

1 *pound crab meat*
1 *tablespoon prepared horseradish*
¼ *cup chili sauce*
2 *tablespoons chopped green pepper*
2 *tablespoons chopped pickle*
1 *tablespoon chopped scallion*
1 *tablespoon lemon juice*
½ *cup mayonnaise or boiled dressing*
½ *teaspoon salt*
⅛ *teaspoon pepper*
Dash Worcestershire sauce

Mix all ingredients except crab meat and add salt and pepper to taste. The quantity of salt and pepper will depend on how highly

seasoned the dressing is. Bone the crab meat and mix carefully into the sauce. Serve on lettuce leaves in avocado halves, or in scooped-out tomatoes if you wish.
Makes six servings.

It's different – great for women's luncheons on a hot day.

FROZEN LOBSTER SALAD

½ pound cooked lobster meat
1 package (3 ounces) cream cheese
½ cup mayonnaise or salad dressing
2 tablespoons chopped pimento
½ cup chopped nuts
½ teaspoon salt
5 drops Tabasco
½ cup whipping cream
Lettuce

Cut lobster meat into ½-inch pieces. Cream cheese and mayonnaise. Add the next four ingredients and lobster meat. Whip cream. Fold in whipped cream. Place in a 1-quart ice-cube tray; freeze. Remove from freezer and let stand at room temperature for 15 minutes before serving. Cut into 6 slices and serve on lettuce.
Makes 6 servings.

Bean sprouts add the Oriental touch.

TOSSED TUNA SALAD

2 cans (6½ or 7 ounces each) tuna
1 clove garlic
1 cup drained bean sprouts
½ cup chopped cucumber
1 cup celery crescents
2 cups chopped raw spinach
¼ cup chopped green onion
½ cup French dressing
Tomato wedges

Drain tuna. Break into large pieces. Rub the inside of a salad bowl with the cut surface of a clove of garlic. Combine all ingredients except tomatoes. Garnish with tomato wedges.
Serves 6.

SEA-FOOD SALAD

3 cans shrimp
1½ cans crab meat
1 cup finely chopped onion
1 cup finely chopped parsley
3 small packages cream cheese
1½ cups cold water
3 cups mayonnaise
3 cups tomato soup
3½ tablespoons unflavored gelatin

Combine soup and cheese. Cook until cheese is melted over low temperature. Dissolve gelatin in 1½ cups cold water. Add soup, cheese, and remaining ingredients. Pour into mold. This makes a large mold.

Excellent served as a luncheon entree. Garnish with extra sea food and large ripe olives.

Salmon, peas, and sour cream add style to this sea-food salad. Try it—you'll like it.

SALMON SALAD SUPREME

1 1-pound can salmon, drained
½ cup diced celery
1 17-ounce can green sweet peas, drained
2 tablespoons lemon juice
1 teaspoon minced onion
½ teaspoon salt
⅛ teaspoon pepper
⅛ teaspoon marjoram
1 cup dairy sour cream

Break salmon into bite-size pieces in medium-sized bowl. Add celery and drained canned peas. Combine remaining ingredients; pour over

salmon mixture. Toss lightly with fork. Chill several hours. Serve in lettuce cups. Garnish with chopped chives and lemon wedges if desired.
Yield: 6 servings.

A delight on a warm summer day.

DELICIOUS SEA-FOOD STUFFED AVOCADO

1 *cup of lobster meat, cooked (3-4 ounce lobster tails cooked or 1 can of lobster meat)*
1 *pound fresh shrimp with shells, cooked*
1 *cup fresh lump crab meat (1 can)*

Put sea food in a shallow container and pour over it ½ cup French dressing.

Toss lightly to coat evenly with dressing. Cover and set in refrigerator to chill and to marinate. Toss occasionally.

French Dressing:

Combine in a screw-top jar:

¾ *cup olive oil*
¼ *cup tarragon or cider vinegar*
¼ *teaspoon Worcestershire sauce*
1 *clove garlic cut into halves*
1 *teaspoon sugar*
½ *teaspoon salt*
¼ *teaspoon paprika*
¼ *teaspoon dry mustard*
⅛ *teaspoon pepper*
⅛ *teaspoon thyme*

Shake well, remove garlic. Makes about 1 cup dressing.

Topping for Salad:

Blend together:

1 *teaspoon tarragon vinegar*
¼ *teaspoon salt*

¼ *teaspoon dry mustard*
¼ *teaspoon sugar*

Blend into:

¼ *cup mayonnaise*
¼ *cup sour cream (thick)*

Put into refrigerator until ready to use.

Cut into halves lengthwise and remove pits from 3 ripe avocados. Brush cut surfaces with lemon juice.

Mound the sea-food mixture into the avocado halves. Spoon some of the topping over each.

Sprinkle with finely chopped chives.

Garnish, if desired, with a whole shrimp or claw of lobster meat.

Serve with cheese sticks or hot buttered miniature biscuits.

Salad Dressings

POPULAR GARLIC DRESSING

This is a popular one at the Country House. Try throwing broken, crisply fried bacon and toasted slivered almonds on your greens next time you make a tossed salad. I'm a devoted fan to bib lettuce. Chunks of sea food with bacon and almonds are delicious, too!

2 *cups olive oil or salad oil*
½ *cup vinegar*
¼ *cup tarragon or wine vinegar*
3 *teaspoons salt*
1 *teaspoon dry mustard*
1 *teaspoon sugar*
2 *teaspoons coarse pepper or freshly ground pepper*
2 *or* 3 *cloves of garlic, sliced*

Mix together oil, vinegar, spices, and garlic. Cover and let stand in refrigerator until ready to use. Strain and pour over thoroughly chilled greens. Especially good on bib lettuce.

This is the famous dressing served at the Claridge Hotel, Atlantic City. It is used on either cold shrimp, crab meat, or lobster.

LAMAZE DRESSING

1 *pint mayonnaise*
1 *pint chili sauce*
½ *cup relish, chopped*
1 *hard-cooked egg, chopped*
1 *teaspoon chives, chopped*
1 *pimento, chopped*
½ *green pepper, chopped*
2 *tablespoons celery, chopped*
1 *tablespoon prepared mustard*
1 *tablespoon Worcestershire sauce*
⅛ *teaspoon paprika*
⅛ *teaspoon salt*
Black pepper

Mix well. Chill and serve.
Makes 1 quart. Serves about 12.

It is the rock of cloud that makes the sunset lovely — Christopher Morley

Don't throw up your hands in horror. It's wonderful! Marvelous on fruits.

COTTAGE CHEESE FRENCH DRESSING

1¼ *cups creamed cottage cheese*
¼ *cup sugar*
1 *teaspoon salt*

2 tablespoons dry mustard
1 teaspoon paprika
¾ cup salad oil
¼ cup catsup
⅓ cup mild vinegar
1 tablespoon water
2 teaspoons Worcestershire sauce
1 teaspoon grated onion
1 clove garlic, mashed
Dash Tabasco sauce

Put cottage cheese in mixing bowl and beat until creamy. Blend dry ingredients into cottage cheese. Add other ingredients and mix well. Serve on hearts of lettuce or any other tossed green salad.

Obey the recipe. I agree, 35 to 40 minutes is a long time to mix. However, it pays great dividends.

CELERY-SEED DRESSING

In a medium-sized mixing bowl combine the following ingredients and beat 35 to 40 minutes on mixer.

½ cup white granulated sugar
1 or 2 teaspoons dry mustard
1½ teaspoons salt
½ cup vinegar
1 cup salad oil
1 to 1½ teaspoons celery seed

This salad dressing is delicious served on fresh fruits.

HERB DRESSING

Make this tasty dressing for a vegetable salad with 1 cup of yoghurt, 1 tablespoon lemon juice, 1 teaspoon all-purpose, finely ground herbs, a pinch of curry powder, a few chopped chives, and ½ teaspoon onion juice.

Mix ingredients well in a jar and keep in the refrigerator to blend flavors.

This is John Suur's popular egg dressing.

JOHN'S DUTCH EGG DRESSING

1 cup oil
½ cup white vinegar
2 tablespoons prepared mustard
1 tablespoon finely chopped onion
1 tablespoon chopped chives
1 clove of garlic
1 teaspoon sugar
Salt
Few drops of Tabasco sauce
Juice from one lemon

Mix ingredients, add 3 chopped hard-boiled eggs. This is an excellent salad dressing for all types of greens.

VINAIGRETTE DRESSING

1 clove garlic (chopped fine)
2 tablespoons chopped onion
2 tablespoons tarragon vinegar
5 tablespoons salad oil (olive oil may be used)
Very generous dash dry mustard
Dash Tabasco sauce
Juice of one lemon
Salt to taste

Mix all the above ingredients together (very well). Add 2 tablespoons chopped fresh parsley and 2 chopped hard-boiled eggs.

This salad dressing should be served over the greens in very generous amounts. Also good served over cooked asparagus spears with tomatoes.

Approximately 1 cup.

Any goddess would love this one. It's a favorite of mine. Be sure it's well chilled and ladle generous amounts over salad greens.

GREEN GODDESS SALAD DRESSING

1 garlic clove, finely minced
10 anchovy fillets, or 3-4 tablespoons anchovy paste

2 sprigs parsley
1 pinch tarragon leaves
1 bunch chives, or finely cut green onion tops
1 bottle capers, drained
1 tablespoon lemon juice
1 tablespoon tarragon vinegar
1 cup sour cream
2 cups mayonnaise
Sugar to taste
1 tablespoon freshly ground pepper

Combine all ingredients, blending well. If too sweet, add more vinegar; if too sharp, add more sugar.

This tangy mixture is ideal for topping greens of all kinds in a tossed salad.

DILL DRESSING

1 cup yoghurt
1 chopped hard-cooked egg
1 tablespoon lemon juice
Salt and pepper
1 tablespoon chopped dill
1 small dill pickle, finely minced

Mix thoroughly, chill in refrigerator.

This also makes a delicious barbecue sauce for chicken and steaks.

FRENCH DRESSING

½ cup salad oil
½ cup sugar
½ cup catsup
¼ cup vinegar
¼ cup lemon juice (either fresh or reconstituted [canned])
1 teaspoon salt
1 tablespoon paprika
1 tablespoon finely chopped onion or clove of garlic (optional)

CRANBERRY DRESSING

⅔ cups sugar
1 teaspoon salt
1 teaspoon dry mustard
½ cup vinegar
1 teaspoon onion juice
1 cup oil
1 orange
1 cup cranberries
½ cup sugar

Combine dry ingredients, mix with vinegar to dissolve. Combine onion juice and oil with above and beat until well blended. Wash and cut orange into segments, removing seeds. Grind with cranberries. Stir in sugar and blend with oil mixture.

This is delicious over fresh pear or banana salad. Put in covered jar. Will keep in cool place until used up. Stir well before each serving.

Makes about 1 quart.

For a different and delicious salad dressing to serve over lettuce wedges, try this.

RARE TANG DRESSING

To the desired amount of French dressing, add a spoonful or two of peanut butter, a little chili sauce (according to taste and to improve color), a teaspoon of chopped chives or minced onion, and a bit of chopped parsley. Beat to blend and spoon over lettuce wedges just before serving.

AVOCADO DRESSING

No coaxing to eat vegetables when they are topped with mashed California avocado mixed with a little oil, vinegar, and a dash of garlic salt. This is a very good use for avocados that are soft-ripe.

POPULAR GARLIC DRESSING

2 cups olive oil or salad oil
½ cup vinegar
¼ cup tarragon or wine vinegar
3 teaspoons salt
1 teaspoon dry mustard
1 teaspoon sugar
2 teaspoons coarse pepper or freshly ground pepper
2 or 3 cloves of garlic, sliced

Mix together oil, vinegar, spices, and garlic. Cover and let stand in refrigerator until ready to use. Strain and pour over thoroughly chilled greens. Especially good on bib lettuce.

FRENCH DRESSING

½ cup salad oil
½ cup catsup
1 small onion cut fine
Dash of garlic salt
⅓ cup sugar
¼ cup vinegar
1 teaspoon A-1 sauce
Pinch of paprika

Put all ingredients in a pint jar in any order. Shake until well blended. Store in cool place. Shake well before using.

FRUIT SALAD DRESSING

⅓ cup orange juice
⅓ cup pineapple juice
2 tablespoons lemon juice
2 eggs, slightly beaten
½ cup sugar
¼ teaspoon salt
1 cup heavy cream, whipped

Mix fruit juices. Add 2 beaten eggs and add sugar and salt.

Cook in double boiler for 3 to 5 minutes or until thickened. Cool. Fold in whipped cream.

Makes about 2½ cups.

All Roquefort cheese is made in Roquefort, France, where a special committee samples the cheese before it starts its journey to the United States.

Kings and conquerors, warriors and writers throughout 2,000 years of history have proven that Roquefort is the "king of cheeses."

When you are ready to eat your Roquefort, be sure to let it stand at room temperature for 30 or 40 minutes so that it will soften and regain its full flavor. Neither Roquefort nor any other cheese tastes at its best when cold.

Here are four good Roquefort dressings.

ROQUEFORT DRESSING

6 ounces Roquefort cheese
2 cups mayonnaise
½ cup onion, ground
2 hard-boiled eggs, chopped fine
¼ cup sugar
1 ounce vinegar
1 cup tomato catsup
1 teaspoon paprika

Pour all ingredients into mixing bowl and beat with electric mixer at high speed for 3 minutes. Refrigerate.

ROQUEFORT CREAM DRESSING

1 3-ounce package cream cheese
¼ pound Roquefort cheese
½ pint whipping cream
1 cup French dressing
½ cup mayonnaise

Mix together and serve on chilled lettuce wedges.

ROQUEFORT WINE DRESSING

¾ cup olive oil
2 tablespoons wine vinegar
3 tablespoons cream

½ clove garlic
¼-inch slice of onion
3-ounce package of Roquefort cheese
1 teaspoon salt
½ teaspoon pepper
Dash cayenne

Put all the ingredients into a blender in the order given. Blend for ½ minute. If you like a lumpy dressing, blend half the cheese, mash the rest, and add it later. If you do not use a blender, beat the oil, vinegar, salt and pepper in a bowl until thoroughly blended. Mince the garlic fine and use 1 tablespoon of grated onion. Mash the cheese with this, adding the cream. Then combine the two mixtures and beat hard. This dressing may be kept on hand in refrigerator. It solidifies as it chills, but softens readily at room temperature.
Yield: about 1¾ cups.

SOUR CREAM ROQUEFORT DRESSING

Combine 1 cup sour cream, 1 cup mayonnaise, 1 2-ounce wedge of Roquefort (or to taste), 2 teaspoons lemon juice, 1 teaspoon horseradish sauce, a few drops Worcestershire sauce, a dash of Tabasco sauce, and 2 tablespoons sherry.

SOUR CREAM DRESSING

1 cup mayonnaise
1 small clove of garlic
4 tablespoons chives (chopped)
4 tablespoons chopped parsley
1 tablespoon tarragon vinegar
1 tablespoon lemon juice
½ cup thick sour cream
½ teaspoon salt
Dash of pepper

Combine all ingredients. Mix well. Chill. Serve on greens, sea food, or fruit.

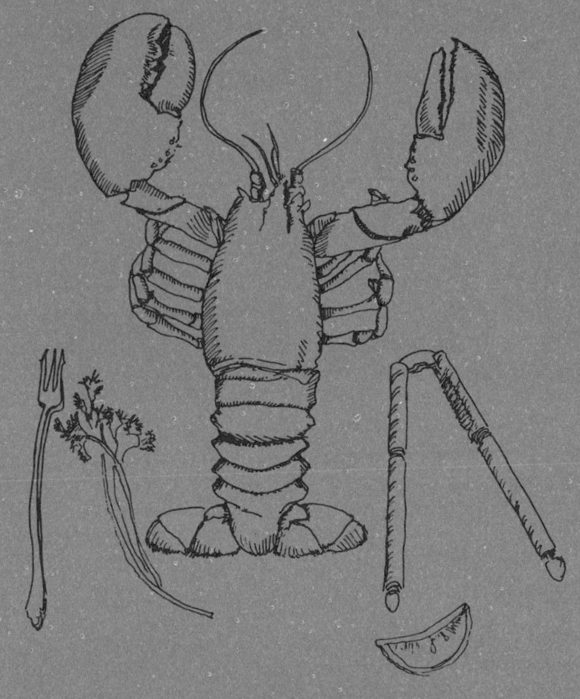

Only the game fish swims upstream
—John Trotwood Moore

Poultry, Game, and Fish

The appeal of the truly good things to eat knows no boundary of race, creed, or country. These are the universal pleasures of the gourmet. May your pleasures be enhanced with the use of the following recipes for poultry, game, and fish.

Always a favorite when served at Kellogg Center, Michigan State University. Excellent for luncheon.

CHICKEN LOAF

- 3 *eggs*
- 1 *cup milk*
- ½ *cup chicken broth, heated*
- 1 *teaspoon finely chopped onion*
- ¾ *teaspoon salt*
- ½ *teaspoon paprika*
- 2 *cups diced cooked chicken*
- ¾ *cup bread crumbs*

Beat eggs, add milk, chicken broth, onion, seasonings, chicken, and bread crumbs. Mix well. Pour mixture into greased loaf pan 9½ x 5¼ x 2¾. Set in pan of hot water. Bake in moderate oven (350 degrees) 45 to 50 minutes, or until done.

Invert loaf onto hot platter. Serve with almond mushroom sauce. 6-8 *servings.*

Almond Mushroom Sauce:

4 tablespoons butter
1 tablespoon chopped onion
1 cup chopped fresh mushrooms
4 tablespoons flour
½ teaspoon salt
Dash of pepper
2 cups chicken stock
2 teaspoons lemon juice
½ cup chopped toasted almonds

Melt butter, add mushrooms, and onion. Sauté, then add flour and blend well. Add salt and pepper, and chicken stock. Cook until thick and smooth. Add lemon juice and almonds. Serve over baked chicken loaf.

PERFECT FRIED CHICKEN

¾ cup enriched flour
1 tablespoon salt
1 tablespoon paprika
¼ teaspoon pepper
1 2½-to-3-pound ready-to-cook frying chicken, disjointed
Fat

Combine flour and seasonings in paper or plastic bag; add 2 or 3 pieces of chicken at a time and shake. Place on rack to let coating dry. Heat fat (¼ inch deep in skillet) till it will sizzle a drop of water. Brown meaty pieces first: then slip in others. Don't crowd (use two skillets, if needed). Brown one side slowly; turn (use tongs so as not to pierce). When lightly browned, 15 to 20 minutes, reduce heat; cover. (If cover isn't tight, add 1 tablespoon water.) Cook until tender, 30 to 40 minutes. Uncover last 10 minutes to crisp.

Note: For extra crustiness, add ½ cup fine dry bread crumbs to flour for coating.

Makes 4 servings.

SAVORY BROILED CHICKEN

2-to-2½-pound ready-to-cook broiler-fryer, cut up
½ cup cooking oil
3 tablespoons vinegar
¼ teaspoon dry mustard
½ teaspoon salt
¼ teaspoon paprika
½ clove garlic, minced

Place chicken in shallow baking pan. Combine remaining ingredients to make a marinade. Pour over chicken. Let stand in refrigerator at least 1 hour; turn chicken once. Remove from marinade. Place skin-side down on broiler rack. Put in preheated broiler 4 to 5 inches from heat. Broil 12 minutes, basting often with marinade. Turn; broil 15 minutes or until tender, continuing to baste.
Makes 4 servings.

Unusual but delicious.

CHICKEN PUFF

⅓ cup flour
2 teaspoon salt
1½ teaspoons ground sage
¼ teaspoon pepper
2-pound frying chicken cut into pieces

Batter:

1 cup sifted flour
1 teaspoon baking powder
1 teaspoon salt
⅓ cup instant non-fat milk
3 eggs, beaten
1½ cups water
¼ cup melted butter or margarine

Turn on oven and set at 400° (hot). Mix flour, salt, sage, and pepper in heavy paper bag. Coat chicken with flour mixture in bag, 2 or 3 pieces at a time. Brown on all sides in ¼-inch hot fat in skillet over medium heat. Place chicken pieces skin-side up in a well greased 11 x 7 x 2 baking dish.

Batter: Sift flour, baking powder, salt and non-fat dry milk together in a 2-quart bowl. Combine in a 1-quart bowl eggs, water, and melted butter. Add to dry ingredients; beat with fork until smooth. Pour batter over chicken. Bake 35-40 minutes or until top is nicely browned. Serve immediately.
Makes 4 servings.

CHICKEN SAVORIES

Combine 1 16-ounce can (1 cup) diced cooked chicken, 2 tablespoons mayonnaise, 2 tablespoons commercial sour cream, 1 tablespoon chopped chutney, and ½ teaspoon curry powder.

Make crisscross cuts in the tops of 12 small brown-and-serve dinner rolls. Gently spread rolls apart and spoon in about 1 teaspoon of the chicken mixture. Place on a flat baking sheet. Bake in a moderately hot oven (400°) 10 to 12 minutes, until brown. An equal amount of lobster, tuna, or shrimp may be substituted for the chicken. All ingredients for these snacks may be kept on hand ready to use.
Makes 12.

Delicate chicken livers served with rosemary and sour cream make a delectable dish — — even served by Rosemary herself.

CHICKEN LIVERS IN SOUR CREAM

¼ cup chicken fat
2 teaspoons Kitchen Bouquet
½ cup thinly sliced onion
1 pound chicken livers
1½ teaspoons salt
¼ teaspoon pepper
⅛ teaspoon rosemary
1 can (6 ounces) sliced broiled mushrooms
1 tablespoon cornstarch
1 cup thick sour cream
Cooked rice or noodles

Heat fat in large frying pan. Add Kitchen Bouquet and onions. Cook over moderate heat about 5 minutes, stirring frequently. Add chicken livers and sprinkle with salt, pepper, and rosemary. Cook, stirring occasionally, until the livers are well browned, about 15 minutes. Drain mushrooms, reserving broth. Combine cornstarch and mushroom broth and add to livers, stirring constantly until thickened. Add mushrooms and sour cream, stirring until smoothly blended. Cover and simmer over low heat until thoroughly hot, about 15 minutes. Serve immediately over rice or noodles.
Makes 4 servings.

CHICKEN PARMESAN

½ cup grated Parmesan cheese
3 broiler-fryer chicken breasts, split
Fat for browning
1 clove garlic, finely minced
3 tablespoons flour
1¾ cups chicken broth
½ cup sherry wine
1 4-ounce can mushroom stems and pieces
1 teaspoon salt
¼ teaspoon pepper
1 8-ounce package spaghetti

Rub cheese on chicken. Brown slowly in medium fat. Remove chicken, save fat. Add garlic. Cook until soft. Blend in flour, add broth, sherry, mushroom liquid, salt and pepper.

Add chicken to sauce, cover and cook until chicken is tender—30 to 60 minutes. Serve on spaghetti.

BROILED CHICKEN HALVES

Select broiler halves, wash and dry. Place skin-side down on broiler rack. Brush generously with a mixture of melted butter, salad oil, lemon juice, and sprinkle with rosemary leaves. Place rack 6 to 8 inches below broiler unit. After 20 minutes turn pieces over and brush with butter mixture. Broil about 20 minutes longer or until fork-tender. The rosemary leaves give these broiled chicken pieces a very delicious and different flavor. A sprinkle of paprika will give the chicken pieces a nice color, too!

CHICKEN BREAST VÉRONIQUE

Split 3 chicken breasts in half, take out bones. Salt and pepper and dredge through flour. Sauté in equal quantities of butter and oil. Place in flat casserole.

Swirl the saucepan with a cup of sherry wine, reduce heat, and add ½ cup of good brown sauce. Reduce heat again and add 1 can #2 muscatel grapes. Pour over chicken and serve.

Brown Sauce:

- 2 *tablespoons butter or meat drippings*
- 1 *tablespoon minced onion*
- 1 *tablespoon minced carrot*
- ½ *bay leaf*
- 2 *tablespoons flour*
- 1 *cup meat stock*
- *Salt and pepper*

Melt the butter or drippings; add onion, carrot, and bay leaf and cook over low heat until butter is brown. Stir in flour and cook until bubbly. Add stock and cook until thick and smooth. Strain and season.

The connoisseur of foods selected this one!

HAWAIIAN STUFFED CHICKEN

- 2 *1½-pound whole broilers*
- 2 *teaspoons salt*
- ½ *teaspoon pepper*
- 4 *slices white bread, trimmed*
- 1 *cup light cream*
- ¼ *pound ground beef*
- ½ *pound ground veal*
- 4 *tablespoons minced onion*
- 3 *tablespoons soy sauce*
- ½ *teaspoon powdered ginger*
- ¾ *cup diced water chestnuts*

2 tablespoons salad oil
1 cup pineapple juice
2 tablespoons honey
½ cup sesame seeds

Wash and dry the chickens. Sprinkle with the salt and pepper.

Soak the bread in the cream; press out the liquid and mash the bread. Mix together the beef, veal, onion, soy sauce, ginger, water chestnuts, and bread. Stuff the broilers and close the openings with skewers, thread, or aluminum foil.

Oil a shallow baking pan and roast chickens in a 400° oven 20 minutes. Mix the pineapple juice and honey and pour over the chicken. Reduce the heat to 350° and roast 35 minutes longer, basting frequently. Sprinkle the sesame seeds on the chicken and roast in a 450° oven 5 minutes, or until browned. Cut each chicken in half and serve with sautéed pineapple.
Serves 4.

Easy, tasty, and rewarding.

BAKED PUNGENT BROILERS

2 1½-pound broilers
½ cup soy sauce
½ cup honey
¼ teaspoon pepper
1 teaspoon ground ginger
2 tablespoons sesame seeds
1 cup chicken broth

Wash, dry, and quarter the broilers. Mix together the soy sauce, honey, pepper, ginger, and sesame seeds. Let the broilers stand 1 hour in the mixture, turning them to coat well.

Arrange the chicken in a shallow greased baking dish. Mix the broth with the soy mixture and pour over the chicken.

Bake in a 350° oven 40 minutes, or until tender and browned, basting frequently.
Serves 4.

The curry adds the glamour touch!

TAHITIAN CHICKEN CURRY

1 3½-pound frying chicken, cut up
4 tablespoons butter
¾ cup minced onion
2 tablespoons flour
1 cup chicken broth
1½ teaspoons salt
¼ teaspoon white pepper
2 tablespoons cognac
1 cup heavy cream
1 tablespoon curry powder

Wash and dry the chicken; brown in the butter with the onion. Sprinkle with flour and stir in the broth, salt, and pepper. Cover and cook over low heat 1 hour, or until tender. Warm the cognac; set it aflame and pour over chicken. Shake the pan until flame dies. Transfer the chicken to a serving dish and keep it warm.

Stir the cream and curry powder into the sauce. Cook over high heat 5 minutes. Pour over the chicken.
Serves 4.

No more ugly duckling.

ROAST DUCK À L'ORANGE

One 5-pound duck
1 teaspoon salt
¼ teaspoon pepper
⅛ teaspoon marjoram
⅛ teaspoon thyme
2 tablespoons olive oil
1 to 2 oranges, peeled and sliced
1 cup dry white wine
4 sprigs parsley
1 bay leaf
¼ clove of garlic, crushed

Garnish:

2 *oranges, peeled and cut in sections*
1 *cup sugar*
1 *cup water*

Gravy:

Grated rind and juice of one orange
2 *tablespoons flour*
1 *cup chicken bouillon*

Rinse duck with cold water. Wipe with damp cloth. Mix salt, pepper, marjoram, and thyme and rub duck inside and out with mixture. Brush with olive oil. Fill with orange slices and truss. Roast duck in white wine with herbs and garlic, first in very hot oven, 450°, 10 minutes. Reduce heat to moderate, 350°, and cook for one hour, basting every 10 minutes with wine in pan. Remove excess fat now and then.

Prepare garnish: Boil orange sections for 5 minutes in syrup.

Arrange on platter around duck. To pan drippings add orange rind and thicken with flour. Stir in stock gradually. When boiling, add orange juice. Season, strain, and serve. *4 servings.*

SESAME FRIED CHICKEN

1 *young frying chicken (cut up for frying)*
1 *egg, beaten*
½ *cup milk*
1 *cup flour*
1 *teaspoon baking powder*
2 *teaspoons salt*
2 *teaspoons paprika*
¼ *teaspoon pepper*
¼ *cup chopped nuts*
2 *tablespoons sesame seeds*
½ *cup butter (¼ pound)*

Dip chicken pieces into egg and milk mixture, then into a mixture of flour, baking powder, salt, paprika, pepper, nuts, and sesame seeds. Melt butter in a shallow baking pan in a hot oven (400°).

Remove baking pan from oven. As pieces of floured chicken are placed in pan, turn to coat with butter, then bake skin-side down in a single layer. Bake in a hot oven (400°) for 30 minutes. Turn chicken. Bake another 30 minutes, or until tender. If chicken cannot be served at once, reduce oven heat and brush chicken with more melted butter.

CRISPY FRIED CHICKEN

Roll potato chips fine. Melt one stick butter in saucepan. Add ¼ teaspoon ground marjoram, thyme, garlic salt, salt, pepper, and Lawry's salt. Dip pieces of chicken breasts, legs, and thighs into seasoned butter and then into potato chip crumbs. Coat chicken pieces well with crumbs. Place on cookie sheet, skin-side up. Bake one hour in 450° oven. Be sure you add plenty of seasonings to the butter.

Regardless of the company, chicken enlivens the dinner, whether baked, broiled, roasted, sautéed, or barbecued. Thanks to the delicate flavor of chicken, the versatile bird combines agreeably with a wide variety of other ingredients.

ROLLED CHICKEN BREASTS WITH DRESSING

3 *broiler-fryer breasts*
3 *slices country ham*
½ *teaspoon salt*
¼ *teaspoon pepper*
½ *cup (¼ pound) butter or margarine, melted*
¾ *cup chopped celery*
½ *cup chopped onion*
3 *cups toasted bread cubes*
½ *cup chopped water chestnuts*
Paprika

Remove bones from chicken breasts and season with salt and pepper. Flatten out chicken breasts and place a slice of ham on each breast side where bone has been removed. Cook celery and onions in two tablespoons butter or margarine until tender, but not brown.

Combine bread cubes, celery, onion, water chestnuts, and two tablespoons additional melted butter or margarine. Toss together lightly and place over ham and chicken breasts. Roll up and tie with cord. Brush with remaining melted butter. Place in shallow baking pan and bake for one hour in a 350° (moderate) oven, or until chicken is fork-tender. Sprinkle with paprika.
Makes 3 servings.

The chicken is cooked in the sauce. Delicious and different. Scatter a few toasted almonds on top.

CHICKEN IN ORANGE SAUCE

3 *broiler-fryer chickens, cut in serving pieces*
2½ *teaspoons salt, divided*
½ *cup butter or margarine*
6 *tablespoons flour*
6 *tablespoons sugar*
½ *teaspoon dry mustard*
1 *teaspoon cinnamon*
¼ *teaspoon ginger*
3 *cups orange juice*
1 *whole orange*

Sprinkle chicken with 1½ teaspoons of the salt. Brown in butter in skillet; remove. Add flour, spices, and remaining 1 teaspoon salt to drippings in skillet; stir to a smooth paste. Gradually add orange juice. Cook, stirring constantly, until mixture comes to a boil. Add chicken; cover; simmer over low heat until chicken is almost tender, about 30 minutes. While chicken is cooking, peel orange in circular

motion removing the rind. Cut rind with scissors into thin slivers. Cover with water and bring to boil; simmer 10 minutes; drain and discard water. Cut membrane from orange; cut out sections. Sprinkle orange rind slivers over chicken; add orange sections; cover, cook 10 minutes longer. Remove chicken to serving platter; spoon sauce over chicken.
Yield: 12 servings.

Chicken Almondine . . . Brunswick . . . Creole . . . Delaware. . . . Don't let the name throw you. Here we recommend Chicken Breasts Romano where the grapes add the flair.

CHICKEN BREASTS ROMANO

4 *chicken breasts*
¼ *cup flour*
1 *teaspoon salt*
¼ *teaspoon pepper*
4 *tablespoons butter or margarine*
½ *teaspoon garlic salt*
½ *cup chopped onion*
1 *pound mushrooms, small button-type*
½ *cup Parmeggiano cheese*
2 *tablespoons chopped parsley*
1 *cup sherry wine*
¼ *pound white grapes, stemmed*

Remove skin and bone from chicken breasts and cut each crosswise, making 8 pieces. Combine flour, salt, and pepper. Coat chicken well with flour mixture. Melt butter or margarine in electric fry-pan. Brown each breast lightly on each side (15 minutes each). Remove to a warm platter and cover with aluminum foil. Lower heat and cook onions in butter remaining in skillet until tender but not brown; then add remaining ingredients except grapes. Cook over medium heat for 10 minutes. Add grapes and cook 10 more minutes. Pour sauce over chicken and garnish with extra grapes.
Serves 4.

Longtime favorite of mine.

OVEN-FRIED CHICKEN WITH BUTTER HONEY SAUCE

1 tender frying chicken, cut up for frying
1 cup flour
2 teaspoons salt
¼ teaspoon pepper
2 teaspoons paprika
¾ cup butter (1½ sticks)
¼ cup honey
¼ cup lemon juice

Dip chicken pieces into mixture of flour, salt, pepper, and paprika. Melt ½ cup (1 stick) butter in a shallow baking pan in a hot oven (400°), remove pan from oven. Arrange chicken in single layer in pan, turning to coat with butter. Bake skin-side down in a hot oven (400°) 30 minutes. Turn chicken.

Pour over chicken a butter-honey sauce made by melting (½ stick) butter in a saucepan and adding honey and lemon juice. Bake another 30 minutes or until fork-tender. Spoon sauce over chicken during last 15 minutes of baking.
Yield: 4 servings.

CORNISH HEN CASSEROLE

4 Cornish hens
⅓ cup butter or margarine
½ teaspoon salt
½ teaspoon onion or garlic salt
¼ teaspoon black pepper
4 tablespoons chopped parsley
1 cup wine (white)
3 firm tomatoes, peeled and diced
6 scallions, chopped
1 cup sour cream

Select medium-sized birds weighing about one to one and one-half pounds each. If frozen, thaw before cooking. Remove giblets and boil until tender in water to cover. Mix soft butter or margarine with seasonings; spread birds with mixture. Mash cooked livers with the chopped parsley and place a generous spoonful of mixture in the cavity of each bird. Place birds in a shallow casserole and roast in a hot oven (400°) 35 minutes. Reduce heat to moderate, 350°, pouring white wine over birds and continue to cook until tender, 30-35 minutes, basting once or twice with juice in pan. Add tomatoes and scallions, cook 10 minutes. Just before ready to serve, blend sour cream into pan gravy and heat through. Serve at once, a bird per portion. *Makes 4 generous servings.*

Your bird is in the bag. An excellent way to roast turkey, capon, and even ham.

TURKEY ROASTED IN A PAPER BAG

Prepare and stuff your turkey the usual way. Try placing a half or whole orange in the neck cavity. The orange will give the meat of your turkey a wonderful flavor. Brush well with at least one stick melted butter. Place bird very carefully inside regular, brown paper bag (head first). Fill Pyrex baking cup half full of water and place *inside paper bag,* being careful to place it beside turkey legs so it will stand upright. Fold edges of bag together and place in shallow roasting pan and roast in low oven – I usually roast my turkey at about 325°. Sometimes I will preheat my oven to 350° and allow the turkey to roast for about ten minutes or so, then reduce to 325°. Never hotter! This is a wonderful way to roast a turkey – requires absolutely no basting and when finished roasting is a beautiful golden brown. To make gravy, tear bag down the center, lift turkey into serving platter. Pour drippings from bag into roasting pan and make gravy the usual way. I make gravy in the roasting pan. In doing it this way, you retain all the goodness of the turkey drippings in your gravy.

TURKEY DIVAN

Cook turkey, or chicken, and slice rather thin. Cook broccoli. Make supreme sauce. In a buttered casserole dish, place a layer of cooked broccoli, a layer of sliced turkey (light or dark meat). Place in layers until you have used all of the turkey and broccoli; pour supreme sauce over top. Place whole button mushrooms and extra Parmesan cheese on top and bake in moderate oven until the mixture is heated through (35 to 40 minutes).

Supreme Sauce:

3 tablespoons butter
3 tablespoons flour
¼ teaspoon salt
Pinch of nutmeg
1½ cups milk (I use part cream)
1 egg yolk
3 to 4 tablespoons Parmesan cheese
3 tablespoons sherry

Melt butter, add flour, stirring briskly. Blend in milk or cream and sherry. Add 1 beaten egg yolk and pinch of nutmeg. If too thick, add more top cream.

Today the game that our forefathers took for granted has become the gourmet's choice for special and festive occasions. Whether you have a hunter in the family who keeps you supplied with game or whether you buy it at the local butcher's, game offers a rare treat.

You have to be "game" to try these.

HASENPFEFFER

2 2-pound rabbits
¾ cup cider vinegar
1½ cups beer
½ cup grated onion
1 tablespoon mixed pickling spice
2 teaspoons salt
¼ teaspoon pepper
½ cup flour
4 tablespoons butter
1 cup thinly sliced onions
1 tablespoon sugar

Have the rabbit cut in serving pieces. Wash and soak the meat in salted water 1 hour. Drain.

In a bowl (not metal) combine the vinegar, beer, grated onion, pickling spice, salt, and pepper. Mix well and add the rabbit. Let marinate 36-48 hours. Remove the rabbit and dry with paper towels. Strain the marinade and reserve. Roll the meat in the flour.

Melt the butter in a casserole or deep skillet; brown the rabbit and sliced onions. Pour off the fat and add 1½ cups marinade and the sugar. Cover and cook over low heat 1½ hours, or until the rabbit is tender. Add more marinade if needed. Delicious with dumplings. *Serves 6-8.*

STUFFED GROUSE

3 tablespoons butter
2 cups finely shredded cabbage
2 cups thinly sliced onions
3 tablespoons dry bread crumbs
3 teaspoons salt
¾ teaspoon freshly ground black pepper
2 1½-pound grouse
4 slices bacon

Melt the butter in a skillet; sauté the cabbage and onions 10 minutes without browning. Stir in the bread crumbs, 1 teaspoon salt, and ¼ teaspoon pepper.

Clean, wash, and dry the grouse; season with the remaining salt and pepper. Stuff with the cabbage mixture, closing the opening with skewers, thread, or aluminum foil. Arrange in a shallow baking pan, breast side up. Place 2 slices of bacon on each. Roast in a 350° oven 40 minutes, or until tender. Baste frequently.

Serves 4.

PARTRIDGE À LA TITANIA

4 partridges
1 tablespoon salt
½ teaspoon freshly ground black pepper
5 tablespoons butter
1 tablespoon cornstarch
½ cup chicken broth
½ cup orange juice
2 tablespoons currant jelly
2 oranges, peeled and segmented
½ cup seedless grapes

Clean, wash, and dry the partridges; season with the salt and pepper. Melt the butter in a casserole and brown the birds on all sides. Mix the cornstarch and broth together and add to the casserole with the orange juice, jelly, oranges, and grapes. Cover tightly.

Bake in a 400° oven 25 minutes, or until tender. Taste for seasoning.

Serves 4.

CORN-CRISPED SALMON CROQUETTES

Salmon Mixture:

1-pound can salmon, drained and flaked
½ cup evaporated milk
½ cup corn-flake crumbs
¼ cup drained pickle relish
¼ cup finely cut celery
2 tablespoons finely cut onion

Dipping Mixture:

½ cup evaporated milk
1 cup corn-flake crumbs
1 teaspoon Accent

Mix salmon mixture and shape into 12 balls or cones. Dip in evaporated milk. Roll in mixture of corn-flake crumbs and Accent. Place in shallow baking pan lined with aluminum foil. Bake in 350° oven (moderate), about 35 minutes. Serve with tartar cream sauce.
Serves 4 to 6.

Tartar Cream Sauce:

⅔ cup evaporated milk
¼ cup mayonnaise or salad dressing
2 tablespoons drained pickle relish
1 tablespoon finely cut onion

Mix all ingredients in 1-quart saucepan. Stir over medium heat to thicken. Do not boil.
Makes about 1 cup.

FISH BAKED IN CREOLE SAUCE

1 *pound fish fillets (if frozen fish is used, thaw as directed on package)*
½ *medium onion, thinly sliced*
½ *medium green pepper, thinly sliced*
2 *tablespoons butter or margarine*
1 *can (10½ ounces) condensed tomato soup.*
1 *teaspoon vinegar*
Dash black pepper
Dash Tabasco

Arrange fillets in single layer in greased shallow baking dish (10″ x 6″ x 2″). In saucepan, cook onion and green pepper in butter until tender. Blend in soup, vinegar, pepper, and Tabasco. Pour sauce over fish. Bake in a moderate oven (375°) about 45 minutes, or until bubbling.
Makes 4 servings.

When the first settlers came to America, one of the most impressive indications of the richness of the new land was the great abundance, large size, and excellence of the oysters they found along the coastline and in the bays. Even the Indians loved them and consumed large quantities of this delicious shellfish.

DEVILED OYSTERS

4 *dozen oysters*
1 *bunch celery*
2 *large onions*
5 *hard-boiled eggs*
1 *cup bread crumbs*
1 *level tablespoon shortening*
2 *teaspoons flour (to be used for roux)*
Liquid of oysters for roux
Salt and pepper and onion tops
1 *tablespoon butter*
12 *cleaned oyster shells or ramekins*

Make a golden brown roux with the shortening and flour. Into this, mix the finely chopped celery, onion tops, and parsley. Cook slowly, then add oyster liquid. Let simmer slowly. Add the chopped oysters,

bread crumbs, five hard-boiled eggs chopped fine. Mix in a generous tablespoonful of butter. When ingredients are well mixed, fill the shells. Sprinkle with toasted bread crumbs. Bake in a quick oven about ten minutes.
Will serve from ten to twelve.

OPEN-FACE CRAB SUPREME

Spread 8 slices lightly toasted bread with tartar sauce. Combine 2 cups flaked crab meat, dash Tabasco sauce, 1 teaspoon Worcestershire sauce, ¼ teaspoon lemon juice, and ¼ cup mayonnaise. Spread bread evenly with crab mixture. Top with 1 cup grated American cheese. Place under broiler till cheese is melted. Cut 4 slices diagonally into halves. For each sandwich, serve whole slice in center with 2 halves on opposite sides.
Makes 4 sandwiches.

DEVILED CRABS

1 can crab meat
½ cup hot water
2 eggs
½ small onion
6 shells
1 tablespoon butter
1 tablespoon vinegar
Red pepper and salt to taste

Rub yolks of hard-boiled eggs smooth with tablespoon of butter. Season with salt and pepper. Add chopped onion and parsley. Add vinegar and chopped whites of eggs. Scald crab meat with ½ cup boiling water, and add egg mixture. Put in shells. Cover with buttered cracker crumbs and brown. Serve garnished with sliced lemon and sprigs of parsley.
Makes 6 servings.

CRAB-MEAT CHEESEBURGER

1 package (1 pound) frozen crab meat
½ cup chopped green pepper
½ cup mayonnaise
2 teaspoons lemon juice
2 teaspoons prepared mustard
½ teaspoon grated onion
2 teaspoons pickle relish
½ teaspoon salt
⅛ teaspoon pepper
8 hamburger buns
⅓ cup butter or margarine
¾ cup (6 ounces) grated natural Cheddar cheese

Let crab meat thaw overnight in the refrigerator. When ready to use, drain crab meat, pick over (for tiny shell bits), and dice. Mix with green pepper. Combine mayonnaise, lemon juice, mustard, onion, relish, salt, and pepper; fold into the crab mixture. Split buns and toast very lightly under broiler. Butter the cut sides, then place top halves of buns in slow oven to keep warm. Spread bottom half of each roll with a scant one-fourth cup of crab mixture. Then sprinkle each with a heaping tablespoon grated Cheddar. Broil slowly, five inches from source of heat, until cheese melts and is slightly browned. Cover with bun tops and serve. For a delicious supper, surround each burger with potato chips, sliced tomatoes, lettuce, and a sprig of water cress.
Serves 8.

CRAB RAREBIT

4-ounce can mushroom stems and pieces
2 tablespoons butter or margarine
¼ cup flour
4 to 5 drops Tabasco sauce
¼ cup chili sauce
1 cup evaporated milk
1 cup grated process cheese (¼ pound)
6½-ounce can crab meat, flaked
⅓ cup sliced stuffed olives

Drain and save liquid from mushrooms. Add enough water to make ½ cup of liquid. Melt butter or margarine in a 2-quart saucepan. Stir in flour until smooth. Gradually stir in mushroom liquid, Tabasco sauce, chili sauce, evaporated milk, and grated cheese. Cook and stir over low heat until cheese melts and mixture begins to thicken. Stir in mushrooms, crab meat, and olives. Heat until steaming, but do not boil. Serve in patty shells or over rice.
Serves 4 to 6.

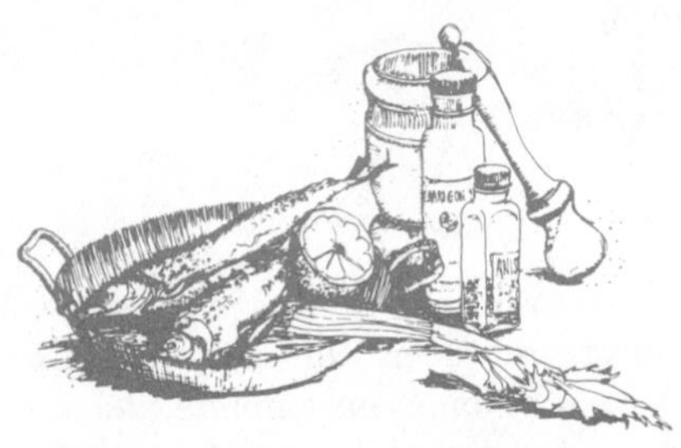

Viewers who have visited Tampa, Florida, know the Columbia Restaurant as a glamorous setting for its delicious food. It's the largest Spanish restaurant in North America, with six marble- and tile-decorated dining rooms. A Cuban family by the name of Hernandez founded it in 1905, and few Tampa visitors fail to eat there. As you can guess, the restaurant was named for the discoverer of America. The picture of Columbus' three tiny sailing vessels plays a large part in the decor. Shrimp is a top favorite with Columbia patrons, and the restaurant prepares a great variety of shrimp dishes daily. One of the most popular is Shrimp Sarapico.

SHRIMP SARAPICO

You prepare each serving individually. Make a paste of 2 ounces creamed cheese, 2 ounces Roquefort cheese, and 1 chopped pimiento. Spread the paste on a piece of aluminum foil about 12 inches square. Place ¼ pound cleaned shrimp on the paste, and on the shrimp put two slices of lemon. Close the aluminum bag by pinching the top together, and bake 30 minutes in a 400° oven. To serve the Shrimp Sarapico, place each hot bag on a plate and let each guest open his own. The aroma's as fine as the taste!

Here is a specialty of our good friend, Howard Finch. Howard and I have made Shrimps à la Finch on Copper Kettle many times. It has always been enthusiastically received by the Channel 6 viewers. The last time we made it, we received approximately 3,000 requests for the recipe.

Howard has great talent, and is also one of the great epicures.

SHRIMPS A LA FINCH

This recipe is excellent to use for buffets and late suppers. Heat chafing dish or electric skillet to about 375°. Place one stick (¼ pound) butter in bottom. When butter is melted and hot (watch butter to prevent excessive browning), add 12 to 16 uncooked, shelled, and deveined medium-sized shrimp which have been dredged in flour. Sauté floured shrimp in melted butter until done: 10 to 15 minutes, depending upon size of shrimps. Remove shrimps from butter, add 2 to 2½ tablespoons of cooking sherry, juice of 1½ lemons, and a dash of salt and pepper to remaining butter in skillet. Stir quickly to make smooth sauce. Pour sauce over shrimps and sprinkle dried parsley flakes or chopped fresh parsley over shrimps and sauce. Very delicious!

The only "just" way to prepare whitefish.

BROILED WHITEFISH

Brush melted butter on cookie sheet or broiler pan. Place whitefish fillets on sheet, skin-side down. Brush with melted butter and lemon juice, sprinkle with salt, pepper, and paprika. Broil only until fish flakes easily. Do not overcook fish; 4 to 8 minutes is sufficient.

SWEET AND SOUR SHRIMP

1 *20-ounce package breaded fantail shrimp*
¾ *cup brown sugar*
3 *tablespoons cornstarch*
1 *teaspoon salt*
⅓ *cup vinegar*
1 *cup water*
1 *green pepper, thinly sliced*
¾ *cup drained pineapple tidbits*

In a saucepan mix the brown sugar, cornstarch, and salt. Add the vinegar and water. Cook over low heat, stirring until thick and smooth. Cover and cook 12 minutes longer. Add green pepper and pineapple. Heat through. Deep-fry breaded shrimp according to package directions. Drain on unglazed paper. Add shrimp to sauce. Heat thoroughly and serve on hot fluffy rice.
Serves 6 people.

Better make lots of these – good!

SHRIMP TOAST

1 *pound cooked shrimp*
¼ *cup minced scallions or onions*
4 *tablespoons mayonnaise*
2 *hard-cooked eggs, chopped*
¼ *teaspoon freshly ground black pepper*
6 *slices buttered toast, quartered*
½ *cup grated Parmesan cheese*

Chop or grind the shrimp and blend in the scallions, mayonnaise, eggs, and pepper. Taste for seasoning and heap on the toast squares. Sprinkle with the cheese.

Broil in a 350° oven for about 5 minutes, or until delicately browned.

An elegant main dish from a can of tuna. For a luncheon, serve with buttered broccoli or asparagus, and a fruit-plate salad.

COMPANY CREAMED TUNA

2 *tablespoons finely chopped onion*
3 *tablespoons butter or margarine*
3 *tablespoons flour*
¼ *teaspoon salt*
Dash pepper
1¼ *cups milk*
½ *cup dairy sour cream*
1 *6½-, 7-, or 9¼-ounce can tuna, drained*
3 *tablespoons cooking sherry*

2 tablespoons chopped parsley
Toasted slivered almonds
Puff-pastry shells

Cook onion in butter until tender but not brown. Blend in flour, salt, and pepper. Add milk; cook and stir until mixture thickens. Stir in sour cream. Add tuna, cooking sherry, and parsley. Heat through. Sprinkle with toasted almonds, if desired. Serve in pastry shells or spooned over toast points.
Makes 4 servings.

BAYOU STUFFED CRABS

1 *pound crab meat*
½ *cup minced onions*
½ *pound mushrooms, coarsely chopped*
3 *tablespoons butter*
2 *tablespoons flour*
1½ *teaspoons salt*
¼ *teaspoon freshly ground black pepper*
1 *cup heavy cream*
1 *tablespoon chili sauce*
1 *tablespoon finely chopped chives or scallions*
⅛ *teaspoon Tabasco*
1 *tablespoon lemon juice*
2 *egg whites, stiffly beaten*
⅓ *cup bread crumbs*
2 *tablespoons melted butter*

Use 6 crab shells or ramekins for baking. Pick over the crab meat, removing any tendons. Preheat oven to 400°.

Sauté onions and mushrooms in the butter 5 minutes, stirring occasionally. Sprinkle with the flour, salt, and pepper. Stir constantly until flour turns golden brown. Gradually add the cream, stirring constantly to the boiling point. Blend in the chili sauce, chives, Tabasco sauce, lemon juice, and crab meat. Cook over low heat 5 minutes. Taste for seasoning. Cool 10 minutes.

Fold in the egg whites. Turn into the shells or ramekins. Sprinkle with the bread crumbs and melted butter.

Bake 10 minutes or until delicately browned.

A love with the first mouthful.

OYSTERS ROCKEFELLER

36 open oysters on half shell
6 tablespoons butter
6 tablespoons minced raw spinach
3 tablespoons minced onion
3 tablespoons minced parsley
3 tablespoons minced celery
5 tablespoons bread crumbs
½ teaspoon thyme
½ teaspoon salt
½ teaspoon mustard powder
Tabasco sauce
3 ounces red wine

Melt butter in saucepan. Add all the ingredients except oysters. Sauté, stirring constantly for 15 minutes. Press through food mill. Cool. Put spoonful of this sauce on each oyster, garnish with pimiento strip. Broil oysters until sauce begins to brown.

SHRIMP BOATS

6 medium baking potatoes
1½ small cans shrimp, chopped
½ cup butter
1 cup grated sharp cheese
Dash cayenne pepper
½ teaspoon salt
⅛ cup grated onion
¾ cup light cream
Paprika

Bake potatoes at 325° until well done, then cut potatoes in half lengthwise, and scoop out inside. Put in mixing bowl and add butter, cream, salt, pepper, onion, cheese, and whip. Mix chopped shrimp with potato. Refill the potato shells and sprinkle paprika over the "boat tops." Reheat in 450° oven about 15 minutes. May be made ahead of time and frozen in foil. To serve, unwrap and reheat in hot oven about 30 minutes.

BATTER-FRIED SEA FOOD AND ONION RINGS

1½ cups pancake mix
2 eggs, slightly beaten
1¼ cups milk
1 pound raw shrimp, shelled, and deveined
1 pound scallops
1 large onion, sliced
About 1 cup milk

Combine pancake mix, eggs, and milk; beat together about 2 minutes. For shrimp and scallops have sea food well drained, dip into batter, drain off excess and fry in deep, hot fat (375°) 3-5 minutes, or until golden brown. Drain on absorbent paper. Soak onion slices, separated into rings, in milk for 15 minutes; drain, dip into batter and proceed as above.
Serves 4-6.

POACHED WHITEFISH WITH EGG SAUCE

Cold water (amount depending on size of pan and fish)
1 or 2 pieces of thyme (not too much)
½ lemon – sliced
1 raw carrot
2 or 3 peppercorns
½ tablespoon salt
½ teaspoon wine or vinegar
(If you boned the fish, put the bones in also.)
1 whitefish – about 4 pounds

Have a shallow oval-shaped pan 1½ to 2 inches deep with a loose perforated inner bottom on which to lay the fish. Combine above ingredients in pan and bring to a boil.

Put fish in hot liquid and reduce the flame. Let simmer slowly until fish is done (time depends on kind and size of fish), about 18 minutes. Do not overcook!

Egg Sauce:

1 cup cream
2 hard-boiled eggs – chopped fine
Salt and pepper to taste
3 teaspoons of water in which fish was cooked

Mix together and bring to a boil. Remove from heat.
Add to sauce: 1 egg yolk, well beaten, and chopped parsley.
Serves 4.

A cool, summery dish – with out-of-this-world flavor.

POACHED SALMON WITH SAUCE VERTE

1 tablespoon salad oil
4 salmon steaks (1½ pounds)
2 tablespoons lemon juice
6 peppercorns
Sprig parsley
2 slices onion
½ cup sauce verte

Rub the salad oil around skillet or flat baking dish. Lay in the salmon steaks. Add lemon juice and enough water to just cover; add seasonings. Cover and poach on top of the stove for 15 to 20 minutes or in a moderate oven, 325°, for the same time – until the salmon is just cooked. Allow to cool in the liquid, as this will keep it moist. Drain well, remove the skin. Arrange on a serving platter, spoon over the sauce verte, and serve with cucumber salad.
Makes 6 servings.

Sauce Verte:

Green onion tops or chives
½ cup chopped green pepper
¼ cup chopped parsley
¼ cup chopped spinach
1 tablespoon lemon juice
1 cup special mayonnaise

Whirl all ingredients except mayonnaise in a blender, or chop together very fine. Add to mayonnaise. Chill before using.
Makes 1¼ cups.

Special Mayonnaise:

1 cup salad oil
¼ cup non-fat milk solids
⅔ cup hot water
1½ teaspoons salt
½ teaspoon mustard
½ teaspoon pepper
2 tablespoons lemon juice
3 tablespoons vinegar
Paprika

Combine thoroughly in blender, or beat in small bowl, at low speed, oil, the non-fat milk solids, and water. Add salt, mustard, pepper. Mix lemon juice and vinegar, add slowly, still beating at low speed. Scrape down sides, and mix at high speed 30 seconds. Color with paprika.

You cannot prevent the birds of sorrow from flying over you, but don't let them build any nests in your hair — Chinese Proverb

Meats

When you are wondering what to plan for dinner, chances are you think first of what the meat shall be. In the following pages you will come across recipes for elegant prime rib of beef served with English Yorkshire pudding, sauerbraten and gingersnap gravy, Swedish and Japanese meat balls, Hawaiian stuffed chicken, and Beef Bordelaise. The ever humble stuffed cabbage rolls along with several other recipes use America's number-one favorite meat—ground beef. Here they are, and we're mighty proud of them, too!

FILLED GREEN PEPPERS WITH SOUR CREAM

6 *medium-sized green peppers*
1 *quart tomato juice*
1 *pint commercially prepared sour cream*
1 *tablespoon flour*
1½ *pounds ground pork*
1 *medium-sized onion, chopped fine*
2 *eggs*
¾ *cup rice*
Salt to taste
Pepper to taste

Mix pork, onion, eggs, rice, salt, and pepper together. Cut the tops off the peppers and clean well. Fill peppers with meat mixture and put in a deep kettle. If some of the meat mixture is left over, make into meat balls and put in same kettle. Pour tomato juice over peppers and let cook 1½ or 2 hours or until meat is done. About ½ hour before serving, in a bowl put sour cream with 1 tablespoon flour and mix. Then take a ladle of hot tomato juice mixture from kettle and put into bowl of sour cream, mix well, and return mixture to kettle, pouring over the green peppers. Let simmer ½ hour or until ready to serve.

SUKIYAKI

One of the most colorful and beautiful parties held at the Country House was the Japanese dinner party, given by Mr. and Mrs. Harold F. Gross for their host of friends. They imported lovely lanterns and intriguing favors; and there were beautiful Japanese girls swathed in gorgeous kimonos. The party menu was complete even to shrimp tempura with its alluring sauce and Japanese sake served warm.

Mrs. Shigemi Honma, East Lansing, was our official consultant for this party. We used her recipe for the sukiyaki. Here it is:

- 1 *to 2 pounds tender beef, pork, or chicken (beef and pork sliced very thin)*
- 2 *to 3 large bulb onions, halved and sliced ⅛" thick*
- 2 *bunches green onions including tender portions of green tops, cut in 2" lengths*
- 2 *bamboo shoots, halved and sliced thin, available in large or small cans*
- 6 *stalks celery, sliced thin on bias*
- 6 *dried mushrooms (soaked in water and sliced very thin) or fresh mushrooms sliced*
- *If available, tofu or fresh bean cake cut up in 1" cubes, about 1 cup (also available in can)*
- ½ *to ¾ cup stock (juice from meat bone or vegetables)*
- ¼ *cup shoyu (preferably Japanese soy sauce)*
- ½ *teaspoon ajinomoto (similar to Accent)*
- 1 *tablespoon sugar (white or light brown)*
- ⅛ *teaspoon grated ginger root or sprinkle of ground ginger*
- 1 *clove garlic grated*

Optional:

- 2 *green peppers cut in 1" squares or*
- 6 *large leaves of fresh spinach cut up*
- 2 *cups bean thread or long rice (a gelatinous vermicelli) soaked in hot water to soften*

Raw fresh ingredients are prepared ahead of time and arranged attractively in groups on a platter, also some of the canned ingredients if not available fresh. The cooking is done preferably at table on hot plate with deep-frying pan or electric frying pan. It can also be done on range.

In pan, heat about 2 tablespoons cooking oil or suet from meat and sauté ½ of meat slices for about 30 seconds, stirring and turning over. Add 5 or 6 tablespoons stock and stir for another 30 seconds. Then move meat to one side of pan. Add half of onions, not green part. Place meat on top of onions and put half of celery where meat was. Now spread cooked meat over it. This keeps meat from over-cooking and puts vegetables which need most cooking where the heat is greatest. Over meat, place other ingredients, half of each in layers or groups with tofu last since they need least cooking. Sprinkle sugar and add more stock; add ginger, garlic, and shoyu. Cook gently for 5 to 10 minutes. Sauce in pan can be spooned for testing. If too salty, add sugar and stock. If flat, add shoyu and stock. If sauce boils down, add more stock. If you use long rice, watch it as it absorbs juice quickly and needs more stock and shoyu.* Vegetables should not be overcooked. Repeat for further servings so it will be hot.

With this you have hot rice in bowl, sukiyaki in small plate; if preferred, raw egg beaten in small container and hot sukiyaki placed in egg mixture and eaten together with hot rice.

*Add this at end so it does not take up all the juice while dish is cooking.

Serves 4-6.

SIMPLY SPECIAL

Toasted blanched slivered almonds sprinkled over hot creamed dried beef served in toast cups turn a simple main dish into something special.

Casseroles need no watching, and they need no pampering either. Toss a salad, heat rolls, and complete a meal for company as well as family affairs. So quick and easy.

STUFFED CABBAGE ROLLS

1 *pound ground beef*
½ *pound ground pork*
3 *cups cooked rice*
1 *teaspoon sugar*
1 *onion, chopped*
1 *can (10½ ounces) cream-of-tomato soup*
1 *teaspoon salt*
¼ *teaspoon pepper*
1 *head cabbage*
1 *tablespoon butter or margarine*
1 *cup hot water*

Combine the beef, pork, rice, sugar, onion, salt, and pepper. Wilt the cabbage leaves by placing in boiling water for a few minutes. Place about ½ cup of the mixture in each cabbage leaf and roll up securely. Place rolls in a baking pan. Dot each with butter. Combine water and soup and pour over the rolls. Bake in moderate oven (350°) one hour.
Yields 6 servings.

This will make you think you're dining in the shadow of the Eiffel Tower.

BEEF BORDELAISE

1 *pound round steak (or flank steak) sliced thin and pounded, or cubed*
1 *hard-cooked egg, chopped fine*
1 *small onion, sliced thin*
About 1 teaspoon salt and ¼ teaspoon pepper
Pinch of nutmeg on each piece of meat
About 2 tablespoons chopped parsley
1 *anchovy cut into small pieces, or a little anchovy paste (optional)*
2 *tablespoons fine-chopped suet or bacon (or small pieces of firm butter)*

Flour
¼ cup hot butter or other shortening
1 cup water or stock

Sprinkle egg, onion, salt, pepper, nutmeg, parsley, anchovy, and suet over pounded meat. Roll carefully and tightly. Hold rolls together with wood pins wherever necessary. Roll them in flour, and shake off loose flour. Brown well on all sides in butter or shortening over medium heat. Season with a little more salt and pepper. Place in a small heavy saucepan or skillet if preparing only 1 pound of meat. Add water or stock, cover tightly, and cook slowly at simmering point, turning them over several times, about 2 hours or until meat is tender when tested with a fork. When meat is done, pour off liquid, measure, and to each cup add about 1 tablespoon cornstarch combined with 2 tablespoons water. Cook until thick and smooth, and simmer about 5 minutes. Now add 1 tablespoon dry wine and about ¼ cup sliced sautéed mushrooms. Taste and season further, if necessary.
Serves 3.

How To Serve Beef Bordelaise. Brush meat with hot gravy; arrange it in center of large round platter. Place individual fruit or vegetable salads around meat, alternately with potato croquettes.

Potato Croquettes:

Wash 1 pound potatoes. If using boiling potatoes, cook with skins on in small amount of boiling water in a tightly covered pan. If using Idaho potatoes, peel them, and cut in uniform large pieces (about 2 inches). Cook 20 to 30 minutes or until soft. Drain well. Mash, and to 2 cups (more or less) add 1 very small beaten egg (only enough to hold ingredients together), 1 teaspoon salt, ⅛ teaspoon white or black pepper, 1 tablespoon (more or less) fresh parsley chopped fine, 1 tablespoon Italian grated cheese, ¼ teaspoon onion or garlic salt. Mix well, and let cool. Then divide into 8 uniform portions (about ¼ cupful each) and form oval croquettes. Roll in fine light bread crumbs, then into beaten egg combined with 1 tablespoon water, then into crumbs again. Let stand on wax paper in room temperature about 20 minutes, turning over several times. Shake off loose crumbs and deep fry at 375° several minutes until golden brown and crisp. May be kept warm in a very, very low oven on cake rack about 15 minutes. Or croquettes may be fried to a lighter color in advance and refried at 350° for several minutes just before serving. Or they may be completely fried and reheated on cake rack with drip pan underneath in a 350° oven about 12 to 15 minutes, but no longer or they are likely to crack. They may be pan-fried in about ⅛ inch of hot shortening several minutes on each side, instead of being fried in deep fat.

Different, but good!

GOULASH WITH SAUERKRAUT

¼ *cup flour*
2 *teaspoons salt*
½ *teaspoon pepper*
2 *pounds veal cut in 2-inch cubes*
2 *pounds pork cut in 2-inch cubes*
3 *tablespoons fat or oil*
3 *onions, sliced*
1 *tablespoon paprika*
2 *pounds sauerkraut*
1 *tablespoon caraway seeds*
½ *pint sour cream*

Mix together the flour, salt, and pepper; toss the veal and pork in the mixture.

Heat the fat in a heavy saucepan or Dutch oven; brown the meat and onions; then sprinkle with the paprika. Cover and cook over low heat 30 minutes. Watch carefully to prevent burning.

Wash the sauerkraut under running water and drain. Add to the meat along with the caraway seeds and a little water if pan is dry. Cover again and cook over low heat 1½ hours, adding a little water, if necessary. Stir in the sour cream and taste for seasoning. Heat but do not let boil.
Serves 6-8.

So English you could swear you hear the chimes of Big Ben.

LONDON BROIL WITH ROQUEFORT CHEESE

1 *2-pound flank steak*
1 *cup salad oil*
2 *tablespoons wine vinegar*
1 *teaspoon soy sauce*
⅛ *teaspoon thyme*
1 *clove garlic, minced*
¼ *pound Roquefort cheese*
2 *tablespoons heavy cream*

Buy a very tender flank steak and have it scored. In a bowl, combine the oil, vinegar, soy sauce, thyme, and garlic. Marinate the steak 12 to 24 hours or overnight, basting and turning it a few times.

Remove from the marinade and place on a greased rack. Broil 2 inches from the heat 5 minutes. Turn and broil other side 4 minutes, then spread with the Roquefort mashed with the cream. Broil 2 minutes longer. Cut diagonally across the grain into very thin slices.

Serves 4-6.

Made the proper way . . . with beef cubes.

CHILI CON CARNE

2 *cups dried red beans*
3 *tablespoons olive oil*
1 *cup chopped onions*
3 *cloves garlic, minced*
2 *pounds beef in ¼-inch cubes*
3 *tablespoons chili powder*
1 *29-ounce can tomatoes*
2 *teaspoons salt*

Wash the beans and soak in water to cover overnight. Drain and add fresh water to cover. Bring to a boil and cook 2 hours, or until almost tender. Drain. (Four cups canned kidney beans may be substituted.)

Heat the oil in a saucepan; brown the onions, garlic, and beef. Add the chili powder, tomatoes, and salt. Cover and cook over low heat 1½ hours. Add the beans and cook 45 minutes longer. Taste for seasoning. Serve with mounds of rice, shredded lettuce, minced onions, and tortillas or crackers.
Serves 6-8.

It's a gourmet's delight prepared this way.

VEAL ROULADES

6 slices veal cutlet (about 2 pounds)
6 slices Swiss cheese
6 paper-thin slices prosciutto or smoked ham
½ cup flour
1½ teaspoons salt
½ teaspoon pepper
2 eggs, beaten
¾ cup dry bread crumbs
6 tablespoons butter

Pound the veal very thin; cut the cheese a little smaller than the meat. Place over the veal and cover with the ham. Roll up and fasten with toothpicks or thread, if necessary. Roll in the flour seasoned with salt and pepper. Dip in the eggs and then in the bread crumbs.

Melt the butter in a skillet and sauté the rolls over low heat until browned on all sides.
Serves 6.

PEPPER STEAK

2 pounds beef tenderloin, sliced in 1-inch strips
2 tablespoons butter
2 tablespoons chopped onion
2 medium-sized green peppers, cut in 1-inch squares
2 medium-sized tomatoes, cut in 1-inch squares
1 pint fresh mushrooms, sliced
Salt and pepper to taste
½ cup sherry wine

Melt butter, sauté onions until transparent, add meat, cook until tender, add green peppers, and sliced mushrooms. Cook for 5 minutes; add sherry wine and tomatoes. Cook for an additional 5 minutes or until done. If needed, thicken sauce with 1 tablespoon cornstarch and water mixture. Add salt and pepper to taste. Can be served with rice pilau or steamed rice.
Serves 6-8.

Pilau:

Wash 1 pound rice in several waters, soak it for 2 hours, and drain thoroughly. Melt ½ pound butter in a deep, heavy pan. Add 1 large onion and 1 clove garlic, both finely chopped, and cook until the onion is soft but not at all colored. Add the rice and cook, stirring occasionally, for 5 to 6 minutes. The pilau may be seasoned to taste with clove, cinnamon, or allspice, or all three. Add salt to taste and, if desired, ½ teaspoon saffron steeped in ½ cup warm water for ½ hour. Add boiling water to cover the rice by 1½ inches. Cover the pan tightly and cook over very slow heat until the water has been absorbed and the rice is tender. Mix in ¼ cup sultana raisins and 2 tablespoons blanched almonds, both tossed in a little butter. Serve the rice on a shallow platter or in a shallow bowl.

Thanks to John Suurs and Archie Tarpoff for

SHISH KEBAB

Cut into 1½-inch squares lean pieces of 1 pound veal and 1 pound lamb that have been marinated the night before in:

2 *tablespoons of olive oil*
1 *onion cut in squares*
2 *cloves of garlic (chopped)*
1 *teaspoon of oregano*
2 *bay leaves*
½ *cup sherry wine for veal*
½ *cup burgandy wine for lamb*

Alternate 2 pieces of lamb, 1 square of onion, 1 square of green pepper and 2 pieces veal on skewer.
Broil slowly on charcoal fire until done. Serve with broiled tomato and wild rice.
Serves 4.

Wild Rice:

1 cup wild rice
3 cups cold water or stock
¼ cup butter
2 tablespoons onion
1 tablespoon chopped pepper
¼ cup chopped celery
Salt, pepper, pinch of sage

Sauté onions, pepper, celery in butter. Add washed wild rice, stock, salt, pepper, and sage. Bring to a boil. Let simmer for 30 minutes, stirring occasionally.

BAYONNE STYLE HAM SOUS LA CENDRE

Soak 10- to 12-pound ham in cold water 4 hours. Place in fresh cold water (enough to cover) and boil slowly until pelvic bone is easy to remove. No spices are necessary.

Remove skin and all black parts from the outside. Sprinkle the ham with powdered sugar mixed with a very little ground cloves. Place under salamander until golden brown. Prepare a paste with rye flour and water, roll same as for pie crust, large enough to enclose the ham. Place ham on center of dough, fat down.

Draw ends together and seal well to retain all flavor. Turn ham over without tearing paste, and place on a pan. Brush with egg yolk, and make a small slit on top.

Place ham in the oven until crust is golden brown. Through slit pour a wine glass of Port or Malaga wine and close slit with a piece of paste.

Let it cook again until crust is hard and dry, about 20 minutes in 350° oven.

Serve very hot with spinach *à l'anglaise,* and a large fresh baked potato.

Different – you may just like it!

CALF'S LIVER IN WINE

8 slices liver, cut ⅛-inch thick (be sure it's skinned)
Flour, salt and pepper
3 tablespoons butter
1 cup consommé
1 cup sherry or Burgundy
1 cup water
2 tablespoons chopped parsley
1 teaspoon salt

Dust liver lightly with seasoned flour and sauté in butter until light brown. Pour over the rest of the ingredients, cover and bake at 350° for 45 minutes. Serve on a thin slice of broiled ham or Canadian bacon.
Makes 4 servings.

VEAL-AND-PORK RAGOÛT

1½ pounds boneless stewing veal
1½ pounds boneless pork shoulder
Flour
3 tablespoons butter or margarine
1 onion, chopped
1 cup hot water
½ cup dry red wine
1 tablespoon salt
½ teaspoon pepper
2 sprigs parsley
½ bay leaf
1 clove garlic, minced
Veal bone, if desired
4 to 6 small potatoes, peeled and quartered
½ pound mushrooms, halved
1 can (1 pound) onions, drained
1 can (1 pound) tiny carrots, drained
½ cup frozen peas

Cut meat in 1½" cubes. Dredge with flour and brown on all sides in butter. Add onion and brown a few minutes longer. Add next 8

ingredients. Bake, covered, in moderate oven (350°) 1½ hours. Remove bone and add potatoes, mushrooms, and enough water to almost cover. Return to oven; cook 40 minutes. Add onions, carrots, and peas; cook 20 minutes.
Serves 6 to 8.

Beef tenderloin is probably one of the most popular and elegant dinner party entrees served. Don't overroast this expensive, delicious cut of meat. High-brow, middle-brow, and low-brow ask for it.

WHOLE ROASTED BEEF TENDERLOIN

Have a large fillet of beef trimmed and larded, ready for roasting. Rub with a cut clove of garlic, garlic salt, seasoned pepper, and salad oil. Pour ½ cup red wine over meat. Allow to stand in marinade for at least 3 hours. Place in a rather shallow roasting pan. Brush with additional oil or butter. Sprinkle with salt, cracked pepper. Roast fillet at 450° for about 20 to 30 minutes. Do not overroast. Remember the meat is hot inside and will continue to cook an additional 5 to 10 minutes after you remove it from the oven.

Make thickened gravy from the drippings in the pan or serve the *au jus* over meat.

Remove meat to serving platter, attractive when left whole. Arrange nests of vegetables, or fresh stalks of cooked broccoli or asparagus around base of meat. Garnish top of meat with large sautéed carved mushrooms.

Sautéed Mushrooms:

Purchase large firm stuffing mushrooms. Wash them well, dry on towels. Slice off stems. Sauté mushrooms with rounded side down first in hot butter over moderate heat. Turn and brown second side.

Cover skillet if mushrooms are very large and thick, and steam about 3 or 4 minutes, but DO NOT overcook. Mushrooms can be prepared in advance and kept covered. Reheat gently. Arrange mushrooms on tenderloin and brush with a little of the gravy.

If you crave the delicious and unusual for a black-tie dinner, you must try Beef Tenderloin Wellington. Simply "c'est magnifique," as the French would say. Members of the Walnut Hills Country Club, Lansing, enjoy fine cuisine carefully prepared under supervision of our friend, Chef Emil Niederer. Thanks, Emil. The Beef Tenderloin Wellington is great!

BEEF TENDERLOIN WELLINGTON

6 six-ounce tenderloins
6 strips bacon
¾ pound chopped veal
1 cup chopped mushrooms
1 tablespoon chopped onions
Salt and pepper to taste
Thyme or oregano to taste
2 ounces sherry or brandy
2 pounds puff paste dough
1 egg

Season, then sauté your tenderloin in hot oil to seal the meat (5 to 6 seconds on both sides). Wrap with bacon.

Sauté onions and mushrooms in 1 tablespoon of butter. Add to veal and mix it well with brandy and seasoning.

Cover your tenderloin on both sides with this (you can call it stuffing) so it looks like a sandwich.

Roll puff paste dough out to thickness of ⅛ inch. Cut first circle 1 inch larger than your meat, second circle 1½ inch larger, which will make the cover. Place your tenderloin on the first one. Brush with egg, so the cover will stick to it. Close it with fork on the edges of the circle. To garnish, you can cut stripes or stars out of the remaining dough. Brush again with egg and place it in hot oven of 375° for 35 minutes if you like it medium done. To test this, stick a knitting needle into the tenderloin and hold the needle between your lips, the temperature should be slightly higher than your lips. This is best served with green vegetables and salad.

Puff Pastry Dough:

5 *pounds pastry flour*
4 *pounds butter*
3 *ounces salt*
1 *quart water*

1. Take flour and 2 pounds butter and mix it with your hands very fine as for pie dough. Add salt and water and finish dough. Roll and form into oblong shape, 10″ x 20″ x 1″ thick. Leave it for 15 minutes.
2. Fold remaining 2 pounds butter into middle of the dough in small flakes. (Butter must be soft.)
Fold dough toward the middle. Leave it for 15 minutes.
3. Roll dough out to its original 10″ x 20″ x 1″ and fold it again.
4. Repeat operation after 20 minutes. Roll out lengthwise. Fold toward the middle.
Dough will be ready to use after 20 minutes. Use 2 pounds of this pastry for Beef Wellington. Remainder may be refrigerated for future use.

FRENCH POT ROAST (Boeuf À La Mode)

4 *pounds beef rump roast*
¼ *pound fat, salt pork*
1 *clove garlic*
Salt and pepper
3 *tablespoons bacon drippings*
2 *onions, sliced*
2 *carrots, sliced*
1 *celery stalk, diced*
1 *sprig parsley, chopped*
1 *bay leaf*
1 *sprig of thyme*
2 *cups dry red wine*
1 *cup tomato purée*
Hot water, if needed

Cut deep gashes in roast. Lard with pork, cut in thin strips. Rub roast with garlic, pepper, and salt. Brown onion in drippings. Remove and brown roast on all sides. Add vegetables and brown. Add parsley, bay leaf, thyme, wine, and tomato purée. Bake, covered, for 3 to 4

hours or until meat is tender. Add small amount of hot water during baking, if needed. Remove meat to hot platter. Keep warm. Strain liquid and serve as gravy. (If desired, the gravy can be thickened.)
8 servings.

TOURNEDOS HUNTER'S STYLE
(Tournedos Chasseur)

Tournedos are 1½" thick slices of beef cut from the narrow part of the tenderloin. This choice cut of beef is expertly fried or grilled and served in hundreds of different ways with some delicious sauce or other accompaniments from which the dish derives its name, i.e., Tournedos Lucullus, Tournedos Rossini, Tournedos Soubise.

1½ *pounds beef tenderloin*
2 *tablespoons butter*
Salt, white pepper

Chasseur Sauce:

1 *cup sliced mushrooms, fresh*
2 *tablespoons butter*
1 *tablespoon finely chopped shallots*
1 *cup dry white wine*
1½ *cups stock, beef or chicken*
1 *cup tomato sauce*
½ *tablespoon cornstarch*
1 *tablespoon chopped parsley*

Sauce Chasseur: Fry mushrooms in butter about 5 minutes. Add shallots, white wine, stock, and tomato sauce. Simmer 5 minutes. Stir in cornstarch, mixed with small amount of stock or water. Add parsley. Season tournedos and sauté in butter about 2 minutes on each side. Remove to hot platter and pour Sauce Chasseur over.
4 servings.

Wouldn't the chicken be surprised!

MOCK CHICKEN

2 *pounds round steak in very thin slices*

Filling:

1 tablespoon butter
¼ cup chopped onion
½ cup bread-crumbs
¾ cup water
¾ cup cream
¼ pound ground veal
¼ pound ground pork
2 eggs
¼ teaspoon nutmeg
1½ teaspoons salt
¼ teaspoon pepper

To braise:

3 tablespoons butter
2 cups stock
½ cup minced celery
1 green pepper, chopped
½ cup sliced mushrooms

Garnish:

Chopped parsley
Lemon slices

Cut steak into serving portions, about 4″ x 2″. Season with salt and pepper. Melt 1 tablespoon butter in skillet and fry onion golden brown. Soak bread-crumbs in water and cream. Add ground veal and pork, onion, eggs, nutmeg, salt and pepper. Mix well. Cover steak slices with filling. Roll them together and tie a string around each to make them keep their shape or fasten with toothpicks. Heat butter in heavy saucepan and brown rolls all around. Add stock, celery, pepper, and cook in slow oven, 300°, 1½ hours. Add mushrooms and cook another 30 minutes. Serve garnished with chopped parsley and lemon slices.
6-8 servings.

BEEF BURGUNDY (Boeuf Bourguignonne)

4 pounds beef tenderloin, cut in 1½" cubes
Salt and white pepper
½ cup cooking oil
3 tablespoons brandy
1 clove garlic, crushed
2 teaspoons Worcestershire sauce
¼ teaspoon thyme
2 bay leaves
2 cups meat broth
1 cup dry red wine
5 tablespoons chopped onion
½ cup sliced mushrooms
3 tablespoons butter
½ cup tomato paste
3 tablespoons chopped parsley

Sprinkle meat with salt and pepper and brown in oil on all sides. Pour brandy over and set it aflame. Add garlic and seasonings. Stir in broth and wine, a little at a time. Cover skillet tightly and simmer for ¾ hour or until meat is almost tender. Fry onion and mushrooms in butter until soft and golden, about 5 minutes. Add with tomato paste to casserole and simmer for another ¼ hour. Sprinkle with chopped parsley.
8 servings.

VEAL CHOPS SUPREME

Inch-thick veal chops with deep pockets
Cube into ¼-inch cubes equal part of cold boiled ham and Swiss cheese.

Stuff chops with this mixture. Place in roaster and cover with cream-of-mushroom soup. Cover and bake in slow oven until tender. Season according to your own taste.

SIMPLE HOME COOKING

There's a lot of homey goodness in this easy Dutch-oven meal. Braise shortribs in bacon drippings until well browned. Add canned stewed tomatoes, chopped green pepper, and a tablespoon or more of instant minced onion. Cover and simmer about 2 hours until tender, adding tomato juice for liquid as needed. About 10 minutes before end of cooking time, add uncooked egg noodles and cook until tender. If you are an herb fancier, a touch of sweet basil and thyme enhances the flavor.

A meal in one dish with cheese and tomato for flavor.

POTATO-FILLED MEAT ROLL

½ cup soft bread crumbs
½ cup milk
1½ pounds ground beef chuck
½ clove garlic, finely chopped
2 eggs, slightly beaten
2 tablespoons chopped parsley
1½ teaspoons salt
¼ teaspoon pepper
3 tablespoons grated Romano cheese
¼ cup fine dry bread crumbs
2 cups dry hot mashed potatoes
1 cup shredded processed American cheese
1 8-ounce can tomato sauce

Soak crumbs in milk until soft; break up with a fork. Combine with meat, garlic, eggs, parsley, salt, pepper, and cheese. Sprinkle the dry bread crumbs on a sheet of waxed paper. Pat out meat mixture on the paper into a rectangle 8″ by 12″. Spread with a layer of mashed potato and a layer of cheese. Lift edge of waxed paper and carefully roll up mixture like a jelly roll. Press ends to seal. Place in a shallow baking pan. Bake in a moderate oven (350°) about 50 minutes. After 30 minutes pour tomato sauce over meat and continue to bake.
Makes 6 servings.

Americans have a fixed notion that veal is indigestible. In France it is regarded as the proper food for invalids.

Veal presents a paradox. It comes from a young animal. It is the flesh of calves from three to twelve weeks old. The whiteness of veal is considered a sign of good quality.

"The gentleman who pays the rent," as the Irish saying goes, may use every part of the veal in cooking.

Almond Veal Imperial requires little effort to make and is a delightful party dish. Try it, won't you?

ALMOND VEAL IMPERIAL

2 pounds veal, cut in 1-inch cubes
2 tablespoons lard or drippings
1 teaspoon salt
2 cups chopped celery
¼ cup chopped green pepper
½ cup chopped onion
¼ cup pimento
1 can (4 ounces) mushroom stems and pieces
1 can (10½ ounces) mushroom soup
¼ cup soy sauce
½ cup water
1 package (8 ounces) noodles, cooked
1 cup dairy sour cream
½ cup sliced almonds

Brown veal in lard or drippings. Pour off drippings. Add salt, celery, green pepper, onion, pimento, mushrooms and liquid, mushroom soup, soy sauce, and water. Cover tightly and simmer 45 minutes or until tender. Combine noodles and sour cream with veal mixture. Place in a greased 2½-quart casserole and top with sliced almonds. Bake in a slow oven (325°) for 30 minutes.
Makes 6 to 8 servings.

JIM GROSS'S SUKIYAKI

My good friend and cohort, Jim Gross, says, "This is an Americanized version of a recipe I brought back from Japan. One of the first times it was served to those other than the immediate family was to a group of forty friends of my parents, Mr. and Mrs. Harold F. Gross. They had hired a Scottish caterer to prepare the meal, and while she was an excellent cook, she was far from happy about the prospect of preparing a meal other than one of her specialties. She was muttering something about the strange eating habits of the Orientals when the stove, probably sharing her sentiments, turned itself off and refused to run again.

"I started a Hibachi we used for a grill and managed to finish cooking the meal. However, not being sure of my talents with Hibachi cooking, I changed into an old comfortable, well-worn sweatshirt. Fortunately the guests did not see the substitute chef, or I fear we would have had an abundance of Sukiyaki left over.

"Despite the adverse conditions, the meal was a huge success; but to this day, I don't know whether this success was due to my culinary efforts of the evening, or the fashionable, 5th Avenue attire of the chef."

2 *tablespoons of salad oil*
5 *pounds of filet of beef (cut into small chunks, not chopped)*
3 *bunches of green onions*
4 *or* 5 *large stalks of celery*
1 *small can water chestnuts*
1 *large frying pan with suitable cover for steaming*
2 *pounds of bean sprouts*
2 *bouillon cubes in cup of water*
½ *cup of soy sauce*
Approximately 2 *tablespoons of sugar*

Cut onions and celery in strips about 2 inches long; keep separate. Mix the dissolved bouillon and soy sauce to make 1½ cups of liquid. Brown beef in the salad oil in large frying pan over medium heat. Add onion strips and allow to simmer for about 4 or 5 minutes. Add bouillon and soya sauce mixture and one tablespoon of sugar. Add cut celery and allow to steam for 2 minutes. Add water chestnuts and bean sprouts and the second tablespoon of sugar and allow to steam until hot.

Note: Vegetables should be steamed. *Do not* allow them to cook thoroughly. They must remain crisp.

This dish may be served over freshly steamed rice. However, I personally prefer the rice (either steamed or fried) served as a side dish.

Thanks, Jim, you're tops!

Many hands make light work and all hands are welcome in the preparation of egg rolls *(Chuen Guen)*—a favorite hors d'oeuvre when Michigan State University's Consumer Marketing Information specialists and guests get together. George and Marcella Stachwick, Mary Zehner, Grace Masuda, and Marie Ferree agree that egg rolls aren't really difficult to make, but all the chopping can be time-consuming and getting ninety wrappers to turn out "whole" is a combination of magic and a miracle.

CHUEN GUEN

Egg-Roll Wrappers:

2 *eggs*
2 *cups water*
½ *teaspoon salt*
1 *cup sifted flour*
2 *tablespoons cornstarch*

Beat the eggs. Add the rest of the ingredients and beat with a rotary beater until smooth (batter will be very thin). Heat a lightly greased 6-inch skillet over very low heat. Pour a scant 2 tablespoons of batter into the skillet. Tip and tilt the skillet so the batter spreads evenly in the skillet. Fry on one side only. Set aside as finished. Save about ¼ cup of batter to use for sealing the edges of the finished rolls.

This recipe makes about 30 wrappers. Repeat 3 times to make enough wrappers for the filling.

Egg-Roll Filling:

2 *cups lean cooked pork, cut into fine shreds*
1 *cup cooked shrimp, diced fine*
1 *cup bamboo shoots, drained and chopped fine*
1 *cup cooked mushrooms, diced fine*
1 *can bean sprouts, drained and chopped fine*
1 *can water chestnuts, diced fine*
1 *large onion, chopped fine*
1 *cup celery, chopped fine*
2 *tablespoons toasted sesame seeds*
1 *teaspoon mei jing (gourmet powder)*

Mix all the ingredients together thoroughly. Put a tablespoon of filling on the cooked side of each wrapper. Fold the ends in and roll up, sealing the roll with a bit of the reserve batter. Fry in deep fat until golden brown.

Cooked egg rolls may be wrapped in moisture-vapor-proof wrap and frozen until needed. To reheat, place frozen rolls on baking sheet and bake for 10 minutes in oven preheated to 475°.

Serve with sour plum sauce made by mixing 2 parts plum jam with 1 part vinegar.

Sauerkraut is an age-old food and did not originate in Germany, as is commonly believed. It dates back to the building of the Great Wall of China.

Originally the Tartars introduced the acid cabbage from the Orient into eastern Europe, and from there kraut went to Germany, Alsace-Lorraine, and France.

COUNTRY HOUSE SAUERKRAUT

Mrs. Charlotte Gross and I were planning the menu for one of the traditional, colorful and gay Football Parties when she said, "Let's have something different for one of our entrees this time." I said, "Great, but what would you suggest?" Her reply, "The sauerkraut dish with sour cream." Her suggestion paid great dividends. The guests raved about it, begged for the recipe, and departed satisfied when assured their morning mail would bring a copy of the recipe.

Be it sauerkraut with sour cream or beef Burgeoise, a Country House Football Party invitation is the symbol, the cachet, of a VIP life.

2 pounds lean fresh pork (cubed)
2 medium-sized minced onions
½ stick butter
1 teaspoon paprika
Salt and pepper to taste
1 quart sauerkraut
1½ to 2 cups sour cream

Brown onions in butter, add meat, partially cover with water, and simmer over low flame until tender.

Cook sauerkraut about one hour, drain, add to meat mixture. Fold in 1½ to 2 cups sour cream. Heat slowly. Do not boil or cream will separate.

Note: Mix a little flour with sour cream before folding into mixture. The flour prevents separation.

Serves 8.

This is good – you must try it!

BEEF SUPREME

2 tablespoons flour
1 teaspoon salt
⅛ teaspoon pepper
1½ pounds top round steak, cut into strips
¼ cup butter or margarine
1 cup sliced onions
¼ cup beef bouillon
1 (15½-ounce) can spaghetti sauce with mushrooms
½ cup thick sour cream

Mix flour, salt, pepper, and coat meat.

In a large aluminum skillet melt butter and cook onions until tender but not brown. Add meat and brown. Add bouillon and spaghetti sauce. Cover and cook over low heat 25 minutes. Remove from heat and stir in sour cream. Serve at once with cooked noodles or rice.

Makes 4 to 6 servings.

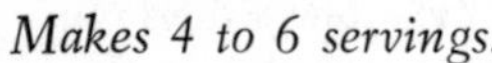

Chinese sweet and pungent pork.

NIW-GOO-YOK

4 green peppers
¾ cup oil
1½ teaspoons salt
1 small clove garlic, minced
2 eggs, beaten

Dash of pepper
1½ *pounds lean pork, cut in ½-inch cubes*
½ *cup chicken stock or canned consommé*
6 *slices canned pineapple cut in ½-inch pieces*
3 *tablespoons flour*

Wash peppers and remove stem and seeds, cut in strips ½ inch wide. Cook in boiling salted water until almost tender. Pour oil into heavy skillet and add 1 teaspoon of the salt and minced garlic. Combine eggs, flour, the remaining ½ teaspoon salt, and pepper, and add to the pork. Mix lightly until every piece of pork is coated. Separate pieces with fork, drain slightly, and drop one piece at a time into skillet. Cook over medium heat until brown on one side. Pour out all but about 1 tablespoon of the oil. Return to heat; add chicken stock, pineapple, and green pepper. Cover and simmer for about 20 minutes. Add the sweet-sour sauce and cook about 10 minutes longer or until juice thickens and ingredients are well blended. Serve immediately with hot boiled rice.

Sweet-Sour Sauce:

2½ *tablespoons cornstarch*
½ *cup vinegar*
3 *tablespoons lemon juice*
1 *tablespoon soy sauce*
½ *cup sugar*
1 *cup chicken stock*
2 *tablespoons water*
¼ *teaspoon salt*

Combine ingredients, mix until smooth, and pour over pork.

BARBECUED PORK CHOPS

8 *rib pork chops, cut 1 inch thick, floured*
¼ *cup shortening*
2 *tablespoons flour*
2 *tablespoons prepared mustard*
¼ *cup chopped onion*
½ *teaspoon ground cloves*
1 *teaspoon salt*
½ *teaspoon pepper*

2 tablespoons Worcestershire sauce
1 cup juice (peach or apple)
Bread-and-butter or sweet pickles
1 cup catsup

Dredge chops in flour. Brown in shortening. Pour off excess fat. Add the 2 tablespoons flour to mustard and make paste. Add remaining ingredients, blend well, and pour over chops. Cover and simmer for 1 hour.
8 servings.

The old stand-by.

BEST MEAT LOAF

1½ pounds ground beef
1 cup cracker crumbs
2 beaten eggs
1 8-ounce can (1 cup) seasoned tomato sauce
½ cup finely chopped onion
2 tablespoons chopped green pepper
1½ teaspoons salt
1 medium bay leaf, crushed
Dash thyme and marjoram
Chili sauce

Combine all ingredients except chili sauce; mix well. Shape mixture in a loaf in shallow baking dish. Score the loaf by pressing top with handle of wooden spoon. Fill the score marks with chili sauce. Bake in moderate oven (350°) 1 hour. Variation: Add ⅔ cup diced process sharp cheese to the meat-loaf mixture.
Serves 6-8.

MUSHROOM-STUFFED MEAT LOAF

¼ cup butter or margarine
1 pound mushrooms, sliced (leave 7 whole)
1 teaspoon lemon juice
1 minced medium onion
4 cups soft bread crumbs (fresh bread)
1 teaspoon salt

⅛ teaspoon pepper
¼ teaspoon dried thyme
¼ cup minced parsley
2 eggs
3 pounds ground chuck
1 tablespoon salt
⅛ teaspoon pepper
¼ cup milk
⅓ cup tomato catsup
1½ teaspoons dry mustard

Early in day: for stuffing, sauté in butter all but 7 small mushrooms with lemon juice and onion 3 minutes. Toss in bread crumbs and next 4 ingredients. Beat eggs; with fork, lightly mix in chuck, then next 5 ingredients. Pack half of chuck into 10" x 5" x 3" loaf pan; pack stuffing on top, then rest of chuck. Press 7 mushrooms into top. Refrigerate.

About 1 hour and 25 minutes before serving:

Start heating oven to 400°. Bake meat loaf 1 hour and 10 minutes. If desired, brush top with heated currant jelly. With 2 broad spatulas, lift onto platter.
Makes 8 servings.

Even meat loaf can be fashionable—in a pastry shell!

MEAT LOAF IN PASTRY SHELL

Combine 1 pound lean ground beef, 1 cup soft bread crumbs, ½ cup chopped onion, 1 teaspoon salt, dash pepper, 1 slightly beaten egg, ⅓ cup catsup, ⅓ cup milk, and 1 tablespoon prepared mustard. Arrange green-pepper rings and pimiento strips in design in bottom of 8¼ x 1¾-inch round baking dish; pat meat mixture into pan to ½ inch from edge. Prepare 1 stick pastry mixture according to package directions. Roll in 9-inch circle ⅛ inch thick. Place over meat, tucking edges down to cover meat completely. Gently press down top till pastry touches sides of pan; prick with fork. Bake in hot oven (400°) 40 minutes or till crust is lightly browned. Let stand few minutes; invert on platter. Garnish with parsley.
Makes 4 to 6 servings.

Company will like minute-steak rolls, with mushroom filling, green beans with almonds, Italian salad, pickled peppers, and apple pie with cheese.

MINUTE-STEAK ROLLS

6 *minute steaks*
1 3-*ounce can (⅔ cup) broiled chopped mushrooms*
1 *cup chopped parsley*
¾ *cup chopped onion*
1 *cup grated or shredded Parmesan cheese*
Salt and pepper
2 *tablespoons fat*
1 *can condensed consommé*
2 *tablespoons cornstarch*

Line up steaks ready to fill. Drain mushrooms, reserving the liquid. Sprinkle chopped mushrooms, parsley, onion, and cheese over steaks; season lightly with salt and pepper. Starting at narrow end, tightly roll up each steak; fasten with toothpicks. Brown steak rolls slowly in hot fat in skillet. Add consommé. Cover: simmer 30 minutes or till tender. Remove steaks to hot platter. Combine cornstarch and reserved mushroom liquid; stir into gravy in skillet; cook, stirring constantly, till mixture thickens. Spoon gravy over meat rolls and sprinkle with additional grated Parmesan cheese. Garnish platter with tomato wedges and celery leaves.
Makes 6 servings.

A must in spring, summer, fall, and winter.

OLD-TIME VEGETABLE STEW

It's the browning—long and lazy—that gives a stew the rich color and flavor men like. Heat 2 tablespoons fat in Dutch oven. Add 2 pounds beef chuck, cut in 1½-inch cubes, and brown on all sides. Keep turning the cubes (use tongs). Don't hurry— this should take about 20 minutes. Next, slice up a nice big onion and add along with a clove of garlic (on toothpick so you can retrieve it!), 4 cups boiling water, 1 tablespoon *each* salt and lemon juice, 1 teaspoon *each* sugar and Worcestershire sauce, ½ teaspoon *each* pepper and paprika, a bay leaf or two, and a dash of allspice or cloves.

Gentle cooking is what makes the meat tender, so cover and simmer (not boil), 2 hours. (Stir now and then to prevent sticking.) When meat is almost done, add the vegetables—6 carrots cut in quarters, 1 pound small white onions (and perhaps a few diced potatoes). For handsome look, cut each kind of vegetable in same-size pieces. Now simmer the stew 30 minutes longer or till everything in the kettle is tender. Discard bay leaf and garlic.

Gravy time. Pour ½ cup cold water into a shaker, then add ¼ cup flour; shake hard to blend. Remove pan from heat, push meat and vegetables to one side; stir in flour mixture. Cook and stir till gravy thickens and boils. Cook gently a few minutes. No lumps!

GOURMET HAM LOAF

1 pound ground veal
1 pound ground smoked ham
1 cup fine dry bread crumbs
½ teaspoon salt
¼ teaspoon pepper
3 tablespoons minced onion
3 tablespoons minced green pepper
2 eggs, beaten
¼ cup tomato catsup
¼ cup water
1 can (1¼ cups) condensed tomato soup

Combine ingredients in order given; mix thoroughly. Pack ham loaf lightly into a greased loaf pan. Bake in a moderate oven (350°) for 1 hour. Pour off juice, loosen edges, and invert on platter. Garnish if desired with green pepper or pimiento or sliced stuffed olives and sprigs of parsley. Serve with sauce below.

Tomato-Horseradish Sauce:

1¼ cups condensed tomato soup
2 tablespoons prepared horseradish
2 teaspoons prepared mustard
Dash of ground cloves
Black pepper to taste

Mix all ingredients well. Serve hot or cold with meats.
Makes about 1½ cups.

Ideal for buffets.

CHUTNEY-BASTED CANADIAN BACON

1½ to 2-pound center-cut Canadian bacon
2 tablespoons brown sugar
1 tablespoon frozen pineapple-juice concentrate
¼ teaspoon ground mustard
1 tablespoon chutney sauce
1 pint ginger ale

Score top of meat in diagonal crisscross pattern. Combine brown sugar, pineapple juice, mustard, and chutney sauce; spread over meat and let stand at room temperature two hours.

Place meat on rack in small roaster; pour ginger ale in pan and cover meat closely with aluminum foil. Roast at 375° for 30 minutes; remove foil and continue roasting 15 minutes longer.

WIENER SCHNITZEL

2 pounds veal, prepared for schnitzel
Lemon juice to cover meat
½ pound butter, melted
12 anchovy fillets, mashed
Pinch of paprika
2 whole eggs
8 tablespoons water
1 cup fine dry bread crumbs mixed with
¼ cup flour

Marinate the schnitzel cuts in lemon juice for 1 hour. Just before sautéing the schnitzel, prepare the sauce by melting the butter and adding the mashed anchovies and paprika. Keep hot. Beat the eggs lightly in a bowl. Add water and dip the schnitzel into the mixture. Dredge with mixed bread crumbs and flour and allow to stand for 15 to 20 minutes. In a good-sized skillet, melt additional butter and let it foam well. Reduce the heat. Add schnitzel and sauté 1 to 1½ minutes for both sides. The slices are done as soon as the coating turns a golden brown. Sprinkle lightly with lemon juice at once and pour the hot sauce over them. Serve immediately with quartered lemons on the side as a garnish. Capers may also be used.

Chops prepared this way are simple and easy to do. I have made them for years. Be sure you use our delicious Michigan apples.

STUFFED PORK CHOPS

Select double-thick pork chops, slash pocket on fat side. Place 5 or 6 slices of apples (skin removed) inside chop. Dredge in seasoned flour. (I use marjoram, thyme, paprika, salt, and pepper.) Brown lightly in frying pan containing approximately 3 tablespoons shortening. When chops are brown, place in baking dish, add ½ to ¾ cup top cream, cover, and bake approximately 45 minutes. These can be baked in frying pan.

The little "birds" will sing when prepared this way.

VEAL BIRDS WITH SAGE STUFFING

2 *veal round steaks, cut ½ inch thick*
4 *slices toasted bread*
2 *tablespoons bacon drippings*
1 *tablespoon grated onion*
¼ *teaspoon sage*
¼ *teaspoon nutmeg*
1 *teaspoon salt*
¼ *teaspoon pepper*
3 *tablespoons flour*
2 *tablespoons lard or drippings*
½ *cup water*

Cut veal into 6 pieces, approximately 3 x 4½ inches. Remove bone and pound veal. Make stuffing as follows: Crush bread. Add melted bacon drippings, onion, sage, and nutmeg. Add enough water so that mixture will hold together when squeezed between fingers. To make birds, spread mixture on center of each piece of veal. Roll and tie with string or fasten with wooden pick. Mix salt, pepper, and flour and roll veal birds in the mixture. Brown in lard or drippings. Add water, cover tightly, and simmer until meat is tender, about 45 minutes to 1 hour.
3 *to 4 servings.*

VEAL PAPRIKA

½ pound pork sausage
2 pounds boneless veal, cut in 1-inch cubes
3 tablespoons flour
⅓ cup chopped onion
¼ cup chopped green pepper
1½ teaspoons salt
1 teaspoon paprika
¾ cup water
1 cup dairy sour cream
3 cups cooked noodles
1 tablespoon butter or margarine
1 teaspoon poppy seeds

Brown sausage lightly. Remove from frying pan. Dredge veal with flour. Sprinkle any remaining flour over meat. Brown on all sides in sausage drippings.

Pour off drippings. Add sausage, onion, green pepper, salt, paprika, and water.

Cover tightly and simmer 1 hour and 15 minutes, or till meat is tender. Add sour cream and heat through. Mix together hot noodles, butter or margarine, and poppy seeds. Serve meat over noodles.
6 servings.

Cheers galore for spring-lamb pie, accompanied by poppy-seed crust.

LAMB PIE WITH POPPY-SEED CRUST

3 pounds lamb shoulder
⅓ cup fat
1 teaspoon salt
⅛ teaspoon pepper
⅓ cup flour
3 cups lamb broth
1 teaspoon Kitchen Bouquet
2 cups cooked green peas
1 cup cooked small white onions
½ recipe pastry
4 teaspoons poppy seeds
About 2 tablespoons water

Cook lamb until tender with 2 cups water and 2 teaspoons salt, about 1½ hours. Cool slightly in broth. Remove meat from bones, cutting in 1-inch cubes. Melt fat in saucepan and stir in salt, pepper, and flour. Pour fat from broth, and add water to make 3 cups broth. Stir broth into flour mixture. Cook, stirring constantly, until gravy thickens. Add Kitchen Bouquet, peas, onions, and cubed lamb. Pour into shallow greased 1½-quart baking dish. Place pastry mix in bowl and stir in poppy seeds. Add water according to directions. Roll out to fit top of baking dish, cutting vents to allow escape of steam. Bake in hot oven, 400°, until crust is done, about 25 minutes.
Makes 4 servings.

BARBECUED SPARERIBS

4 *pounds spareribs*
1 *cup sliced onions*
1 *cup tomato catsup*
½ *cup chili sauce*
2 *teaspoons salt*
1 *cup water*
3 *tablespoons Worcestershire sauce*
¼ *cup vinegar*
½ *cup brown sugar*
2 *teaspoons dry mustard*
1 *teaspoon paprika*
Juice of one-half lemon

Add Tabasco or cayenne pepper for hot sauce

Cut spareribs into serving pieces. Brown them in a baking pan over surface heat. Combine the remaining ingredients and pour over the ribs. Cover. Bake in moderate oven 350° for 1¾ hours. Spoon the sauce over the ribs two or three times during the baking. Bake uncovered 20 minutes.

You'll like the cheese.

LIVER AND BACON FROMAGE

1 *pound beef liver, sliced ½ inch thick*

Cook 4 slices of bacon until crisp. Remove and drain. Then mix together three tablespoons flour, ½ teaspoon salt, ⅛ teaspoon of garlic salt, and ⅛ teaspoon pepper. Dredge the liver in this seasoned flour and sprinkle any remaining flour over the liver. Brown the meat slowly on both sides in the bacon drippings. While the meat is browning, crumble the crisp bacon into bits and grate ¼ cup of American cheese. Then sprinkle the cheese over the meat and top with bacon. When cheese is slightly melted, remove the liver and serve.

The biscuit dumplings will surprise you.

SPICED BEEF WITH BISCUIT DUMPLINGS

3 to 4 pounds beef arm or blade pot roast
1 1-pound can (2 cups) tomatoes
¼ cup wine vinegar
¼ cup water
1 clove garlic, minced
6 whole cloves
½ teaspoon mixed pickling spice
1 teaspoon salt
¼ teaspoon pepper
1 package refrigerated biscuits
1 tablespoon snipped parsley

Trim excess fat from roast. Heat fat in Dutch oven or large skillet. When you have about 2 tablespoons melted fat, remove trimmings. Slowly brown meat on all sides in hot fat.

Add next 8 ingredients. Cover; cook slowly 2½ hours or until tender. Place biscuits on meat; sprinkle with parsley. Cover tightly and steam 15 minutes or till "dumplings" are done. Remove meat and dumplings to warm platter.

Gravy:

Skim excess fat from liquid. Add water to liquid to make 1½ cups. Blend 2 tablespoons flour and ¼ cup cold water to a smooth paste; gradually stir into liquid. Cook and stir till gravy thickens.
Makes 6 to 8 servings.

Don't gasp when you see brown sugar with the beef! It's delicious!

SWEET-SOUR POT ROAST

4 or 5 pounds boned pot roast
2 tablespoons shortening
½ cup sliced onion
1 cup vinegar
¾ cup brown sugar
¼ teaspoon nutmeg
½ teaspoon salt

Melt shortening in heavy kettle. Brown meat in melted fat. Remove meat. Add onions and cook until transparent. Return meat to kettle. Add remaining ingredients. Cover and simmer until meat is tender, 1½ to 2 hours. If gravy is desired, thicken broth. Use 1½ tablespoons flour for every cup of broth.
Yield: 8 to 10 servings.

Where there is patience and humility there is neither anger nor worry — St Francis

Pot roasts rate high on the totem pole.

ITALIAN BEEF POT ROAST

4 pounds boneless pot roast (chunk, round, or rump)
1 tablespoon olive oil
3 large onions, sliced
1 clove of garlic, minced
1½ teaspoons salt
½ teaspoon thyme
¼ teaspoon pepper
1 can (6 ounces) tomato paste
½ cup water

Brown meat on all sides in oil in Dutch oven or large heavy kettle; add remaining ingredients; cover tightly.

Simmer 2 to 2½ hours, or until meat is fork-tender (add a little water during cooking, if needed); remove meat to serving platter; keep hot.

Strain liquid through sieve, pressing onions through; let stand until fat rises to top; skim; measure liquid and return to kettle; heat to boiling.

For each 1 cup, blend 1 tablespoon flour with 1 tablespoon cold water during cooking, if needed); remove meat to serving platter; stirring constantly until gravy thickens, and boil 1 minute. Season to taste.

These are favorites at the WJIM Country House. This is our Swedish cook Ruth Aspgren's special recipe. I think you'll agree they are tops.

SWEDISH MEAT BALLS

Grind together twice:

1 *pound ground beef*
½ *pound lean ground pork*

Mix together beef, pork, and all the following ingredients:

3 *slices soft broken bread*
¾ *cup milk*
1 *egg*
1 *medium onion, grated*
1 *teaspoon whole allspice, crushed*
1½ *teaspoons salt*
1 *cup consommé, with ½ cup water*

Roll into small balls and brown. Pour over consommé mixture and simmer 45 minutes.

The name is misleading but don't be misled and don't overlook this one. You will make it often!

MEATZA PIE

In a 9-inch pie plate mix:

1 *pound lean ground beef*
½ *cup soft bread crumbs*
⅔ *cup evaporated milk (6-ounce can)*
¼ *teaspoon garlic salt (optional)*

Press meat into pie-shell shape. In bottom of shell spread ⅔ cup tomato paste or catsup. Add 2-ounce can mushroom pieces, drained, and 1 cup grated sharp Cheddar cheese. Sprinkle with ¼ teaspoon oregano and 2 tablespoons Parmesan cheese. Bake at 375° for 25 minutes. Cut into six wedges.

A good and uncomplicated chili con carne.

CHILI CON CARNE CON FRIJOLES

½ *cup chopped onion*
½ *clove garlic, minced*
1 *pound ground beef*
2 *tablespoons shortening, if not enough fat in meat*
2 *cups cooked or canned kidney beans (2 cans, size No. 303)*
2 *cans tomato sauce*
1 *teaspoon salt*
2 *teaspoons chili powder*

Cook and stir onions, garlic, and meat in hot fat until meat loses red color. Stir in undrained beans, tomato sauce, and remaining ingredients. Simmer over low heat, stirring occasionally, until chili is desired thickness, about 45 minutes.
Makes 4 servings.

Serve with corn bread, green salad, fruit.

HAMBURGER RAREBIT

You will need 1½ pounds of ground beef for 4 servings. Form the meat into rather flat cakes and broil or sauté them quickly. Arrange each meat cake on a piece of toast and top with a rich rarebit sauce.

Rarebit Sauce:

Blend 3 tablespoons of butter with 3 tablespoons of flour in a skillet and let it brown slightly. Slowly stir in 1 cup of light cream and continue stirring until the mixture is smooth and thickened. Add 1 teaspoon of freshly ground black pepper, ½ teaspoon of salt, and a few specks of cayenne pepper. Stir in ¼ cup of grated sharp Cheddar cheese and let it melt and blend thoroughly with the cream sauce. Add a dash of Tabasco or Worcestershire sauce if you like.

With hamburger rarebit serve black olives, a big tossed salad of romaine and sliced radishes.

Good at all times.

BEEF STROGANOFF

1 *tablespoon flour*
½ *teaspoon salt*
1 *pound beef sirloin, cut in ¼-inch-wide strips*
2 *tablespoons butter*
1 *cup thinly sliced mushrooms*
½ *cup chopped onion*
1 *clove garlic, minced*
2 *tablespoons butter*
3 *tablespoons flour*
1 *tablespoon tomato paste*
1¼ *cups beef stock or 1 can condensed beef broth*
1 *cup dairy sour cream*
2 *tablespoons cooking sherry*

Combine 1 tablespoon flour and the salt; dredge meat in mixture. Heat skillet, then add 2 tablespoons butter. When melted, add the sirloin strips and brown quickly, flipping meat to brown all sides. Add the mushroom slices, onion, and garlic; cook 3 or 4 minutes or till onion is barely tender.

Time to make the rich sauce – easiest if you first remove the meat and mushrooms from skillet. Add 2 tablespoons butter to pan drippings; when melted, blend in 3 tablespoons flour. Add the tomato paste. Now slowly pour in cold meat stock – cook, stirring constantly until mixture thickens. No lumps!

Return browned meat and mushrooms to skillet. Stir in sour cream and sherry; heat briefly.

Serve browned rice, noodles, or rice pilau with your Stroganoff.

CHINESE PICKLED SPARERIBS WITH PINEAPPLE

Have the butcher cut 1½ pounds of spareribs crosswise through the bone, in approximately 1-inch lengths. Make a paste of soy sauce and flour (enough to coat the amount of ribs you have). Add a handful of cracked ginger, dried ginger root or fresh ginger root, peeled. If either cracked or dried ginger is used, soak it a few minutes in enough boiling water to cover the ginger, to bring out the flavor, then add ginger and water to soy sauce and flour paste. Separate the ribs into the 1-inch pieces and stir in the marinade. Marinate overnight in the refrigerator.

When ready to cook, sift through and remove *all* the little pieces of ginger. These are very hot and not pleasant to bite into while eating the ribs. Sauté the ribs in oil, just lightly. Drain off oil and add a sauce made of:

2 *tablespoons flour*
½ *cup vinegar*
1 *tablespoon soy sauce*
½ *cup sugar*
½ *cup pineapple juice, drained from No. 2½ can of pineapple chunks or tidbits*

Allow to simmer slowly about 30 minutes or until tender. Add pineapple pieces 5 minutes before serving. Serve over hot rice.

LAMB CURRY

1½ *pounds boneless lamb stew, cut in 1-inch pieces*
1 *cup water*
½ *cup diced onion*
1½ *cups sliced tart apples, unpared*
1½ *tablespoons curry powder*
⅛ *teaspoon cinnamon*
⅛ *teaspoon nutmeg*
⅛ *teaspoon ground cloves*
¼ *cup shortening*
6 *tablespoons enriched flour*
1 *to* 2 *cups milk*
2 *teaspoons salt*
Few grains red pepper
3 *cups cooked rice*

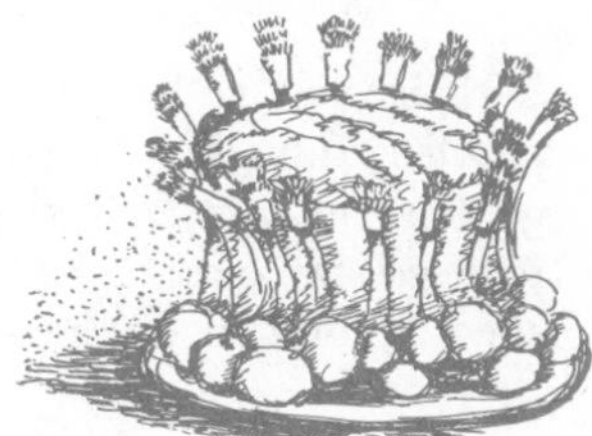

Add water to lamb, cover closely, and cook slowly on top of range or in slow oven (300°) until meat is almost done, about one hour. Add onion, apples, and spices and continue cooking until meat is tender and vegetables are done, about 20 minutes. Drain meat and vegetables. Add enough milk to cooking liquid to make 3 cups. Make a white sauce of shortening, flour, cooking liquid, and milk. Add white sauce to lamb mixture. Cook slowly until heated through.

Serve on hot rice. Shredded coconut, whole or chopped peanuts, raisins, crisp bacon, and finely chopped hard-cooked eggs may be served as accompaniments.
6 servings.

Sweetbreads are the thymus glands of calves. Allow one pair for two people. Sweetbreads should always be parboiled before using.

1 *pair sweetbreads*
1 *teaspoon vinegar*
½ *teaspoon salt*

Wash sweetbreads in cold water; place in saucepan, cover with boiling water and add vinegar and salt. Simmer for 15 minutes, or until tender. Drain, plunge in cold water, drain and remove membranes and tubes — you will have no trouble finding them.

SWEETBREADS SAUTÉED IN WINE

1 *pair sweetbreads, prepared as above*
Salt and paprika
Flour
4 *tablespoons butter*
4 *tablespoons dry sherry*

Parboil, and split sweetbreads. Sprinkle with salt and a pinch of paprika, dust lightly with flour, and sauté slowly in butter until golden brown on all sides. Add wine to the butter and cook until reduced by one half. Spoon over the sweetbreads and serve on slices of broiled Canadian bacon or sautéed ham.
Serves 2.

SWEETBREADS SUPREME

1½ cups cooked sweetbreads
2 tablespoons vinegar to each quart of water used
4 eggs – slightly beaten
2 cups cream
Salt and pepper to taste
Individual slices of tenderized ham – lightly browned

To cook sweetbreads, let stand for 1 hour in cold water. Cook slowly in boiling salted water for 20 minutes, adding the vinegar. Blanch in cold water.

Mix eggs with sweetbreads. Add cream, salt, and pepper to sweetbreads and place in buttered molds. Bake in pan of water in 350° oven for about 20 minutes, or until firm.

Serve on ham slices and cover with cream sauce.

Cream Sauce:

2 tablespoons butter
2 tablespoons flour
¼ teaspoon salt
A few grains of pepper
⅓ cup minced pimiento
1 cup milk

Melt butter. Blend flour, salt, and pepper into the butter, making a smooth paste. Add milk and pimiento slowly to the paste and stir until the sauce thickens. Boil 3 minutes.
Serves 8 to 12.

Different, interesting, and good.

JAPANESE MEAT BALLS

1 pound ground beef
¼ cup fine dry bread crumbs
⅔ cup chopped onion
1 teaspoon salt
Dash of pepper
⅔ cup evaporated milk
2 tablespoons butter

1 *can (1 pound, 3 ounces) bean sprouts*
¼ *cup cornstarch*
¼ *cup water*
½ *cup soy sauce*
1½ *cups thinly sliced onions*
1 *cup sliced mushrooms*
1 *cup shredded raw spinach*

Mix together ground beef, crumbs, onion, salt, pepper, and evaporated milk in a medium-sized mixing bowl. Shape into 12 meat balls. Melt butter in a large skillet over medium heat. Add meat balls, turning occasionally to brown all sides. While meat balls are browning, drain bean sprouts, saving liquid. Mix cornstarch and water in a small bowl to make a smooth paste. Stir in the liquid from the bean sprouts (there should be 1½ cups; if not, add water to measure that amount of liquid), then stir in the soy sauce, mixing well. Pour over browned meat balls. Bring to a boil over medium heat. Cover skillet tightly. Turn heat to low and simmer until thickened and sauce is clear, about 20 minutes. Add sliced onions, mushrooms, spinach, and bean sprouts. Cover and simmer 5 minutes longer. Serve over hot cooked rice.
Makes 6 servings.

Serve mammoth wedges of lemon meringue pie for dessert when you make Joe's spaghetti and meat balls.

My long-time good friend, Mr. Joe Manser, now manager of Gilbert's Steak House, Jackson, gave me this recipe many years ago. It's excellent.

SPECIAL ITALIAN SPAGHETTI AND MEAT BALLS

2 *medium-sized onions, cut fine*
6 *pieces celery, cut fine*
¼ *pound mushrooms, sliced (fresh or canned)*
½ *cup fresh parsley*
2 *cloves garlic, cut fine*

Cook the above ingredients in 3 to 4 tablespoons olive oil and butter—about 5 minutes.

Add 1 bay leaf, 2 crushed peppers, 1 whole allspice. Continue to cook for 10 minutes very slowly.

Add 1 can tomato paste, 1 No. 2½ can tomatoes. Cook for about one hour or longer. Slow cooking brings out the flavor.

Meat Balls:

1½ *pounds ground beef*
1 *cup milk*
1 *onion (cut fine)*
2 *tablespoons chopped parsley*
½ *cup bread crumbs*
½ *cup grated Parmesan cheese*

Mix all together and form into small balls. Place meat balls in spaghetti sauce and cook for additional 30 minutes.

Serve sauce and meat balls over cooked spaghetti. Top with more Parmesan cheese. Three ounces of red wine may be added.
Serves 6.

SAUERBRATEN

3 *to* 4 *pounds of beef of round*
1½ *cups vinegar*
1½ *cups water*
2 *bay leaves*
12 *whole cloves*
¼ *teaspoon pepper*
¼ *teaspoon mace*
1½ *teaspoons salt*
1 *tablespoon sugar*
2 *large onions, sliced*
½ *cup salad oil*
½ *cup enriched flour*
3 *tablespoons shortening*
½ *cup red wine*

Heat vinegar, water, spices, salt and sugar to boiling point. Pour over sliced onions and allow to stand until cool. Stir in oil. Pour marinade over pot roast and allow to stand in refrigerator 2 to 4 days, turning meat once a day so it will marinate evenly. Remove meat from marinade and drain. Dredge with flour and brown on all sides in shortening. Place rack under meat and add 1 cup

of strained marinade. Save remaining marinade. Cover meat closely and simmer 3 to 4 hours or until meat is tender. Remove to hot platter and make gingersnap gravy.
6 to 8 servings.

Gingersnap Gravy:

2 cups marinade and drippings
3 tablespoons enriched flour
Salt
Pepper
½ cup crumbled gingersnaps

Add enough strained marinade to liquid in pot-roast kettle to make 2 cups. Make a smooth paste with flour and 3 tablespoons of cold marinade. Add flour-marinade mixture to liquid in pot-roast kettle. Bring to boiling point, stirring constantly. Cook until thickened. Season. Add gingersnap crumbs just before serving.

RIB ROAST OF BEEF WITH TRIMMINGS

Place roast fat side up in a shallow open pan. Do not cover. The rib bones form a natural rack to hold the meat out of the drippings. Insert point of roast-meat thermometer into center of meat. Roast in a slow oven (325°) until the thermometer indicates the desired doneness.

Crusty Brown Potatoes:

Pare and boil medium-sized potatoes 15 minutes. Drain. About ½ hour before roast is done, place the hot potatoes into the meat drippings around the roast. Turn to coat on all sides. Use tongs to avoid breakage. Finish cooking potatoes with the roast. Season potatoes with salt and pepper before serving.

Cherry Peach Garnish:

Fill centers of 8 peach halves with 1 tablespoon crushed pineapple and 1 teaspoon lemon juice in each. Top peach halves with 1 table-

spoon cherry preserves. Heat in oven or broiler until preserves are bubbly. Arrange peaches on platter with roast beef.
For a very special treat, try making the "English Yorkshire Pudding." Your family will love you forever!

Yorkshire Pudding:

Yorkshire pudding is a favorite English accompaniment with roast beef. It is a thin batter like popovers baked in the meat drippings, cut into squares, and served hot with the roast. Many folk prefer to bake spoonfuls of this batter in a little of the beef drippings in muffin pans so the rest of the drippings may be made into gravy. The trick is to have drippings, pan, and oven hot so the batter puffs and gets crusty brown. Start the Yorkshire pudding about 40 minutes before serving time and serve as soon as it is done.

1 *cup sifted flour*
1 *teaspoon salt*
2 *eggs*
1 *cup milk*

Combine the flour and salt in a 1-quart bowl. Beat the eggs well with an electric or rotary beater, then beat in the milk. Pour this into the flour and continue beating until the thin batter is smooth. Pour ½ cup of the meat drippings from the roasting pan into an 8 x 8-inch pan (or into 6 deep muffin pans). Heat the pan in the oven. Add the pudding batter and bake in a hot oven 30 minutes. Cut into squares to serve. This means that the roast and batter bake in the same oven for 15 minutes, then the roast is removed to "set" before carving.
Yield: *6 servings.*

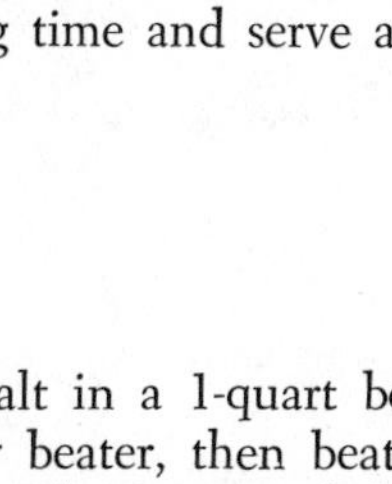

Happiness is best attained by learning to live each day by itself. The worries are mostly about yesterday and tomorrow — M. Nolan

Sauces for Meats, Fowl, Fish, Vegetables

A well-prepared sauce or gravy adds richness and the finishing touch to meat, fish, poultry, and vegetables. To be perfect, it must be smooth, glossy, and distinctive in flavor. It takes patience to make a sauce that will enhance, not disguise. A good sauce takes time to blend thoroughly. A rule in blending is to follow your sauce recipe, but let your imagination inspire your seasoning.

Don't be fooled by the simplicity of this recipe. My good neighbor of many years ago, Mrs. Russell Goodrich, Jackson, Michigan, gave it to me. It is wonderful when spread on plain meat loaves the last few minutes of baking.

MEAT SAUCE

1 *cup brown sugar*
2½ *tablespoons flour*
1 *teaspoon dry mustard*

Add vinegar to make a paste. Spread on meat loaves last 20 minutes of baking.

SPICY HAM SAUCE

Simmer canned fruit cocktail in its syrup with orange and lemon slices, whole cloves, and stick of cinnamon. Thicken with cornstarch blended with a little water. Serve hot with ham slices.

A famous sauce used at the hunt suppers in Cumberland County in Merrie Olde England.

CUMBERLAND SAUCE

1 *cup currant jelly*
1 *tablespoon hot water*
1 *teaspoon dry mustard*
1 *tablespoon orange juice*
¼ *teaspoon grated orange rind*

Heat the jelly until it just simmers. Add hot water and beat until well combined. Remove from heat. Dissolve the mustard in a little cold water and stir to a smooth paste. Add to mixture. Add orange juice and rind.

Serve slightly warm. A wonderful combination with ham or wild game. Excellent with breakfast ham for a Sunday brunch party. *Serves 8.*

SIMPLE BARBECUE SAUCE

1½ *tablespoons salad oil*
1 *onion, minced*
1¼ *cups chili sauce*
⅓ *cup steak sauce*

Heat salad oil in 8-inch frying pan. Add onion and cook until tender. Add sauces. Serve hot over frankfurters. Makes 2 cups spicy sauce, enough for 12 servings.

SAUCE FOR STEAK SUPREME

½ *pound mushrooms*
Enriched flour
3 *tablespoons butter*

½ teaspoon soy sauce
Salt and pepper

Wash mushrooms in small amount of water; don't soak or peel. Cut off tip of stem. You can slice mushrooms or leave whole. Sprinkle lightly with flour. Cook, covered, in butter, over low heat till tender (8-10 minutes), turning occasionally. Add soy sauce and seasoning to taste.
Makes about 4 servings to go with broiled steak.

MUSTARD SAUCE

1 cup brown sugar
¼ cup dry mustard
1 tablespoon flour
¼ teaspoon salt

Dissolve 1 beef bouillon cube in ½ cup hot water. Add, with ½ cup vinegar, to dry ingredients. Mix well. Add 2 beaten eggs and cook in the top of a double boiler over hot water until consistency of a soft custard. Cool. Serve with ham and cold meats.

HORSERADISH SAUCE, COLD

¼ cup grated horseradish
1 tablespoon lemon juice
1 teaspoon vinegar
¼ teaspoon salt
Dash of cayenne pepper
½ cup heavy cream

Drain horseradish to remove any excess liquid. Combine horseradish, lemon juice, vinegar, salt, and cayenne pepper. Chill. Just before serving, whip the cream and fold in horseradish mixture. Serve with baked ham or cold meats.
Yield: about one cup.

ORANGE SAUCE

For ham or duck.

- *½ cup sugar*
- *2 tablespoons flour*
- *⅛ teaspoon salt*
- *½ cup water*
- *½ cup orange juice*
- *2 tablespoons lemon juice*
- *2 tablespoons orange rind, grated*
- *1 tablespoon butter*

Mix flour, sugar, and salt. Add water and boil until thick. Add orange and lemon juice, rind, and butter and let come to a boil. Serve hot.

Always associated with boiled meats is

HORSERADISH SAUCE, HOT

- *1 tablespoon chopped onion*
- *3 tablespoons butter*
- *2 tablespoons flour*
- *1 cup milk or light cream*
- *¼ cup prepared horseradish*

Brown onion slightly in butter; add flour, then milk or cream to make a sauce. When thick, add horseradish. It is especially good on boiled brisket of fresh beef and corned beef.

Variation:

Mustard Sauce: In place of the horseradish, substitute 3 tablespoons prepared mustard and ½ teaspoon Worcestershire sauce. Serve over fresh pork, spareribs, pork butts, and regular hams.
Makes 1 cup.

A rather hot sauce, delicious with lamb.

LAMB SAUCE ANITA

½ cup brown sugar
½ cup currant jelly
1 tablespoon dry mustard
3 egg yolks
½ cup vinegar

Mix brown sugar, jelly, dry mustard, and egg yolks and cook in double boiler until thick. Add vinegar slowly, beating after each addition.
Makes 1 cup.

LOUIS SAUCE, HOT

2 tablespoons butter or margarine
1 tablespoon very finely chopped onion
2 tablespoons flour
½ teaspoon salt
Dash pepper
Few drops Worcestershire sauce
1 cup milk
½ cup mayonnaise
⅓ cup chili sauce
2 tablespoons chopped stuffed olives
½ teaspoon grated horseradish

Melt butter in saucepan; add onion and sauté until onion is tender but not browned. Stir in flour, salt, pepper, Worcestershire sauce, and milk; cook, stirring, until mixture thickens and comes to a boil. Remove from heat, stir in mayonnaise, chili sauce, olives, and horseradish. Serve hot on shrimp that have been heated according to directions on package.
Makes about 2 cups.

LOUIS SAUCE, COLD

1 cup mayonnaise
2 tablespoons French dressing
⅓ cup chili sauce

1 tablespoon grated onion
1 tablespoon chopped parsley
2 tablespoons chopped stuffed olives
1 teaspoon grated horseradish
½ teaspoon Worcestershire sauce

Combine all ingredients; chill. Serve as dip or dressing for breaded shrimp heated according to package directions. Makes a fine first course or party nibbler; or, served on shredded lettuce with chunks of chilled seafood, a delicious luncheon main dish.

CELERY SAUCE FOR FISH

1 can (1¼ cups) condensed cream-of-celery soup
1 teaspoon prepared mustard
¼ cup milk
3 tablespoons sweet-pickle relish
1 hard-cooked egg, chopped

Empty soup into a saucepan; blend in mustard and milk. Add relish and egg; heat over low heat. This sauce is excellent with fish, fish cakes, and other sea food.
Makes about 1¾ cups sauce.

CUMCUMBER SAUCE FOR FISH

1 cup finely chopped, peeled cucumbers
½ teaspoon salt
1 tablespoon sugar
1 tablespoon cider vinegar
⅛ teaspoon ground white pepper
½ cup heavy cream, whipped

Combine cucumbers and salt. Let stand in a covered jar in refrigerator for at least 1 hour. Drain and mix with sugar, cider vinegar, and white pepper. Just before serving, fold in heavy cream. Serve over baked salmon steaks, broiled fillet of haddock, sword fish, or other fish.
Yield: ½ cup.

Wonderful!

SHERRY SUPREME SAUCE

2 tablespoons flour
2 tablespoons butter
½ cup cream
½ cup chicken broth
¼ cup grated Swiss or Gruyère cheese
2 tablespoons sherry
Salt

Make a cream sauce with the flour, butter, cream, and chicken broth. Add cheese and stir until thoroughly blended. Add sherry and season to your taste.

This sauce is delicious served over thin slices of white meat of turkey or chicken, over rice seasoned with a very faint suspicion of curry.
Makes 1 cup.

SPAGHETTI SAUCE

½ cup finely chopped onion
1 teaspoon finely chopped garlic
1 teaspoon finely chopped celery
1 teaspoon finely chopped parsley
½ cup olive oil
2 cups canned tomatoes
2 cups tomato purée
⅛ teaspoon paprika
Salt and pepper
¼ cup sherry

Sauté finely chopped onion, garlic, celery, and parsley in olive oil until celery and onions are soft. Add tomatoes, purée, and paprika. Cook until well blended and thick and season with salt and pepper. Add sherry and serve at once. Combined with fresh crab flakes or chicken, it is a good buffet supper dish. Serve with a dish of grated Parmesan cheese nearby.
Makes 4 cups.

The sauce of all sauces—fit for a king. Wonderful on steaks or tenderloins!

BÉARNAISE SAUCE

Combine 1 cup white wine, 1 tablespoon tarragon vinegar, 1 tablespoon finely chopped shallots, 1 small sprig of parsley, 2 small stalks of tarragon herb, coarsely chopped, 1 small sprig of chervil, finely chopped, and 2 bruised peppercorns. Cook over a hot fire until reduced to ⅔ of its original volume. Cool it a little before adding 3 egg yolks gradually, stirring constantly and vigorously, alternating with ½ pound melted butter, or as much as the sauce can hold, until it has the consistency of heavy cream. Blend thoroughly over a slow fire, strain through a fine sieve, and finish with a dash of cayenne and 1 teaspoon each finely chopped tarragon leaves and chervil.

SOUR-CREAM CUCUMBER SAUCE

1 *cup sour cream*
1 *tablespoon vinegar*
1½ *tablespoons lemon juice*
½ *to 1 teaspoon sugar*
Few grains of pepper
½ *onion passed over grater 2 to 3 times*
1 *cucumber, seeded, peeled, and diced*

Blend ingredients and chill.

This sauce will do as the name implies—"never fail." I'm as pleased with making a batch of smooth creamy Hollandaise as I am with the purchase of a new Lilly Daché creation.

NEVER-FAIL HOLLANDAISE SAUCE

¼ pound butter (½ cup)
2 egg yolks
½ teaspoon salt
Dash of cayenne
1½ to 2 tablespoons lemon juice

Melt butter. Beat the egg yolks until thick. Add the salt, cayenne, and 3 tablespoons of melted butter. Beat until well mixed and stiff. Continue beating and add lemon juice and rest of melted butter, a few drops of each alternately, until all has been added. *Makes 1 cup.* To use sauce, heat in top part of double boiler over hot water, stirring constantly, serve at once on hot broccoli or other greens.

To know how to make a smooth cream sauce, thick, or thin, or medium, is a necessity. Here is a good one.

BASIC CREAM SAUCE

1 tablespoon butter
1 tablespoon flour
¼ teaspoon salt
1 cup milk (or half-milk and half-cream)

Melt butter in top part of double boiler, add flour and salt, and cook until bubbly. Slowly add milk and stir briskly. Cook over hot water until thick and smooth, stirring occasionally. (A French whip or wire whisk is, or ought to be, a must in the kitchen drawer, especially for stirring sauces of all kinds.) All cream sauces should be cooked until there is no starchy taste remaining. Use more or less milk for desired consistency.

MEDIUM CREAM SAUCE

2 tablespoons butter
2 tablespoons flour
¼ teaspoon salt
1 cup milk

Variations of Medium Cream Sauce:
Sea-Food Sauce for Fish:

Add ½ cup sautéed oysters and shrimp with 1 teaspoon lemon juice.

Add ½ teaspoon grated onion and 1 teaspoon anchovy paste for a sauce for fish or asparagus.

Egg Sauce:

Add 2 chopped hard-cooked eggs, 1 tablespoon chopped parsley, 1 teaspoon chopped chives or grated onion. Serve with fish.

Supreme Sauce:

Add 1 slightly beaten egg yolk with ¼ cup heavy cream and a pinch of nutmeg. ½ cup sherry may be added. Serve with fish or chicken croquettes or soufflés.

In the long run, men hit only what they aim at. Therefore ... they had better aim at something high – Thoreau

Relishes and Fruits to Accompany Meat and Fowl

ROSEMARY PEACH PUFFS

1 can (1 pound, 13 ounces) cling peach halves
2 tablespoons soft butter or margarine
½ teaspoon seasoned salt
½ teaspoon crushed rosemary
Dash garlic powder
½ cup dairy sour cream
2 tablespoons fine dry bread crumbs
2 tablespoons grated Cheddar cheese

Drain peaches and pat dry with paper towels. Work soft butter, seasoned salt, rosemary, and garlic powder together. Stir into sour cream. Place peach halves, cut-side up, in shallow pan. Fill and spread each half with sour cream mixture, covering completely. Sprinkle lightly with crumbs, then cheese. Broil about 5 inches from heat until fruit is hot and flecked with brown, 5 to 7 minutes. *Makes 6 or 7 servings.*

HOLLY-BERRY PEACHES

1 No. 2½-can cling peach halves
½ cup water
¾ cup sugar
½ cup vinegar
1 tablespoon mixed pickling spices
Red food coloring
Water cress or butter lettuce
Seedless green grapes
2 teaspoons prepared horseradish
Dash of salt
½ cup commercial sour cream

Drain peaches and to the syrup add the water, sugar, vinegar, and spices. Color bright holly-berry red with about ¼ teaspoon food coloring. Boil 5 minutes. Add peaches and simmer 5 minutes longer. Refrigerate peaches in the syrup overnight.

At serving time, arrange water cress in wreath on large serving platter (milk glass would be effective). Top with the peach halves. Heap center of ring with clusters of green grapes. Beat horseradish, salt, and 1 tablespoon pickling syrup into sour cream. Put a spoonful in each peach.

These Holly-Berry Peaches are perfect as a relish for roast turkey or ham. We gave them this name for their beautiful red color. They make a spectacular salad or fruit wreath for a buffet table. Stick cinnamon can replace the pickling spices.

DELICIOUS HORSERADISH RELISH

1 package lemon Jello
1 cup boiling water
2 tablespoons vinegar or lemon juice
¼ teaspoon salt
¾ cup horseradish (drained)
1 cup cream, whipped

Mix Jello, water, vinegar, salt. Let cool. When this begins to thicken, fold in cream and horseradish, pour in a mold, and chill until firm. This is very good with ham or roast pork.

TEN-MINUTE CRANBERRY SAUCE

2 *cups sugar*
2 *cups water*
1 *pound (4 cups) cranberries*
Dash ground cinnamon
½ *teaspoon vanilla flavoring*

Combine sugar and water in saucepan; stir to dissolve sugar. Heat to boiling and boil 5 minutes. Add cranberries and cook till skins pop, about 5 minutes. Serve warm or chilled.
Makes 4 cups.

STUFFED ORANGES

6 *oranges*
½ *cup chopped dates*
½ *cup chopped nuts*
½ *cup shredded coconut*
1 *egg white*
½ *cup powdered sugar*

Cut a slice from the top of each orange and carefully remove pulp. Discard all tough membrane. Mix dates, nuts, orange pulp, and coconut together. Refill orange shells. Beat egg white until stiff, and add sugar gradually. Continue beating. Pile on top of oranges. Brown in 400° oven. Serve hot. Serve around ham or other meats.

RHUBARB-PINEAPPLE RELISH

1⅓ *cups minced rhubarb*
⅓ *cup minced celery*

⅔ cup minced fresh pineapple
⅔ cup granulated sugar

Combine ingredients and chill for one hour. Serve with chicken or lamb.

Delicious with roast pork and baked pork chops, especially during the winter months. Be sure you are generous with butter and sugar.

FRIED APPLES

6 tart apples
¼ cup butter or more
4 tablespoons white sugar
4 tablespoons brown sugar (more if needed)
½ teaspoon salt

Core apples, pare if desired. Slice and cook in butter over medium heat. Cover and steam 5 minutes. Turn, add sugar and salt. Cover and cook until tender.
Serves 6.

My greatest inspiration is a challenge to attempt the impossible. —Albert A. Mickelson

Vegetables

There's no better bargain than vegetables. Their bright colors add appeal to the meal, plus the flavor-fresh goodness. They are easy and fun to fix. Use your imagination and add extra touches, such as toasted almonds, crisp croutons, lemon butter, or a dramatic swoop of sour cream.

We love broccoli prepared this way. Nice with cauliflower, too.

BROCCOLI WITH SHRIMP SAUCE

In saucepan, blend ¼ cup chive cream cheese (about 2 ounces) and ¼ cup milk. Add 1 can frozen condensed cream-of-shrimp soup.

Heat and stir till hot. Add 2 teaspoons lemon juice; pour over hot drained broccoli. Sprinkle with 2 tablespoons toasted slivered almonds.

Makes 1½ cups sauce.

Corn pudding with the curried top. Excellent . . . if you like curry. We do!

CURRIED CORN PUDDING

1 *tablespoon butter or margarine*
¼ *cup flour*

- 2 *cups milk*
- 1 *cup cream*
- 4 *egg yolks, beaten*
- 1 *teaspoon salt*
- *Dash of pepper*
- 2 *teaspoons sugar*
- 1 *tablespoon mild curry powder*
- 6 *ears fresh corn, kernels removed, or 4 cans (12 ounces each) whole kernel or cream-style corn*
- 4 *egg whites, beaten stiff*

Melt butter. Stir in flour to make a smooth paste. Add milk. Cook over low heat, stirring, until mixture comes to a boil and thickens. Slowly stir in cream. Simmer, stirring a few minutes. Cool. Add egg yolks, salt, pepper, sugar, and curry powder. Blend. Stir in corn. Fold in beaten egg whites. Turn into buttered 2-quart casserole. Place in pan of hot water. Bake at 300° for 1 hour or until set. *Makes 8 servings.*

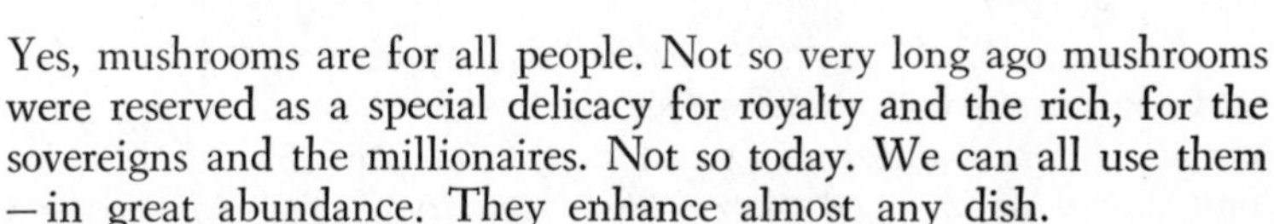

Yes, mushrooms are for all people. Not so very long ago mushrooms were reserved as a special delicacy for royalty and the rich, for the sovereigns and the millionaires. Not so today. We can all use them – in great abundance. They enhance almost any dish.

MUSHROOMS AND GREEN PEAS

In heavy saucepan having tight lid, make a nest of outside lettuce leaves, dipped out of cold water and still dripping. Into this, center a pound of frozen peas. Add a chunk of butter, a dash of salt and pepper, and a dash of nutmeg, freshly grated if you have it. Cover with more lettuce leaves and cook gently for about fifteen minutes. Keep lid on saucepan also. When ready to serve, remove all lettuce leaves and discard them, and stir into the peas 4 to 6 finely diced mushrooms lightly sautéed in butter. If you like, use a 4-ounce can sliced mushrooms (drained) in this serving. Serve from heated bowl. Delicious and different.

Don't be fooled—these are corn oysters. Good!

CORN OYSTERS

1 cup fresh corn, sliced from the cob
1 egg, separated
¼ cup sifted all-purpose flour
½ teaspoon double-acting baking powder
1 teaspoon salt
1/16 teaspoon ground black pepper
½ teaspoon grated onion
Bacon fat or shortening

Combine corn and egg yolk. Mix well.

Thoroughly mix flour with baking powder, salt, black pepper, and grated onion and stir into the corn and eggs. Beat egg white stiff and fold into the corn mixture. Drop from a teaspoon onto a hot griddle greased with bacon fat or shortening. Cook until brown. *Yield: 5 servings or 20 corn oysters.*

If bacon fat is used, fry out 4 strips of bacon for sufficient fat to fry the mixture.

The Texans scramble for this.

TEXAS CORN SCRAMBLE

Beat 6 eggs lightly with 1 teaspoon salt, ¼ teaspoon pepper, then add 1½ cups whole-kernel sweet corn, 4 tablespoons young green onion, chopped, one small green pepper cut into tiny short strips, one pimiento, chopped. Turn into large frying pan containing 6 slices bacon chopped into tiny pieces, fried a delicate brown. 3 to 4 tablespoons bacon fat should remain in pan or use half bacon fat, half butter, for scrambling. Heap on warm platter for serving.

This tangy sauce gives sunshine carrots a flavor lift.

HARVARD CARROTS

½ cup sugar
1½ tablespoons cornstarch
¼ cup vinegar

¼ cup water
4 cups cooked, sliced carrots
¼ cup butter or margarine

Mix sugar and cornstarch. Add vinegar and water. Cook until thick, stirring constantly. Add carrots and let stand over low heat 5 to 10 minutes. Add butter.
Serves 6.

SWEET POTATOES ON PINEAPPLE

Boil 6 or 8 sweet potatoes. Peel and mash and add butter and salt to taste. Place a scoop of the potatoes on slices of pineapple. Bake in 350° oven for 15 minutes or until heated through. Remove from oven and place a marshmallow on top. Return to oven until marshmallows melt and spread over sweet potatoes.

SWEET-POTATO AND ORANGE CASSEROLE

5 large sweet potatoes
⅓ cup brown sugar
¼ cup butter
2 unpeeled oranges (seedless)
½ cup orange juice
¼ cup honey
¼ cup bread crumbs
2 tablespoons sugar
1 tablespoon butter

Boil potatoes or use canned sweet potatoes. Slice and place one layer in buttered casserole. Sprinkle with brown sugar; dot with butter. Cover with layer of orange slices. Repeat until potatoes and oranges are used up. Pour honey and orange juice over contents. Cover with bread crumbs mixed with brown sugar, and bake at 350° for about 30 minutes. Remove cover last 15 minutes.

LADIES' CABBAGE

Boil a firm cabbage for 15 minutes, changing the water after the 15-minute boiling period. Add fresh water and boil until head of cabbage is tender. Drain, set aside to cool.

After the cabbage is cool, chop fine and add 2 well-beaten eggs, 1 tablespoon butter, salt and pepper to taste. Add 3 tablespoons rich cream, mix all together, and bake in a buttered dish at 350° until brown.

Place a few crushed cornflakes on top with a few drops of melted butter.

REQUEST GREEN BEANS

1 can (1 pound) cut green beans
1 can (3½ ounces) French-fried onions
1 can condensed cream-of-mushroom soup
1 can (3 to 4 ounces) mushrooms
2 tablespoons toasted almonds, or water chestnuts, sliced
½ cup grated Cheddar cheese

Put alternate layers of drained beans and onions in a casserole. Mix soup, mushrooms with the liquid and almonds; pour over beans and onions. Sprinkle cheese over top. Bake in a moderate oven (375°) about 30 minutes.
Six servings.

SNAPPY BEAN BAKE

2 (1-pound) cans cut blue lake green beans
1 (10½-ounce) can cream-of-mushroom soup
½ cup milk
1 teaspoon Worcestershire sauce
½ teaspoon prepared mustard
½ cup sliced ripe olives
1 cup crushed potato chips

Drain beans and put half of them in a 1½-quart casserole. Blend soup, milk, Worcestershire sauce, mustard, and ripe olives. Turn half of it over beans; sprinkle with half the potato chips. Repeat with beans, soup, and chips. Bake in moderately hot oven (375°) 25 to 30 minutes.
Serve bubbly hot to 4 or 5.

GREEN BEANS WITH HOT MUSTARD SAUCE

½ teaspoon dry mustard
½ teaspoon flour
¼ teaspoon salt
2 beaten egg yolks
¾ cup milk, scalded
2 tablespoons vinegar
3 cups hot green beans

Mix mustard, flour, and salt in a double boiler. Add egg yolks and beat well. Add hot milk slowly and cook until thick. Add vinegar and stir slightly. Pour sauce over hot green beans.
Yield: 6 servings.

SWEET-SOUR BEANS OR SPINACH

Brown until crisp 2 strips bacon. Cook in the bacon fat until yellow 1 cup minced onion. Stir in 1 tablespoon flour. Add and bring to boil:

¾ cup vegetable liquid
¼ cup vinegar
2 tablespoons sugar
1 teaspoon salt
¼ teaspoon pepper

Stir in 2 cups cooked green or waxed beans or spinach. Serve with bacon on top.

GOLDEN CARROTS

2 cups sliced carrots
½ teaspoon salt
1½ cups water
2½ cups (1 pound, 4 ounce can) pineapple chunks
3 tablespoons butter
2 tablespoons cornstarch
¼ teaspoon salt
Dash of nutmeg

Add salt to 1½ cups water; add carrots; cook until tender. Drain, reserving 1 cup of the water in which the carrots were cooked. Drain pineapple chunks, reserving the pineapple juice.

Melt butter; stir in cornstarch. Slowly add carrot and pineapple juices, stirring constantly. Bring to boil. Add salt and nutmeg. Fold in the drained carrots and pineapple. Heat to serve.
Serves 6.

BAKED CHEESE-STUFFED POTATOES

- 4 *large Idaho potatoes*
- 2 *tablespoons hot heavy cream*
- 3 *tablespoons tangy grated cheese*
- 2½ *tablespoons butter*
- 1 *well-beaten egg*
- ½ *teaspoon salt*

Scrub and dry the potatoes, then bake for forty-five minutes in 425° oven. Cut off tops lengthwise and scoop out the middles. Mash with the salt, butter, cheese, cream, and a well-beaten egg. Beat until fluffy and replace in the shells. Brush the tops with more melted butter. Return to oven and bake ten minutes longer, until the tops are delicately browned.
Serves 4.

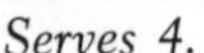

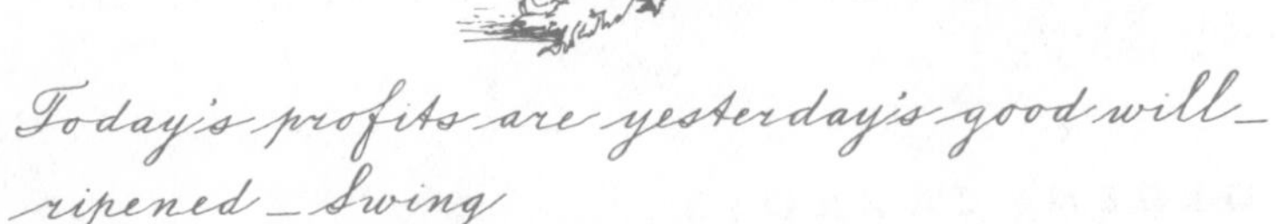

Don't frown. Hominy is wonderful served this way.

HOMINY AND MUSHROOM CASSEROLE

- 2 *cups canned hominy*
- 1 *cup canned mushroom soup*
- 1 *teaspoon Worcestershire sauce*

½ teaspoon salt
Corn flakes rolled into crumbs
1 tablespoon butter

Mix the hominy, mushroom soup, Worcestershire sauce, and salt. Pour into a buttered casserole, sprinkle with the crushed corn flakes, and dot with butter. Bake at 300° until brown.
Serves 6.

You'll not recognize cabbage dressed in this fashion. Excellent!

CURRIED CABBAGE

Cut or chop one medium-sized head of cabbage (about 6 cups). Cook in a small amount of salted water until tender. Drain. Meantime make two cups rich white sauce, using about 3 tablespoons butter to 2½ tablespoons flour. Blend together, adding about 2 cups rich milk. Cook until thickened and free of lumps. Add salt, pepper, and a generous ½ teaspoon curry powder (more if you like curry). Place cooked cabbage in buttered casserole dish. Pour cream sauce over cabbage. Sprinkle well-buttered crumbs over cabbage and bake for 25 minutes in 350° oven.

KIDNEY BEAN AND HERB CASSEROLE

1 large onion, finely chopped
2 cloves garlic, finely chopped
1 green pepper, finely chopped
¼ cup shortening
1 tablespoon flour
2 cups canned tomatoes, drained
2 20-ounce cans cooked kidney beans, drained
1 teaspoon salt
½ teaspoon pepper
½ teaspoon oregano or thyme
2 tablespoons chopped parsley
¼ cup shredded cheese

Fry onion, garlic, and pepper in hot shortening until vegetables are tender. Add flour and stir until blended. Stir in tomatoes and bring to a boil. Add kidney beans, salt, pepper, oregano or thyme, and parsley and put mixture into a 2-quart casserole. Bake at 350° for 40 minutes. Sprinkle with cheese and cook for 5 minutes longer. *Serves 6.*

BUTTER-BEAN CASSEROLE

2 No. 2 cans butter beans (4 cups)
4 slices bacon, cut up in pieces
1½ cups chopped celery
½ cup chopped onion
⅔ cup light molasses
⅔ cup tomato catsup
2 tablespoons prepared mustard
½ teaspoon salt
¾ cup liquid

Brown the bacon and break into small pieces. Remove bacon from pan and brown the celery and onion in the bacon drippings. In 2-quart casserole combine the beans, bacon, celery, onion, molasses, catsup, mustard, salt, and bean liquid. Bake uncovered at 375° for 1½ hours. Cover when the beans and sauce seem to have thickened enough.

These are wonderful for buffet suppers.

COUNTRY HOUSE GREEN BEANS AU GRATIN

4 tablespoons butter
4 tablespoons flour
1 teaspoon salt
¼ teaspoon dry mustard
1½ cups milk
½ cup processed cheese, diced or grated
3 cups cooked fresh or frozen green beans, slivered
Parmesan cheese
Paprika

Melt the butter; add flour, salt, and mustard. Cook over low heat until bubbly. Add milk and cook until thick and smooth. Add cheese and stir until completely melted. Add beans, which have been cooked in boiling salted water until just underdone. Pour into buttered casserole, sprinkle with grated Parmesan cheese and paprika. Bake at 350° for 30 minutes, until bubbly. Add slivered almonds.

Sometimes I sprinkle one can French fried onions on top. Men like onions while ladies enjoy the almonds. They are both delicious!

MICHIGAN BAKED BEANS

1 *large can of beans*
½ *pound sausage*
½ *cup brown sugar*
½ *teaspoon dry mustard*
3 *tablespoons molasses*

Fry the sausage and drain off the fat. Add remaining ingredients. Put in a bean pot and bake in a moderate oven 350° for a half-hour. Leave uncovered the last 15 minutes.
Serves 8 to 10.

If you are not on good terms with zucchini, become acquainted at once!

STUFFED ZUCCHINI

4 *young zucchini, split lengthwise*
2 *tablespoons butter or margarine*
1 *clove of garlic, cut*
1 *cup (about 1 pound) chopped, cooked, fresh spinach*
2 *tablespoons grated Parmesan cheese*
3 *tablespoons evaporated milk*
1 *teaspoon flour*
½ *teaspoon salt*
⅛ *teaspoon pepper*
2 *tablespoons buttered bread crumbs*

Cook zucchini in small amount boiling salted water 12 to 15 minutes, or until tender. Drain; place in baking pan; brush well with butter or margarine melted with cut garlic. Heat spinach, evaporated milk, flour, cheese, salt, and pepper in small saucepan, stirring constantly. Spoon on top of zucchini; sprinkle with buttered crumbs; broil about 7 minutes, or until hot.

BAKED EGGPLANT WITH TOMATOES

Cut into halves a small eggplant; scoop out the pulp, and chop. Leave a shell ¼ inch thick. Mince and heat in a skillet 2 strips bacon. Add to it and sauté until the bacon is cooked, ¼ cup minced onion, ¼ cup minced green pepper; add the eggplant pulp and 2 cups canned tomatoes and ¼ cup diced celery. Simmer these ingredients until the eggplant is tender. Beat them with a fork until they are well blended. Thicken with ⅓ cup bread crumbs; season with salt and freshly ground pepper. Add ½ cup sautéed mushrooms. Fill the eggplant shells with the mixture. Cover with bread crumbs, cheese, and dot with butter. Place the eggplant in a pan with very little water in a moderate oven (350°) until it is very hot.

Great combination.

CRAB-STUFFED MUSHROOMS

2 dozen large, firm mushrooms
1 tablespoon instant minced onion
2 tablespoons butter or margarine
2 tablespoons green onion, chopped
Dash red pepper and cayenne
1 tablespoon prepared mustard (English)
1½ teaspoons salt
3 tablespoons lemon juice
1 tablespoon Worcestershire sauce
1 pound crab meat
¼ cup sherry
¼ cup cream
2 tablespoons flour

Rinse mushrooms in cold water. Remove stems. Drain. Cut tender part of stems into thin slices. Sauté stems and minced onion in butter, but do not brown. Add remaining ingredients. Mix thoroughly. Cook over low heat about 5 minutes. Brush the caps lightly with melted butter and pile them high with this mixture. Bake in a 375° oven in a buttered baking dish about 10 minutes.
Note: Tops may be brushed with a mixture of ½ mayonnaise and ½ cream if desired.

MELT-IN-THE-MOUTH POTATOES

Pare 6 potatoes and cook in rapidly boiling salted water for 20 minutes, or until almost tender. Drain. Place in a small casserole, add 1 cup chicken stock and dot with butter. Bake in moderate oven (375°) for 20 minutes, or until stock is absorbed, turning potatoes occasionally.
Serves 6.

BAKED CREAM POTATOES

1 *medium onion, finely chopped*
3 *tablespoons chopped green pepper*
4 *tablespoons butter or margarine*
1 *tablespoon chopped pimiento*
3 *cups cubed, cooked potatoes (¾-inch cubes)*
2½ *tablespoons flour*
2 *cups milk*
Salt and pepper
¾ *cup shredded sharp cheese*

Cook onion and green pepper in butter 5 minutes. Stir in pimiento and flour. Add milk gradually, stir and cook until thickened. Season to taste. Add potatoes. Pour into 1½-quart casserole. Top with cheese. Bake at 350° about 30 minutes or until bubbly. *Note:* This can be combined early, stored in refrigerator, and baked just before serving.
Serves 4-6.

TOP-STOVE SCALLOPED POTATOES

Pare and slice 6 medium-sized potatoes. Put in covered saucepan with 1 tablespoon instant minced onion, salt and pepper to taste. Cover just to top with half table cream, half milk, about 2½ cups. Cook gently about 25 to 30 minutes, or until potatoes are done but still hold shape and sauce is thick as cream. Turn into shallow baking dish. Top with crumbled corn flakes and crisp bacon bits. Broil until bubbly brown, 4 to 5 minutes.

If we may be so bold as to use the adjective "elegant" for our Wine Creamed Onions . . . we have, and are proud of it!

WINE-CREAMED ONIONS

2 pounds small white boiling onions
2 cups water
1 cup California sauterne or other white dinner wine
Salt
4 tablespoons butter or margarine
4 tablespoons flour
1 cup cream or undiluted evaporated milk
2 tablespoons minced parsley
Pepper
2 tablespoons grated Parmesan cheese

Peel onions. (The skins will slip off more readily if the onions are first covered with boiling water, drained, and rinsed with cold water.) Put water, wine, and ½ teaspoon salt in a saucepan; heat to boiling; add onions and cook, uncovered, for 20 minutes. Drain, reserving liquid. Melt butter and stir in flour; add cream and 1 cup of the liquid from the onions; cook, stirring constantly, until mixture is thickened and smooth. Add parsley, salt and pepper; add onions. Turn into a greased casserole, sprinkle cheese over the top; bake in a moderately hot oven (375°) for 20 to 25 minutes.

Serves 5 *or* 6.

I'm a lover of fresh mushrooms. You will be, too, after you prepare them this way!

MUSHROOMS IN CREAM

½ pound butter
8 small green onions
2 pounds large fresh mushrooms

Melt butter in large iron skillet. Dice onions fine and brown in butter. Wipe mushrooms clean but do not peel. Stir into skillet and simmer all together for about 7 minutes.

1 cup heavy cream
½ cup sherry
¼ cup brandy

Add cream, sherry, and brandy to mushrooms and cook for 20 minutes over low heat. Serve on toast. May also be served on a thin slice of baked ham which has been slightly warmed in a little butter.

Serves 4.

Chick-peas, *garbanzos,* are a favorite vegetable in Spain, served fried, stewed, in casserole dishes, and even used in making cakes.

FRIED CHICK-PEAS

2 *cups chick-peas*
Water
Salt and pepper
Olive oil

Soak peas overnight in water to cover, drain. Cover with fresh salted water and cook until tender, about ½ hour. Sauté peas lightly in hot olive oil. Season with salt and pepper. Served with poached eggs.

4 *servings.*

BROCCOLI ROMAN STYLE

1 *bunch (1 pound) broccoli*
¼ *cup olive oil*
½ *teaspoon salt*
¼ *teaspoon pepper*
1 *cup dry white wine*
Grated Parmesan cheese

Sauté broccoli in olive oil about 5 minutes. Sprinkle with salt and pepper. Pour wine over and simmer until tender. Serve sprinkled with Parmesan cheese.
4 servings.

TWICE-STUFFED BAKED POTATOES

6 baking potatoes. Bake potatoes. Remove centers. Whip with ½ cup rich milk or cream. Add piece of butter and 1½ teaspoons sweet basil, 1½ teaspoons parsley (fresh or dry), 2 tablespoons grated onion, 1½ teaspoons dry tarragon. Whip all together, return mixture to shells. Sprinkle with paprika. Bake for 25 minutes in 400° oven. If you like, sprinkle grated cheese over top of potatoes.

STUFFED ONIONS

Clean 6 medium-sized Spanish onions and boil in salted water until soft; cool and remove the center and fill with any mixture; put in a buttered casserole dish and bake covered until brown. A good filling to experiment with is this:

½ cup minced celery
4 tablespoons melted butter
2 tablespoons chopped parsley
1½ cups bread crumbs
½ cup chopped pecans (you may omit)
Salt and pepper

Mix and stuff. Sprinkle with potato chips crushed fine, and bake at 350° for 30 minutes.
Makes 6 servings.

BOILED SPINACH WITH WHIPPED SOUR CREAM

Wash 2 pounds fresh spinach and cook in its own moisture until tender, seasoning with about 1 teaspoon salt.

Whip ¾ cup sour cream, season with salt, pepper, and a generous grating of nutmeg, and toss with the well-drained spinach. Transfer to a hot platter, garnish with sliced hard-cooked eggs, small triangles of bread, fried in butter and drained.

TARRAGON CARROTS IN SPINACH NESTS

4 medium carrots, cut in small chunks (1⅓ cups)
1 tablespoon butter or margarine
⅛ teaspoon crumbled dried tarragon or ½ teaspoon minced fresh tarragon
Dash garlic salt
1 10-ounce package frozen leaf spinach
4 lemon wedges

Cook carrots in small amount of boiling salted water till tender. Drain; add butter and tarragon; sprinkle with garlic salt. Meanwhile cook spinach according to directions on package. Drain well.

On platter or plates, shape spinach roughly into 4 nests and fill with carrots. Garnish with lemon wedges.
Makes 4 servings.

HORSERADISH BEETS

2 cups diced beets
3 tablespoons sugar
1 tablespoon cornstarch
1 tablespoon horseradish
½ teaspoon salt
1½ teaspoons vinegar
1 tablespoon butter

Drain beets. To beet juice add remaining ingredients. Cook until juice is thickened and cornstarch cooked. Add beets and heat.
6 servings.

BEETS IN ORANGE SAUCE

½ cup orange juice
2 tablespoons lemon juice
1 tablespoon vinegar
½ teaspoon salt
Dash of pepper
1 tablespoon sugar
1 tablespoon cornstarch

1 tablespoon cold water
1 No. 2 can small, whole beets
2 tablespoons butter

Combine in double boiler orange juice, lemon juice, vinegar, salt, pepper, and sugar. Mix cornstarch and water to a smooth paste. Add to juice. Cook until slightly thickened, stirring constantly. Add beets and heat thoroughly. Add butter and blend. Serve hot. *Serves 4.*

SWEET-POTATO BALLS

2 cans sweet potatoes
½ stick butter
½ teaspoon almond flavoring
1 cup sugar
1 cup raisins
Corn flakes or cereal flakes

Drain the potatoes and mash thoroughly. Add sugar, butter, raisins, and flavoring. Mix well. Shape into balls (2 or 3 inches in diameter) and roll in corn flakes until well coated. Top each ball with your favorite meringue recipe. On top of meringue add chopped nuts and ½ marischino cherry. Bake at 350° or 400° until meringue is light brown and balls are heated through. (You may have to experiment with oven temperature, as the meringue shouldn't brown too quickly if balls are to be hot.) Excellent with ham or chicken.

Try this delicate sweet potato soufflé as an added attraction with baked ham for your next dinner party. This combination will give an authentic touch of the Deep South.

SWEET-POTATO SOUFFLÉ

2 cups boiled, mashed sweet potatoes
¾ teaspoon salt
1½ cups rich milk
½ cup honey
2 tablespoons cornstarch
3 eggs, beaten
¾ cup pecans, coarsely chopped

Blend all ingredients in order given. Place in buttered 1½-quart casserole. Bake in slow oven (300°) 30 to 40 minutes until set. *Makes 6-8 servings.*

Note: If the sweet potatoes have a tough grain, it is better to sieve them after cooking.

The light touch of cinnamon and the dates give this sweet-potato dish a distinct flavor all its own.

SWEET POTATOES WITH DATES

3 *pounds sweet potatoes*
¼ *cup cream*
¼ *teaspoon cinnamon*
¾ *teaspoon salt*
¾ *cup chopped pitted dates*
¼ *cup butter, melted*

Cook sweet potatoes until tender. Peel and mash while hot. There should be no lumps. Add cream, cinnamon, salt, dates, and butter. Mix well and turn into buttered 1½-quart casserole and bake in moderate oven (350°) 20 to 25 minutes or until light brown. Serve with roast chicken or turkey.
Makes 6 to 8 servings.

COMPANY PEAS WITH WATER CHESTNUTS

2 *10-ounce packages frozen peas*
1 *5-ounce can (about ⅔ cup) water chestnuts, drained and diced*
3 *to* 4 *tablespoons butter or margarine*
Salt and pepper to taste

Cook frozen peas according to package directions. When barely tender, add chestnuts. Heat briefly; drain. Add butter, salt, and pepper.
Makes 6 to 8 servings.

My good friend Mrs. Tom Layman in Jackson makes the most delicious creamed celery casserole dish. I asked for her recipe. I'm not sure she'll agree to the amounts we've used in our recipe, but it's good. Thanks, Alathena!

DELICIOUS CREAMED CELERY

Slice celery crosswise. Boil in salted water till firm but quite tender. Make a rich cream sauce by using:

2 *tablespoons butter*
2 *tablespoons flour*
1½ to 2 *cups milk (part cream)*
Dash salt, pepper, and ground mace

Add ½ cup grated cheese with 2 or 3 dashes of Tabasco and 1 teaspoon Worcestershire sauce. Pour over celery in buttered casserole, top with generous amount of buttered bread crumbs, and bake in moderate oven for 25 minutes.

Happiness adds and multiplies as we divide it with others – A. Nielsen

Rice, Noodles, and Dumplings

Pot roast of beef demands poppy-seed noodles.

POPPY-SEED NOODLES

Cook 3 cups noodles in 3 quarts boiling salted water (1 tablespoon salt). Drain. Melt 3 tablespoons butter; add 1 tablespoon poppy-seed and ¼ cup chopped blanched almonds. Add drained noodles and toss.

Serve with all meats. Nice for buffets. No potatoes when noodles Romanoff are served.

NOODLES ROMANOFF WITH CREAM CHEESE

8-ounce package cream cheese
1 cup dairy sour cream
1 small onion, minced
½ teaspoon Worcestershire sauce
¼ teaspoon garlic salt
Dash Tabasco sauce

½ teaspoon salt
8-ounce package fine noodles, cooked
½ cup bread crumbs

Stir cream cheese, cream, onion, and seasonings into hot cooked noodles. Mix until blended. Turn into a shallow baking dish. Top with crumbs. Bake at 350° for 25 minutes. Serve hot or cold.
6 servings.

NOODLES ROMANOFF WITH COTTAGE CHEESE

Cook 1 pound of wide noodles until tender. Drain. Mix with 2 cups cottage cheese, 2 cups thick sour cream, ¼ cup finely minced onion, ⅛ teaspoon garlic salt, 3 teaspoons Worcestershire sauce, 1 teaspoon salt, and a dash of Tabasco sauce. If the mixture appears too dry (it should not be at all runny), add a little milk. Place in a buttered baking dish and bake for 30 minutes in a 350° oven. Remove from the oven and top with grated cheese, about ½ to ¾ of a cup. It all depends on the area to be covered. Return to the oven for 10 minutes so the cheese can melt and bubbles.
8 servings.

These are fascinating to make. Be sure the cover fits tightly.

THREE-MINUTE DUMPLINGS

1¼ cups all-purpose flour (unsifted)
3 teaspoons baking powder
1 teaspoon sugar
½ teaspoon salt
1 egg
½ cup cold water

Stir everything together. Dip spoon in hot broth and spoon in about a teaspoon of dough at a time, leaving plenty of room for rising. Cover and boil exactly 3 minutes.
Makes about 10.

GREEN RICE

2 *cups cooked rice (¾ cup uncooked)*
1 *cup grated sharp cheese*
¼ *cup butter, melted*
Salt and pepper
2 *tablespoons chopped onion (half of one small onion, minced)*
1 *cup chopped parsley*
3 *beaten egg yolks*
3 *stiffly beaten egg whites*

Combine all ingredients except egg whites and yolks. Blend thoroughly. Cook rice in morning. Leave in pan. Blend other ingredients with rice. Before baking mix in egg yolks and fold in egg whites. Put in greased baking dish in moderate oven 350°. Bake about 30 minutes; use deep pan. Serve with creamed crab meat, shrimp, or cream of mushroom soup.
6-8 servings.

HEARTY NOODLES

2 *cups noodles*
4 *slices bacon, chopped*
3 *hard-cooked eggs*
2½ *tablespoons butter*
2½ *tablespoons flour*
¼ *teaspoon salt*
¼ *teaspoon paprika*
1 *cup milk*
½ *teaspoon Worcestershire sauce*
1 *cup grated American cheese*
2 *tablespoons pimento*
2 *tablespoons finely chopped parsley*

Cook noodles in salted water; drain. Sauté bacon until crisp and remove from skillet. Sauté noodles in bacon grease until lightly browned. Separate whites and yolks of hard-cooked eggs. Chop whites and force yolks through wire sieve. To make sauce, melt butter, add flour, salt, and paprika; cool 1 minute. Add milk and cook over low heat, stirring constantly until thickened. Remove from range; cool. Add Worcestershire sauce, cheese, pimento, and chopped egg white; blend and reheat for 1 minute. Pile noodles on platter and pour sauce over noodles. Garnish with parsley, riced egg yolks, and bacon strips.
Makes 6-8 servings.

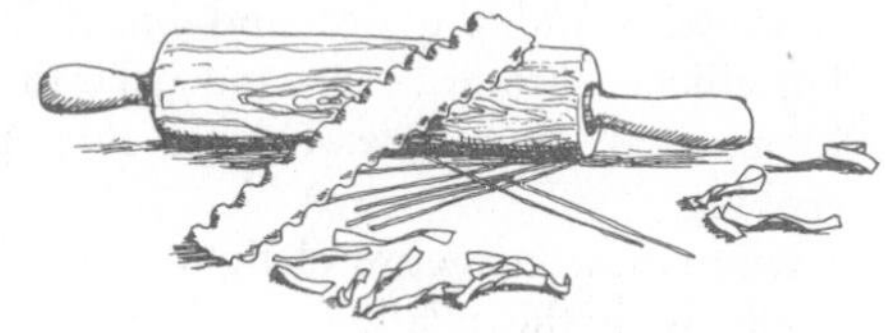

Everyone must try

ALMOND TOKAY PILAF

2 tablespoons instant minced onion
¼ cup water
¼ cup butter or margarine
1 cup regular long-grain rice
2 cups chopped celery and tops
1½ cups chicken stock or broth
1 teaspoon salt
1 teaspoon dried chervil
1 teaspoon dried marjoram
Freshly ground pepper
1 cup toasted almonds, chopped
1½ cups flame Tokay grapes

Stir onion into water; let stand a few minutes. Heat butter till bubbly; toss in rice, onion, and celery. Cook and stir 2 to 5 minutes—just until rice becomes a pale wheat color. Add broth and salt. Cover tightly and simmer over very low heat about 25 minutes, until all the liquid is absorbed. Stir in herbs, pepper—plenty of it—almonds and the grapes, halved and seeded. Mix lightly and stuff into game hens, capon or turkey, or serve separately with meat, fowl, or game.

RICE PILAF

2 cups long grain rice
5 cups chicken broth
1 medium onion, diced
4 stalks celery, diced
6 chicken livers, chopped
½ teaspoon oregano
½ teaspoon salt
½ pound butter or margarine (1 cup)

Melt the butter and brown the onions, celery, chopped chicken livers, oregano, and salt. Add the rice and brown a few minutes more. Add the hot chicken broth, cover, and bake in 350° oven for approximately 40 minutes. Stir at least twice during baking time to insure even cooking.

Cook 1 cup of wild rice to two cups of lightly salted water. When done, drain and mix with the pilaff.

RISOTTO WITH MUSHROOMS

¼ cup olive oil
2 tablespoons chopped onion
1 cup mushrooms, sliced
1 cup rice
1½ cups beef stock
Salt and pepper
½ cup grated Parmesan cheese
2 tablespoons butter

Heat olive oil and sauté onion until golden. Add mushrooms and cook gently for 5 minutes. Add rice and sauté until light golden, stirring constantly. Pour stock over and simmer until tender and liquid absorbed. Season. Remove to serving dish. Sprinkle with cheese and dot with butter.
4-6 *servings.*

CURRIED RICE

Cook rice according to directions on package. Make a rich cream sauce using approximately 2 tablespoons butter to 2 tablespoons flour and 1½ to 2 cups milk or cream. Add salt, pepper, and curry powder to taste. A dash of ground mace is optional to all white sauces. If too thick, add more milk. Place cooked rice in casserole dish and pour medium thick curry sauce over rice. Bake at 350° for about 25 minutes. You can use ½ cup mushrooms in sauce if you like. This amount of sauce will take about 4 cups cooked rice. This rice is delicious served with beef, pork, veal, or fowl.

John Suurs makes wonderful tasting wild rice. Here is how he does it:

WILD RICE

1 *cup wild rice*
3 *cups chicken or beef stock*
¼ *cup butter*
2 *tablespoons onion*
3 *tablespoons chopped green pepper*
¼ *cup chopped celery*
Salt, pepper, pinch of sage

Sauté onions, pepper, celery in butter. Add washed wild rice, stock, salt, pepper, and sage. Bring to a boil. Let simmer for 30 minutes, stirring occasionally. Excellent with all fowl and meats.
Serves 6.

He who would eat the kernel must crack the shell – Platus

Eggs and Cheese

Eggs have been important to man for centuries. History reveals that eggs were a food delicacy in ancient and Biblical times, and a staple food wherever abundant. Eggs were revered as a sacred symbol by the ancients, who believed the egg represented the world and its elements. The breaking of the egg was a ceremony and a means of augury. Men of early times hung eggs in Egyptian temples of worship. Today they are playing an even more important role in the modern homemakers' menu-planning.

QUICK CHEESE-CHICKEN SOUFFLÉS

Do you ever make a soufflé, that impressive concoction, hiding airy lightness under a crown that's golden brown? Delectable, indeed. Yet, women hesitate to make soufflés because they think it is difficult. This recipe is almost failure-proof. Canned chicken soup is used to make the basic sauce. The bits of chicken add additional flavor. Here's what you'll need for six individual cheese-chicken soufflés — 10½-ounce can of condensed cream of chicken soup, 8-ounce package of sharp natural Cheddar cheese, shredded, ⅛ teaspoon of pepper, and 6 eggs, separated. Heat the soup, add the cheese and pepper, and stir until the cheese melts. Remove from heat and cool slightly, beat the egg yolks until thick, beat the egg whites until stiff but not dry, blend the yolks into the cheese sauce, then fold in the beaten egg whites. Pour the mixture into 6 1½-cup ungreased casseroles. Bake in a slow 300° oven for 50 minutes or until golden brown. Serve with buttered asparagus and a good crisp mixed green salad.

Like the grape with its various vintages, caviar has its differences of quality and flavor.

Four kinds of sturgeon give their eggs for caviar. Beluga is the largest. It weighs around 1,000 pounds and only 10% represents the eggs. It's the height of luxury when it is served in its original container, surrounded by cracked ice, minced egg white, sieved egg yolk, onion, and toast rounds. Thin little French crêpes are good served with caviar, too.

Poached eggs and caviar – just a different approach! It is good.

POACHED EGGS, CAVIAR

1 *piece buttered toast*
1 *slice nearly-ripe tomato*
1 *poached egg*
½ *teaspoon caviar*
1 *fillet anchovy*
Sprig parsley

Cut a large round out of the piece of toast. On it place the slice of tomato. On the tomato place a poached egg. Garnish with caviar, top with anchovy fillet and parsley. (A thin slice of ham may be put under tomato slice.) *Makes 1 serving.*

One day during the time I was dietitian at the Cat Key Club on Cat Cay in the Bahamas, we featured on our luncheon menu elegant "strawberry omelet." This met with great disapproval on the part of one of our most distinguished guests. His remarks were, "Who ever heard of such a thing, strawberry omelet." However, our French maître d' hôtel, Paul Coté, urged him to try just a half. The distraught gentleman consented and in a matter of minutes he sent word he would like an entire order, saying it was the best thing he'd eaten in a long time. He is now a loyal and devoted follower of strawberry omelet.

Hope you will be, too!

STRAWBERRY OMELET WITH SOUR CREAM

3 *eggs*
1 *tablespoon light cream*
¼ *teaspoon salt*
2 *tablespoons butter*
¼ *cup sour cream*
½ *cup frozen or fresh strawberries*
Powdered sugar

Beat the eggs in a bowl, add the cream and salt. Beat with a fork for ½ minute. Heat the butter in a skillet until it sizzles. Pour in the beaten eggs. Stir once or twice with a fork. Lift the edges as the eggs begin to cook and let the liquid part run under. Shake the pan back and forth to keep the omelet free. When cooked but still soft on top, add ½ of the sour cream and ½ of the berries. Slide the omelet well to the right edge of the pan and fold over.

Pour remaining sour cream and berries on top, sprinkle lightly with powdered sugar, and run under a hot broiler for 10 seconds. *Serves 1.*

For a change in macaroni dishes, try this one. It's delicious, especially with the sauce.

MACARONI MOUSSE

1 *cup cooked broken elbow macaroni*
1½ *cups scalding milk*
1 *cup soft bread crumbs*
⅓ *cup melted butter*
1 *pimento (chopped fine)*
1 *tablespoon parsley*
1 *medium-sized onion (chopped fine)*
1½ *cups American cheese (grated)*
3 *teaspoons salt*
Dash paprika
⅛ *teaspoon pepper*
3 *eggs*

Cook macaroni in boiling water until done, drain, rinse in cold water. Pour scalding milk over bread crumbs; add butter, pimento, parsley, onion, grated cheese, salt and pepper; then add well-beaten

eggs. Pour cooked macaroni in well-buttered loaf pan (quite large). Then pour the above mixture over macaroni. Bake about 1 hour in slow oven or until loaf is firm. Serve with mushroom sauce.
Serves 8 very nicely.

Mushroom Sauce:

- 3 *tablespoons butter or margarine*
- ½ *pound fresh mushrooms, sliced*
- 1 *tablespoon all-purpose flour*
- 1 *teaspoon soy sauce*
- ¾ *cup light cream*

Melt butter. Add mushrooms; sprinkle with flour; toss. Cook over medium heat, stirring occasionally, 8 to 10 minutes, or till tender. Add soy sauce, slowly stir in cream. Cook and stir till mixture bubbles and thickens. Season to taste. Serve with steak or on toast.

One of my favorite combinations.

DEVILED EGGS AND ASPARAGUS EN CASSEROLE

- 6 *hard-cooked eggs*
- ¼ *teaspoon dry mustard*
- ¼ *teaspoon celery salt*
- 2½ *tablespoons salad dressing*
- ¼ *teaspoon salt*
- ⅛ *teaspoon pepper*
- 3 *tablespoons butter*
- 3 *tablespoons flour*
- ½ *teaspoon salt*
- 1½ *cup milk*
- 1 *cup grated American cheese*
- 1 *teaspoon grated onions*
- 2 *tablespoons minced pimento*
- 1 *pound fresh or frozen asparagus, cooked (use spears—not cuts of asparagus)*
- 1 *cup corn flakes*
- 1 *tablespoon butter, melted*

Cut eggs in half lengthwise. Remove yolks and combine with mustard, celery salt, salad dressing, salt and pepper. Fill egg whites with yolk mixture.

Melt butter in heavy saucepan; stir in flour and salt. Add milk gradually, stirring constantly. Cook until thickened, stirring occasionally. Add cheese and onions, stir until cheese is melted. Stir in pimento.

Crush corn flakes into fine crumbs; combine with melted butter. Spread half the asparagus in bottom of greased 1½-quart casserole; arrange eggs on top (cut-side up). Put remainder of asparagus on top. Cover with cheese sauce. Sprinkle crushed corn-flake mixture on top. Bake about 20 minutes at 350° or until browned on top.

EGG AND BACON RINGS

Slowly broil or pan-fry bacon strips about two minutes. (Allow 2 slices for each egg.) Grease muffin pans and line the sides of each with 2 bacon slices. Gently drop 1 egg into each muffin pan and sprinkle with salt. (For a spicy flavor, add 1 tablespoon chili sauce before adding egg.) Bake in moderate oven (325°) for about 15 minutes or until eggs are set. Loosen the egg and bacon rings with a knife, then lift out of muffin pan. Serve immediately with cinnamon toast and sliced oranges.

CUSTARD MACARONI AND CHEESE

½ *pound macaroni*
1 *tablespoon butter*
1 *egg, beaten*
1 *teaspoon salt*
1 *teaspoon dry mustard*
3 *cups grated sharp cheese*
1 *cup milk*

Boil the macaroni in water until tender and drain thoroughly. Stir in the butter and egg; mix the mustard and salt with 1 tablespoon

hot water and add to the macaroni. Add the cheese, leaving enough to sprinkle on the top. Pour into a buttered casserole, add the milk, sprinkle with the cheese, and bake at 350° for about 45 minutes, or until the custard is set and the top crusty.
Serves 8.

Now have great fun with your fondue, but remember this Swiss tradition:

If a lad should drop his bread, his penalty is wine around; but if a lassie should lose her cube, then to her neighbor she owes a kiss!

FONDUE RECIPE

1 *pound Swiss cheese, shredded*
1 *clove fresh garlic*
2 *cups dry, white wine*
1 *teaspoon cornstarch*
3 *tablespoons kirsch, or 4 tablespoons cognac*
Nutmeg, pepper, or paprika to taste
2 *loaves Italian or French bread cut in bite-size pieces*

Rub cooking utensil with garlic. Pour in wine; set over slow heat. When air bubbles rise to surface in wine, add cheese by handfuls, stirring constantly with wooden fork or spoon. Keep stirring until cheese is melted. Dissolve cornstarch in kirsch. Add to cheese mixture. Stir for 2 or 3 minutes, add spices. Serve bubbling hot.
Serves 4.

AUSTRIAN EGGS

8 *hard-cooked eggs*
4 *tablespoons anchovy paste or caviar*
4 *tablespoons cold, cooked chicken, finely chopped*
4 *tablespoons cooked celery, finely chopped*
5 *tablespoons mayonnaise*
Salt and cayenne
Dry mustard

Cut eggs into halves lengthwise. Remove yolks and mash. Mix anchovy paste (or caviar), chicken, celery, mayonnaise, and blend well with mashed yolks. Season with salt, cayenne, and dry mustard.

Fill egg halves. Sprinkle with paprika. Serve on lettuce leaves or toast.
6-8 servings.

Surprise — oysters in the rarebit!

WELSH RAREBIT WITH OYSTERS

3 *tablespoons butter*
3 *cups (¾ pound) grated American cheese*
1 *teaspoon salt*
1 *teaspoon dry mustard*
½ *teaspoon paprika*
1 *cup beer*
24 *small oysters, shucked*

In a saucepan or chafing dish, combine the butter, cheese, salt, mustard, and paprika. Cook over low heat, stirring constantly until cheese begins to melt. Gradually add the beer and continue stirring constantly until almost smooth. Add the oysters; cook 3 minutes. Serve on toast.
Serves 6.

EASY WELSH RAREBIT

4 *tablespoons butter*
1 *teaspoon salt*
½ *teaspoon paprika*
¼ *teaspoon cayenne pepper*
½ *teaspoon prepared mustard*
1 *teaspoon Worcestershire sauce*
1 *pound sharp processed cheese, grated*
About 1 cup beer or ale
2 *eggs, slightly beaten*

In double boiler, melt butter, add seasonings and cheese. Stir until cheese is soft. Add some beer, tablespoon by tablespoon, stirring gently. Mix the slightly beaten eggs with a little of the beer and add last, stirring until the rarebit is smooth. Serve on French bread cut rather thick and oven-toasted, or slices of broiled tomatoes.
Serves 6.

ESCALLOPED CHEESE

6 slices bread
2½ cups sharp cheese (grated)
½ teaspoon salt
¼ teaspoon cayenne pepper
2 cups milk
3 eggs
Dry mustard

Remove crusts from bread. Butter and cut in cubes. Cover bottom of casserole or pan. Cover with grated cheese. Beat eggs well, add milk, salt, mustard, and cayenne pepper. Pour over double layer of bread cubes and cheese and let stand 20 minutes to ½ hour before baking in 350° oven. Bake ¾ to 1 hour. This can be served plain or with tomato or mushroom cream sauce, or topped with crushed corn flakes.

MAIN DISH SOUFFLÉ

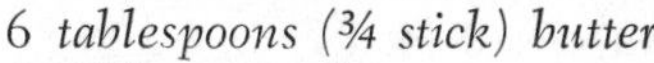

6 tablespoons (¾ stick) butter
6 tablespoons flour
¾ teaspoon salt
⅛ teaspoon pepper
1½ cups milk
2 cups shredded Cheddar cheese or
1 cup (7-ounce can) tuna or
1 cup (10-ounce can) spinach, well-drained
6 egg yolks, slightly beaten
6 egg whites

In saucepan melt butter; blend in flour, salt, and pepper to form a smooth paste. Gradually stir in milk; heat, stirring constantly, until thick. Add cheese or tuna or spinach; heat, stirring constantly, until cheese is melted or tuna or spinach is heated through. Cool slightly; blend in egg yolks. Beat egg whites until stiff; fold sauce into egg whites. Pour into 2-quart soufflé dish; bake 40-50 minutes in 350° oven. Serve immediately. 4-5 *servings.*

Note: Spinach or tuna soufflé may be served with a cheese sauce.

You are sure to please with this.

EXCELLENT CHEESE SOUFFLÉ

3 tablespoons butter
¼ cup flour
1⅞ cups milk
1 teaspoon salt
Dash of cayenne pepper
1 teaspoon prepared mustard
2 drops Worcestershire sauce
1 cup grated American cheese, packed
6 eggs

Make a cream sauce by melting the butter and blending into the flour. Cook until bubbly. Add the milk, salt, cayenne, mustard, and Worcestershire sauce, and bring to a boil, stirring constantly. Boil 1 minute. Remove from heat and cool slightly. Add the cheese. Beat the egg yolks until thick, and add the cheese mixture, stirring constantly. Beat the egg whites until stiff. Fold into the cheese mixture carefully; pour into a well-buttered baking dish (¾ full). Bake at 300° in a hot-water bath for 2 hours, or until a silver knife inserted into the center comes out clean. This soufflé keeps a day in the refrigerator after baking, so it can be a leftover successfully. Use this as a base for creamed chicken or sea food.

BREAD-AND-CHEESE PUFF

8 slices buttered enriched bread
½ pound package sliced American cheese (8 slices)
Salt and pepper
4 eggs, beaten
1 quart milk
1 teaspoon Worcestershire sauce
Dash of Tabasco

Set oven for moderate 350°.

Place 4 slices bread on bottom of shallow baking dish, cutting to fit. Cover bread with half of the cheese; sprinkle with salt and pepper. Repeat. Combine remaining ingredients; pour over bread and cheese. Bake 40 minutes or until top is golden brown, and puffed. *Makes 6 servings.*

The burden becomes light which is cheer-fully borne – Ovid

Casseroles and One-Dish Meals

We all love casseroles and one-meal dishes—and why not! They're fast to fix, flavorful, easy, glamorous, and good-tasting. The main dish is in the oven while you put a salad and dessert together. Wonderful for modern homemakers on the go!

BAKED EGGPLANT AND MEAT CASSEROLE

Syrians who settled in the area probably are responsible for the popularity of this casserole combination. It appears both as a vegetable dish and as a main course at easy, one-dish meals.

1 *medium-sized eggplant*
½ *pound ground beef*
5 *tablespoons margarine*
½ *cup minced onion*
¼ *cup chopped green pepper*
2 *cups cooked rice*

1 *teaspoon salt*
½ *teaspoon pepper*
½ *cup bread crumbs*

Peel eggplant and cut into cubes. Cook in boiling salted water until tender (about 15-20 minutes). Drain; mash eggplant with a fork.

Brown ground beef in 3 tablespoons margarine. Add minced onion and chopped pepper; cook until vegetables are tender. Stir in mashed eggplant, cooked rice, salt, and pepper.

Spoon into a 10 x 6 x 2-inch baking dish. Sauté bread crumbs in remaining 2 tablespoons margarine. Sprinkle over eggplant mixture. Bake in moderate oven (375°) for about 20 minutes. *Makes* 4-6 *servings.*

CASSEROLE SANS SOUCI

Combine cut blue lake green beans in a casserole dish with baked-ham strips and cream-of-mushroom soup sauce. Top with mounds of mashed potato mixed with grated cheese. Bake in a moderate oven until heated thoroughly.

DRIED BEEF-BROCCOLI CASSEROLE

2 *packages frozen broccoli—cook until tender*
½ *package (8-ounce size) noodles—cooked and drained*
4 *tablespoons butter*
3 *tablespoons flour*
2 *cups milk*
1 *jar or 14-ounce package dried beef*
½ *teaspoon Worcestershire sauce*
½ *teaspoon salt*
¼ *teaspoon pepper*
½ *cup bread crumbs*

Make white sauce with butter, flour, and milk. To assemble: pull dried beef into shreds, cut cooked broccoli into chunks, and add beef, broccoli, Worcestershire sauce, salt, and pepper to sauce. Put cooked noodles in the bottom of the casserole and spoon dried beef-broccoli mixture on top.

Melt remaining 2 tablespoons butter and fry bread crumbs. Sprinkle over casserole mixture and bake at 375° for 20 minutes.

An unusual casserole dish for potluck.

RICE AND CHICK-PEA CASSEROLE

½ *pound dried chick-peas or 3 cups canned*
1 *pound lean pork*
1 *cup sliced onions*
2 *cloves garlic, minced*
3 *tablespoons olive oil*
2 *teaspoons salt*
½ *teaspoon freshly ground black pepper*
1 *teaspoon Spanish paprika*
1½ *cups raw rice*
4 *cups chicken broth*
2 *Spanish or Italian sausages, sliced*
3 *eggs, beaten*

Soak the dried chick-peas overnight in water to cover. Drain, add fresh water, and cook 1 hour. Drain.

Cut the pork in narrow strips. Brown the pork, onions, and garlic in the olive oil. Add the salt, pepper, paprika, rice, broth, sausages, and chick-peas. Cover.

Bake in a 375° oven 1 hour. Taste for seasoning. Gently mix the eggs in and bake uncovered until eggs set, about 10 minutes.
Serves 6.

PARTY HAM CASSEROLE

3 *cups diced cooked ham*
3 *medium potatoes, cooked and sliced*
1 *No. 303 can or 1 pound green beans, cooked*
¼ *cup butter or margarine*
¼ *cup flour*
2 *cups milk*
1 *cup grated American cheese*
¼ *cup slivered, blanched almonds*
2 *tablespoons melted butter or margarine*
1½ *cups soft bread crumbs*

Melt ¼ cup butter or margarine. Stir in flour. Gradually add milk, stirring constantly until thickened. Add cheese and cook very slowly until melted. Add almonds. Arrange potatoes in a greased 2½-quart casserole; cover with green beans. Pour half of cheese sauce over green beans. Add ham and remaining sauce. Mix melted butter or margarine with bread crumbs. Sprinkle crumbs over casserole. Bake in a moderate oven (350°) for 30 to 35 minutes or until crumbs are lightly browned. *7 to 8 servings.*

Be daring and make the cheese blintzes; you'll hit an all-time high in popularity, I know!

CHEESE BLINTZES

2 eggs
½ cup sifted flour
¾ cup milk and water mixed
1 tablespoon melted butter
Pinch of salt

Make a thin batter. Beat the eggs and then add the flour alternately with the liquid. Beat with a fork until smooth, then add the melted butter and salt. Beat again until smooth.

Heat a heavy skillet and butter well before pouring in a thin stream of batter, starting at center and tilting pan to spread the mixture evenly across the bottom. Reduce the heat immediately after pouring in the batter. When brown on the underside, turn out and start the next blintz.

Long-range goals keep one from being frustrated by short-range failures—Noble

Spread the following mixture on the browned side of each blintz.

Filling:

1 *pound cottage cheese*
1 *egg yolk*
2 *tablespoons sugar*
Pinch of salt
Few drops of vanilla and cinnamon, or brandy

Mix with a fork to a nice spreading mixture. Spread evenly on each blintz and roll up, folding in the ends. Brown in butter until browned on all sides. Serve with sour cream, canned berries, cherries, or delicious with fresh strawberries.

TUNA FLORENTINE

3 *tablespoons butter or margarine*
1 *onion, sliced*
1 *1-pound can (2 cups) tomatoes*
1 *8-ounce can (1 cup) seasoned tomato sauce*
1 *teaspoon salt*
1 *6½-, 7-, or 9¼-ounce can tuna*
4 *ounces (2 cups) medium noodles, cooked*
1 *10-ounce package frozen chopped spinach, cooked and drained*
¼ *cup shredded Parmesan cheese*

Melt butter; add onion and cook till tender. Add next 3 ingredients. Simmer uncovered about 20 minutes. Break tuna in chunks; add with noodles. Turn into 2-quart casserole. Spoon spinach around edge and sprinkle with cheese. Bake in moderate oven (375°) about 25 minutes. *Makes 6 servings.*

TUNA FISH, NOODLE, AND ASPARAGUS CASSEROLE

6 *tablespoons butter*
6 *tablespoons flour*
1 *teaspoon salt*
¼ *teaspoon pepper*
3 *cups milk*

1½ *cups grated sharp cheese*
1 *teaspoon Worcestershire sauce*
1 *13-ounce can tuna fish*
2 *cups cooked fine noodles*
2 *packages frozen asparagus*

Melt the butter, stir in the flour, salt, and pepper. Add milk slowly and cook until thick. Add the cheese and Worcestershire sauce, and when blended, put tuna fish, noodles, and asparagus in layers in a well-buttered 2-quart casserole and pour the sauce over. Dot with 2 pimentos cut in small pieces and bake at 350° until brown and bubbly.
Serves 8.

You can't miss on this one. It's an old stand-by.

EASY TUNA LOAF

2 *eggs*
1 *can mushroom soup*
1 *scant tablespoon grated onion*
1 *scant tablespoon chopped celery*
3 *cups corn flakes*
1 *small can tuna fish*
1 *tablespoon butter*

Mix and bake in regular meat loaf pan at 350° for 30-40 minutes.

Easy Mustard Sauce for Tuna:

2 *tablespoons butter*
2 *teaspoons prepared mustard*
5 *teaspoons flour*
1 *teaspoon salt*
2 *egg yolks*
1½ *cups milk*
1 *tablespoon lemon juice*

Melt butter in boiler, add flour, salt, and mustard. Whip eggs, add milk, then add this to the first ingredients. Cook until thick, then add lemon juice.

The lowly tuna dressed up gourmet style.

TUNA FISH PIE

3 tablespoons butter
½ cup chopped onions
1 medium stalk celery, chopped
3 tablespoons flour
½ teaspoon salt
⅛ teaspoon curry powder
Dash of pepper
Double-crust pie pastry
2 cups milk
1 7-ounce can tuna, drained and flaked
1 cup canned peas, drained
3 tablespoons chopped dill pickles

Line 9-inch pie pan with pastry. Sauté onions and celery in butter until tender and clear but not brown. Remove from heat. Blend in flour, salt, curry powder, and pepper; slowly stir in milk. Return to low heat, cook until sauce thickens and boils one minute. Stir in tuna, peas, and dill pickle, heat to boiling, stirring constantly. Pour into the pie pan, place upper crust on top, crimp and seal. Cut gashes in crust. Bake in hot 425° oven 25-30 minutes.

Please don't neglect the little dab of curry powder and the chopped dill pickles. They are the ingredients that lift this dish out of the ordinary. If you don't trust yourself with pie crusts or are in a hurry, you can pour the tuna mixture in a greased 1½-quart baking dish, top it with refrigerated biscuits and bake in a 400° oven for about 20 minutes until the biscuits are brown. But if you have the time, it's really much better as a pie.

BAKED OYSTERS AND MACARONI

2 cups cooked macaroni
1 pint oysters
4 tablespoons butter
½ cup grated cheese (I use more)
½ cup light cream
Salt, pepper, paprika
Crumbs

Place a layer of cooked macaroni in a greased baking dish. Sprinkle with grated cheese. Add a layer of oysters; sprinkle with crumbs, salt, pepper, paprika, dot with butter. Repeat. Have a layer of oysters and crumbs on top. Pour the heated cream into the side of the dish. Bake in hot oven (400°) about 30 minutes.
Serves 6.

SALMON MOUSSE WITH SOUR-CREAM CUCUMBER SAUCE

3 cups cooked salmon
½ tablespoon salt
1½ tablespoons sugar
½ tablespoon flour
1 teaspoon dry mustard
Few grains of cayenne
2 egg yolks
1½ tablespoons melted butter
¾ cup milk
¼ cup vinegar
¾ tablespoon granulated gelatin soaked in 2 tablespoons cold water

Separate salmon into flakes. Mix dry ingredients, add egg yolks, butter, milk, and vinegar. Cook over boiling water, stirring constantly until mixture thickens. Add soaked gelatin. Add entire mixture to salmon. Mold, chill, and serve with sour-cream-cucumber sauce.

Sour-Cream-Cucumber Sauce:

1 cup sour cream
1 tablespoon vinegar
1½ tablespoons lemon juice
½ to 1 teaspoon sugar
Few grains of pepper
½ onion passed over grater 2 or 3 times
1 cucumber, seeded, peeled, and diced

Blend ingredients and chill.

Pretty on the buffet table is delicious salmon served gourmet style.

SALMON À LA RITZ

2 cans (1 pound each) salmon
1 envelope unflavored gelatin
¼ cup cold water
1 cup mayonnaise
2 teaspoons prepared mustard
Capers
Pimiento strips
Salad greens
Lemon wedges

Chill cans of salmon thoroughly. Sprinkle gelatin over water to soften; set in a pan of hot water and heat until dissolved. Cool. Mix with mayonnaise and mustard; cool until it begins to thicken. Remove both ends from the cans of salmon and ease from can without breaking; drain on paper toweling. Place salmon end to end on a serving platter. Spread generously with the mayonnaise mixture. Decorate with capers and pimiento. Chill. Serve garnished with greens and lemon wedges. *6 to 8 servings.*

Lovely gleaming chafing dishes encourage party-giving. Salmon prepared this way is party fare!

CHAFING DISH RECIPE

2 cups medium white sauce
¼ cup butter
1 can mushrooms, drained

1 green pepper, diced
3 tablespoons chopped onions
1 cup grated cheese
1 teaspoon salt
⅛ teaspoon pepper
1 box frozen asparagus
1 cup salmon, flaked
Chow mein noodles

Make white sauce in advance. Melt butter, add onion, green pepper, and mushrooms, cook until tender. Add to white sauce. Add cheese and seasonings. When hot, add salmon and asparagus. Serve with chow mein noodles (put noodles on top).
Serves 6.

Of all salmon recipes, this is tops. Of course, we are fond of curry. If you are not, cultivate the taste for this unusual Indian flavor.

SALMON LOAF WITH CURRY SAUCE

1 pound can salmon
1 cup fine bread crumbs
2 tablespoons chopped parsley
2 teaspoons lemon juice
1 cup milk
1 egg, slightly beaten
2 tablespoons chopped onion
¼ teaspoon salt
Dash of pepper

Drain salmon, remove bone and skin, and break into flakes. Combine all ingredients. Place in greased loaf pan or casserole. Bake in 375° oven for 25 to 30 minutes or until loaf is set in center. Remove from oven, cool 5 minutes in pan. Turn out on heated serving platter. Serve with hot curry sauce.

Curry Sauce:

1 tablespoon butter
1 tablespoon onion
1 10½-ounce can cream-of-celery or cream-of-mushroom soup
¼ teaspoon curry powder

Melt butter in saucepan. Chop onion and sauté in butter until golden brown. Blend soup into above and add curry powder. You may add more curry powder if you like. Heat thoroughly and serve immediately over salmon.

CRAB RAREBIT

4-ounce can mushroom stems and pieces
2 tablespoons butter or margarine
¼ cup flour
4 to 5 drops Tabasco sauce
¼ cup chili sauce
1 cup evaporated milk
1 cup grated process cheese (¼ pound)
6½-ounce can crab meat, flaked
⅓ cup sliced stuffed olives

Drain and save liquid from mushrooms. Add enough water to make ½ cup of liquid. Melt butter or margarine in a 2-quart saucepan. Stir in flour until smooth. Gradually stir in mushroom liquid, Tabasco sauce, chili sauce, evaporated milk, and grated cheese. Cook and stir over low heat until cheese melts and mixture begins to thicken. Stir in mushrooms, crab meat, and olives. Heat until steaming, but do not boil. Serve in patty shells or over rice.
Serves 4 to 6.

Bread, beauty and brotherhood are the three great needs of man – Edwin Markham

Sandwiches

An encyclopedia published about 1900 defines a sandwich as "an article of food consisting of a slice of meat, fish, fowl, or other food placed between two slices of bread which may be plain or buttered." This is indeed not the case today. From this simple beginning the sandwich has developed in all directions.

ALMOND CHEESE EXOTICA

Stir roasted diced almonds into cream cheese softened with a little crushed pineapple. Add a dash of curry powder for an exotic sandwich spread.

FRENCH BEEF SANDWICHES

2 cups ground cooked beef
½ cup thick gravy or ½ can condensed mushroom soup
2 teaspoons grated onion
½ teaspoon salt
Butter or margarine
12 slices bread
2 eggs
½ cup milk

Heat gravy or mushroom soup and combine with ground cooked beef, grated onion, and salt. Spread each of 6 slices of bread with butter or margarine and approximately ⅓ cup meat mixture. Top with remaining bread. Beat eggs and add milk. Dip sandwiches in egg mixture. Set oven regulator to broil. Place sandwiches on broiler rack. Insert broiler pan and rack so the top of sandwiches is about 2 inches from the heat. Broil until lightly browned, about 5 minutes. Turn and brown on other side. Serve hot.
4 to 6 servings.

Even if you don't like crab meat, try it! Scrumptious!

BARBECUED CRAB-MEAT SANDWICHES

½ cup chili sauce
3 ounces cream cheese
*1 cup crab meat**
½ teaspoon horseradish
½ teaspoon Worcestershire sauce
1 teaspoon finely chopped onion
2 teaspoons lemon juice
4 round buns
½ cup American cheese, grated

Mix chili sauce with cream cheese. Add crab meat and other ingredients, except cheese. Add more seasonings, if desired. Cut buns in two. Butter cut surface.

Heap crab-meat mixture on buns. Sprinkle with grated cheese on each one. Put under broiler or in hot oven (425°) to melt cheese.
8 Servings.
*Tuna fish may be substituted for crab meat.

For a crowd these are sensational! Can be made ahead, too!

DELICIOUS BURGERS

1 pound ground beef
1 cup Munster cheese
⅔ cups tomato sauce
¾ teaspoon salt
¼ teaspoon garlic salt
¼ teaspoon sliced olives

Brown meat and add other ingredients. Slice hard rolls and fill. Wrap in foil. Prepare ahead if desired, and keep in refrigerator. Put in 400° oven for 15 to 20 minutes. (Add oregano if desired.)

Dads and boys alike will rave for "Denvers."

DAD'S DENVERS

6 hamburger buns, split and toasted
One 4½-ounce can deviled ham
4 eggs
¼ cup milk
¼ teaspoon salt
Dash pepper
¼ cup chopped green onion
2 tablespoons butter, margarine, or bacon drippings
6 thin tomato slices
6 slices sharp process American cheese

Spread lower half of buns with deviled ham. Combine eggs, milk, salt, and pepper. Beat slightly for gold-and-white effect, thoroughly for all-yellow eggs. Add onions. Heat butter in skillet till just hot enough to make a drop of water sizzle. Pour in egg mixture. Reduce heat and cook, lifting and folding occasionally, till eggs are set, but still moist. Pile egg atop deviled ham and add tomato and cheese slices. Place on cooky sheet; broil about 4 inches from heat just till cheese melts. Cover with bun tops.
Makes 6.

This is one of the popular sandwiches served for luncheon at the Country House. Many of our clients, guests, and staff members request it. It's called many names. We prefer to call it

SPECIAL COUNTRY-HOUSE SANDWICH

On dinner plate, place slice of buttered rye bread. Add the following: slices of Swiss cheese, lettuce, tomatoes, turkey, or chicken. I prefer white meat, thinly sliced. Make your sandwich as high as you like.

On top of sandwich, ladle well-seasoned Thousand Island dressing. Be generous with it, too! Garnish with two strips of crisply fried bacon and slices of hard-cooked egg. This is a delicious, hearty sandwich and of course must be eaten with a fork. It's important that your dressing be tasty. Allow your own taste buds to determine the flavor of the dressing. We recommend the following Thousand Island dressing:

Thousand Island Dressing:

1 pint mayonnaise or salad dressing
1 12-ounce bottle chili sauce
2 tablespoons chopped green onion or chives
2 tablespoons chopped stuffed olives
2 tablespoons sweet pickle relish
2 hard-cooked eggs, chopped fine
½ teaspoon salt
¼ teaspoon pepper
1 tablespoon Worcestershire sauce
Generous dash of Tabasco sauce

Blend all the above ingredients together. Pour in covered container and place in refrigerator until serving time. Serve chilled.

Imagine sauerkraut in a sandwich! It's good, too!

KRAUT ROUND DOGS

8 franks
8 round sandwich buns
Butter or margarine
1¼ cups sauerkraut

Mustard
Catsup
Mayonnaise or pickle relish

Cut franks on one side three-fourths of the way through at half-inch intervals. Simmer in water 5 minutes, grill, or broil. As the franks heat, they will curl into a ring. Toast and spread split sandwich buns with butter. Heat sauerkraut. Place a hot frank on the bottom half of each bun. Fill centers of round franks with drained, hot sauerkraut, and top with mustard, catsup, mayonnaise, or pickle relish. Cover with bun tops and serve hot.
Yield: 8 sandwiches.

CHICKEN-AND-CHEESE SANDWICHES

Blend 2 cups canned chicken (removed from bones) with 6 ounces creamed cheese, 1 teaspoon Worcestershire sauce, ½ teaspoon celery salt, ¼ teaspoon black pepper, 1 tablespoon meat sauce, and 1 teaspoon prepared mustard. Mix thoroughly, spread on fresh white bread, trim crusts. Form into sandwiches cut into triangles.

DELICIOUS HAM SANDWICH

Toast bread on one side. Turn over and place slice of ham, generous serving of flaked crab meat, mustard, and mayonnaise on bread. Place under broiler and broil until bubbly and light golden brown. Serve with chip dill pickles.

You can preach a better sermon with your life than with your lips — Goldsmith

Stuffings for Fowl

Don't be mislead into thinking the turkey will stand on its own. Confidentially, it will; but it's far more regal to serve your tastiest stuffing with Mr. Tom Turkey or Milady Hen Turkey.

OYSTER STUFFING

½ *cup chopped celery*
½ *cup chopped onion*
1 *bay leaf*
¼ *cup butter or margarine*
6 *cups dry bread crumbs*
1 *tablespoon chopped parsley*
3 *cups chopped raw oysters*
1 *teaspoon poultry seasoning*
Salt and pepper
2 *beaten eggs*
1¾ *cups oyster liquor and milk*

Cook celery, onion, and bay leaf in butter until tender but not brown. Discard bay leaf. Add crumbs and parsley to butter mixture. Mix thoroughly. Add oysters, seasonings, and eggs. Add enough of the liquid mixture to moisten.
Makes enough stuffing for a 10 to 12 pound turkey.

WILD-RICE STUFFING

1 cup wild rice
Giblets (liver, gizzard, and heart)
2 cups hot broth or water
½ cup finely chopped onion
½ cup butter or margarine
2 quarts oven-toasted dry bread crumbs
1 teaspoon salt
¼ teaspoon ground sage
¼ teaspoon pepper
2 eggs, beaten

Cook the rice according to directions on the package. Chop the giblets fine and cook in water until done. Sauté onion in the butter until yellow in color, add the bread crumbs with the giblets and broth. Add the seasonings and mix lightly. Cover and let stand until the bread is moist. Add the wild rice and eggs, and mix lightly. Pour into a buttered baking dish and bake for 25 minutes at 325°, or stuff whatever fowl you are roasting and cook during the last 20 minutes of its cooking.

CHESTNUT DRESSING

1 pound chestnuts, chopped
½ loaf white bread
3 cups water
½ cup chopped Virginia ham
½ stalk celery, chopped
2 medium onions, chopped
1 tablespoon parsley

Soak bread in water; add chopped ham. Brown celery and onions lightly; add bread and ham with chestnuts, freshly boiled. Stir thoroughly. Bake at 300° for 15 minutes.

Serve with your holiday turkey which has been roasted separately after having been stuffed with celery, chopped onion, and carrots.

SAUSAGE STUFFING

- 2 *pounds pure pork sausage meat*
- 2 *cups water*
- 14 *cups dry bread cubes*
- ¼ *cup chopped onion*
- ½ *cup chopped parsley*
- 2 *cups chopped celery*
- 2 *teaspoons salt*

Pan-fry sausage until brown and well cooked. Combine all ingredients, mixing well. Stuff bird just before roasting. Poultry seasoning may be added.
Yield: 12 cups (enough to stuff 16-pound bird).

This is truly a gourmet's delight. I have been making it for years.

GOURMET TURKEY STUFFING

Simmer until soft and transparent 2 cups of finely sliced or chopped onions in ½ pound of butter. And it must be butter. When onions are sufficiently cooked, add 1 quart of milk and continue to simmer until milk is hot. In a large mixing bowl have ready 8 cups of slightly stale white bread cut into small cubes. I trim most of the crust. On top of the bread throw 1 generous handful of finely chopped parsley, 1 teaspoon of poultry seasoning, 1 teaspoon of salt, ½ teaspoon garlic salt, ½ teaspoon white pepper, ½ teaspoon celery salt, ½ teaspoon of curry powder. Pour the hot milk and onion mixture over the seasoned bread and mash and mix well with a potato masher.

When thoroughly mixed, add four eggs well beaten first. The dressing should be soft but not runny when it goes into the turkey as it hardens during the cooking process. If dressing is too soft, add a bit more bread. If too hard, increase the milk. In stuffing a turkey, I fill the main cavity only, and keep the dressing in place with a couple slices of bread which in turn are held firmly by tightly tying the legs to the tail. The wings simply lock back towards the pan.

In the neck cavity I put a quartered California orange, skin and all. This imparts a delicate flavor and aroma to both bird and gravy.

BREAD STUFFING

1½ cups finely chopped onion
1½ cups finely chopped celery
⅓ cup butter
8 cups dry bread cubes (½″)
1 egg, well beaten
1½ teaspoons salt
⅛ teaspoon pepper
½ teaspoon poultry seasoning
½ teaspoon sage
¼ cup water

Cook onion and celery in butter in a skillet until tender. Add mixture to bread cubes which have been placed in a large pan. Sprinkle with seasonings which have been mixed together. Combine. Add water and egg. Toss together with forks. Stuff bird immediately and roast.
Yield: 9 cups (enough to stuff 12-pound bird).

Chestnut Stuffing:

Add 1 cup chopped cooked chestnuts to bread stuffing. Combine as for bread stuffing.

Corn-Bread Stuffing:

Omit 8 cups dry bread cubes in bread stuffing. Add 8 cups crumbled corn bread. Combine as for bread stuffing.

Give us this day our daily bread (Matt. 6:11)

Breads

Local tradition and taste peculiarity determine the character of many homemade breads. New England has its steamed Boston brown and its extra crusty spider corn bread, made in an old-fashioned frying pan. The South has its batter bread. The "Tall-Corn Belt" smacks its lips over fresh corn bread (and many sections recall pioneer days with hoe cakes, no longer baked on the blade of a hoe). But the entire nation of homemakers unites in making the palate-proved favorite, old-fashioned white bread.

Golden-crusted, warm, and flaky, Win Schuler's Homemade Bread is served in small loaves on individual breadboards as a pre-dinner taste tempter at the famous Schuler's Restaurants in Michigan. Once tried, you will want to serve the large-sized loaves to your family.

WIN SCHULER'S HOMEMADE BREAD

Blend well on low speed 6 cups flour and one teaspoon salt.

Scald 2 cups of milk. To scald milk, use double boiler. When a thin film forms on top, milk is ready to remove from heat. Lift off film, and let milk cool to lukewarm. Add ¼ cup of oil, ¼ cup sugar, and 2 beaten eggs.

Dissolve 2 cakes of moist yeast in ¼ cup lukewarm water and add this to milk and egg mix. Add liquid mixture to flour and beat.

Remove from mixer and place on floured board. Weigh 5 ounces for small loaves and mold like a bun (for large loaves, 15 ounces). Pyrex pans may be used, although we use tin. Fold over sides and tuck in ends. Butter generously and let double in size. The dough is kept at room temperature while rising. This is done after it is placed in the pans. Bake small loaves 30 minutes in 350° oven, large loaves 55 minutes. *Makes 10-12 small loaves, or 3-4 large loaves.*

OATMEAL BREAD

¾ *cup boiling water*
½ *cup rolled oats*
3 *tablespoons butter*
¼ *cup light molasses*
1 *teaspoon salt*
¼ *cup warm water (110°-115°)*
1 *egg*
1 *package dry granular yeast*
2¾ *cups sifted flour*

In large mixing bowl, stir together boiling water, oatmeal, butter, molasses, and salt. Cool to lukewarm. Dissolve yeast in lukewarm water. Add egg, yeast, and half the flour to first mixture. Beat two minutes with mixer, medium speed, or with wooden spoon until smooth. Add rest of flour and mix with spoon until blended. Spread batter evenly in greased loaf pan, 9 x 5 x 3 inches. Smooth top and pat into shape with floured hand. Let rise in warm place until batter is 1 inch from top of pan (about 1½ hours). Bake in 375° oven for 50-55 minutes.

For a loaf of bread excitingly different and delicious, try this chocolate cinnamon loaf. After making this bread on the Copper Kettle Show one day, we received hundreds and hundreds of requests for it. It's good!

CHOCOLATE CINNAMON LOAF

¾ *cup warm water (not hot—110°-115°)*
1 *package active dry yeast*

¼ cup shortening
1 teaspoon salt
¼ cup sugar
1 egg
⅓ cup cocoa
2¼ cups sifted enriched flour
1 to 2 tablespoons butter, melted and cooled
1½ teaspoons cinnamon
3 tablespoons sugar

In mixer bowl dissolve yeast in warm water. Add shortening, salt, sugar, egg, cocoa, and 1 cup flour. Beat 2 minutes medium speed on mixer or 300 vigorous strokes by hand. Scrape sides and bottom of bowl frequently. Stir in remaining flour with spoon, blend until smooth. Scrape batter from sides of bowl. Cover with cloth and let rise in warm place (85°) until double in bulk, about 1 hour. (If kitchen is cool, place dough on rack over a bowl of hot water and cover completely with a towel.) Stir down batter by beating 25 strokes. Turn out on well-floured, cloth-covered board (dough will be soft). Divide dough into 8 equal portions. Shape each into a ball; roll in butter, then cinnamon-sugar mixture. Place balls of dough in well-greased loaf pan, 9 x 5 x 3 inches, 4 lengthwise, 2 crosswise. Let rise in warm place (85°) until double in bulk, about 40 minutes. Heat oven to 375° (quick moderate). Bake 35 minutes. Remove from pan and frost top immediately with browned butter icing.

Browned Butter Icing:

1½ tablespoons butter, ¾ cup sifted confectioners' sugar, 1 table-spoon cream, ½ teaspoon vanilla. Brown butter in saucepan over medium heat until a delicate brown. Blend with sugar; add cream and vanilla and blend until smooth.

Ruth Aspgren, our popular Swedish cook at the Country House, makes this delicious Swedish rye bread. It's a favorite with our staff. They beg for it. Hope you like it!

RYE BREAD

6 *cups rye flour*
2 *cups white flour*
2½ *cups milk*
2 *yeast cakes*
1½ *teaspoons salt*
⅓ *cup shortening or butter*
¾ *cup molasses*
2-3 *teaspoons fennel seed or anise seed, pounded*

Dissolve yeast cakes in ½ cup lukewarm milk. Melt shortening, add remaining milk, and heat until lukewarm. Pour into big bowl, add molasses and half of rye flour and mix well. Then add yeast, salt, seeds, and remaining flour gradually. Beat well until smooth and firm. Cover with towel and allow to rise in warm place until almost doubled in bulk. Turn out onto floured baking board and knead well.

Shape into 3 loaves, prick with fork, and let rise. Bake in moderate oven (375°) 30 minutes. Brush with warm water when half done and again when ready.

P.S. Ruth uses 4 cups of rye and 4 cups of white flour instead of the 6 cups of rye and the 2 cups of white. She also, upon removing bread from oven, brushes with a mixture of:

1 *egg*
1 *tablespoon sugar*
1 *tablespoon of cream*

This gives the bread a shiny sweet crust.

Mrs. Geahan's homemade bread is delicious. She's been making it for years and has taught hundreds of others to turn out a golden brown loaf of homemade bread. She's tops on our list. Don't be afraid to try her recipe. Remember, to do anything well requires a certain amount of practice! Good luck!

MRS. GEAHAN'S HOMEMADE BREAD

6 cups scalded milk (use water or potato water, if you prefer), 3 heaping tablespoons sugar, 3 tablespoons melted shortening, 3 packages dried yeast, 5 teaspoons salt, approximately 10 to 12 cups enriched unsifted flour.

Scald milk, cool to lukewarm, and add sugar, salt, melted shortening, and yeast. Stir until well blended. Next add flour until it is a soft dough—non-sticky—or until you can handle dough easily. Place on floured bread board and knead for about 5 minutes. Toss in the air several times during the kneading process, letting it drop soundly on the floured bread board. Return dough to mixing bowl. Cover with damp cloth and let rise until doubled in size (about 1 hour). Punch down and divide into 4 or 5 loaves. Place in well-greased bread pans or make into clover leaf rolls. Let rise until double. Bake for 30 minutes at 400°. Remove from oven and place on cake racks, brush with melted butter, and cover with tea towel at once. Delicious! *Makes 4-5 loaves.*

The secret of life is not to do what one likes, but to try to like what one has to do – Dinah Muloch Craik

Quick Breads

Quick breads are easy, and fast to mix. Make several loaves at one time and store them a day or so. Flavors mellow and slicing is easier.

Notes on Nut Breads:

1. A crack down the center of loaf is no mistake—it's typical.
2. When bread comes from the oven, turn out of pan and cool on rack.
3. Most nut breads are better if stored at least a day. Place the thoroughly cooled bread in air-tight container—or wrap in aluminum foil or saran wrapping. Nut breads stay nice several days.
4. Nut-bread sandwiches take to simple fillings: soft butter or margarine, softened cream cheese, jam or jelly.

I've made this one for years. A favorite at Thanksgiving and Christmas.

CRANBERRY ORANGE NUT BREAD

Sift together

2 *cups sifted all-purpose flour*
½ *teaspoon salt*

1½ teaspoons baking powder
½ teaspoon soda
1 cup granulated sugar

Grate the rind of one orange, extract the juice, and add 2 tablespoons melted shortening (or salad oil) and buttermilk to make ¾ cup of liquid. Beat 1 egg well, combine with above liquid, and add to the dry ingredients. Add ½ cup chopped nuts and 1 cup raw cranberries, chopped or coarsely ground. Mix well. Pour in greased bread pan. Bake at 325° for one hour. Store 24 hours before cutting.

This keeps well in the refrigerator or can be frozen successfully. Doubling the recipe to make either two large loaves or three smallish ones works fine.

It is "elegant eating" with cream cheese, or just as a bread-and-butter treat.

Simple, but simply delicious! Delightful addition to salad luncheon or afternoon tea.

LEMON BREAD

½ cup shortening
1 cup sugar
2 eggs, slightly beaten
1⅔ cups flour
1 teaspoon baking powder
½ teaspoon salt
½ cup milk
½ cup nuts, chopped fine
Grated peel of 1 lemon

Topping:

¼ cup sugar
Juice of 1 lemon

Cream shortening with sugar; add slightly beaten eggs. Sift flour, measure, and sift again with baking powder and salt. Alternately add the flour mixture and the milk to the shortening mixture, stirring constantly. Mix in nuts and lemon peel. Bake in greased 5 x 9-inch pan in 350° oven for 1 hour.

Combine the ¼ cup sugar with lemon juice and pour over the top of the loaf when it comes from the oven. Cool, slice, and serve. Then wait for compliments galore!

Thanks to Doris Wetters.

ALMOND-HONEY BREAD

Blend bits of candied cherries and slivered almonds with whipped honey. Spread on split English muffins and slip into broiler for quick toasting to make an easy hot bread. Delicious for breakfast or served with cups of hot chocolate for afternoon snacks.

February is the month for cherry breads.

CHERRY-NUT BREAD

2½ cups sifted flour
1 cup sugar
2 teaspoons baking powder
½ teaspoon salt
½ cup shortening
12 chopped maraschino cherries
¾ cup chopped nuts
2 eggs, beaten
½ cup milk
¼ cup maraschino cherry juice

Sift dry ingredients together into bowl; cut in shortening. Stir in cherries and nuts. Combine liquid ingredients. Add liquid ingredients to dry ingredients. Stir only until all flour is moistened. Pour into greased 9 x 5 x 3-inch loaf pan. Bake at 350° for 60-70 minutes. Cool on rack. *Yields 1 loaf.*

Marmalade bread is a delight to serve at the holiday time or anytime of the year! Please try it!

MARMALADE BREAD

3 *cups sifted enriched flour*
3 *teaspoons baking powder*
1 *teaspoon salt*
¼ *teaspoon soda*
1 *cup broken California walnuts*
1 *1-pound jar (1½ cups) orange marmalade*
1 *beaten egg*
¾ *cup orange juice*
¼ *cup salad oil or melted shortening*

Sift together dry ingredients. Reserve ¼ cup of the marmalade. Combine remaining 1¼ cups marmalade, the egg, orange juice, and salad oil; add to flour mixture, stirring till moistened. Stir in nuts. Turn into greased 9½ x 5 x 3-inch loaf pan. Bake in moderate oven (350°) about 1 hour or till done. Remove from pan and place on baking sheet; spread top with reserved marmalade and return to oven about 1 minute or till glazed. Cool on rack.

Don't fail to try this amazingly delicious lemon bubble loaf. It's spectacular coffee cake.

LEMON BUBBLE LOAF

1 *cup granulated sugar*
¼ *teaspoon mace*
Grated rind of 2 lemons
1 *cup milk*
1 *teaspoon salt*
¼ *cup butter or margarine*
½ *cup very warm water*
3 *packages or cakes yeast, active dry or compressed*
2 *eggs, well beaten*
5¾ *to* 6¼ *cups sifted all-purpose flour*
2 *tablespoons melted butter or margarine*

Mixing dough: In a small bowl combine ½ cup sugar, mace, lemon rind; set aside. In small saucepan, scald milk; stir in ½ cup sugar, salt, ¼ cup butter or margarine; cool till lukewarm. Meanwhile, in large bowl, measure very warm water; sprinkle or crumble in yeast; stir until dissolved. Stir in milk mixture, beaten eggs, and 3 cups flour; beat until smooth.

Kneading, raising dough: Stir in 2½ cups more flour, or enough to make soft dough that just cleans sides of bowl. Sprinkle a board with half of remaining flour, turn dough onto it, and knead until smooth and elastic, with small blisters under surface. Place dough in large greased bowl, turning to grease all sides. Cover with towel; let rise in warm place (85°) about 45 minutes or until double in bulk. Punch dough down.

Shaping, baking bubble loaf: Turn dough onto floured surface; cover; let rest 10 minutes. Cut dough in half; cut each half into 16 equal pieces. Shape 16 pieces into balls. Place balls in layer in greased angel-loaf pan, 15½ inches long. Brush layer with half of melted butter; sprinkle with half of lemon mixture. Shape rest of pieces; arrange as second layer; brush and sprinkle as before. Let rise, covered, in warm place, 45 minutes, or until double. Bake at 350° for 35 minutes or until done. Cool in pan 5 minutes; turn out on wire rack to finish cooling. *Makes 1 long loaf.*

Lovers of peanut butter will go for this one. It's good!

PEANUT-BUTTER LOAF

1¾ *cups sifted enriched flour*
2 *teaspoons baking powder*
½ *teaspoon salt*
¼ *teaspoon baking soda*
⅓ *cup shortening*
¾ *cup crunchy peanut butter*
⅔ *cup sugar*
2 *eggs, slightly beaten*
1 *cup mashed ripe bananas (2 or 3 medium bananas)*

Set oven for moderate 350°. Mix and sift first 4 ingredients. Cream shortening and peanut butter; add sugar gradually while creaming. Continue to cream until light and fluffy. Add eggs; beat well. Stir in dry ingredients alternately with mashed bananas; mix well, but do not beat. Spoon batter into well-greased loaf pan, 8 x 4 x 3 inches. Bake 1 hour.

CHOCOLATE CINNAMON TOAST

Mix together ½ cup of cocoa, 5 tablespoons of melted butter, 1 teaspoon of cinnamon, and 6 tablespoons of sugar. Spread on hot crisp toast or English muffins.

The great pleasure in life is doing what people say you cannot do — Bagehot

Biscuits and Rolls

POPOVERS

Popovers, feather-light, are a treat whenever served, for breakfast, luncheon, dinner, afternoon tea, or evening party. And they are versatile, too.

From a standard recipe can be made many variations. But popovers, even more than biscuits and muffins, must be so hot that they burn your fingers when you break them open. They must be baked long enough to have a deep brown crust and be thick enough to prevent falling when they are removed from the pans. The inside, however, should not be too dry lest the flavor be entirely lost.

Popovers will always double when baked; so when pouring batter, fill only ½ to ⅔ full.

Although popovers have a reputation for trickiness, they are the easiest of hot breads to make and bake. The heat of the oven has a great deal to do with success or failure. It must be hot enough to generate the steam that leavens the batter. Once the popovers have risen and popped, the heat is reduced (unless otherwise indicated) to moderate to drive out all moisture and bake the little breads until they hold their shape.

The reason why the cold batter is poured into sizzling hot iron, custard cups or glass cups is to provide more steam than cold cups. No baking powder or soda is needed in any popover recipe; steam is the raising agent.

1 cup sifted all-purpose flour
¼ teaspoon salt
2 eggs
⅞ cup milk
1 tablespoon melted butter

Mix the flour and salt. Beat eggs until light, add milk and butter and add slowly to the flour. Stir until well blended. Beat 2 minutes with rotary beater if by hand, or 1 minute with an electric beater. Heavily butter muffin tins or custard cups and put in the oven to get hot. Fill the cups ½ to ⅔ full. Bake 20 minutes at 450°, then reduce heat to 350° and bake 15 minutes more. Don't peek! Serve hot with marmalade.

CHEESE POPOVERS

1 cup bread flour, sifted twice
½ teaspoon salt
1 whole fresh egg, well beaten
1 cup sweet milk
1 cup grated cheese
A few grains of cayenne pepper

Sift salt with flour. Combine egg with milk, mix well and gradually add to the flour mixture, beating briskly until smooth. Add cayenne pepper. Make muffin pans very hot; then grease or butter generously. Into each greased hot pan, spoon 1 tablespoon of batter, then 1 teaspoon grated cheese, then 1 tablespoon of batter, and again cheese, repeating until pans are ⅔ full. Set in a very hot oven (450°) and bake 30 minutes; reduce oven temperature to moderate 350° and continue baking 10 to 15 minutes longer until popovers have risen and are delicately brown. Serve very hot. *Makes 8 popovers.*

The famous monument called the "Uneven Dozen" in Sucre, Bolivia, was built with money collected from bakers who were fined for not selling a "baker's dozen" (13 pieces to the dozen).

BASIC SWEET DOUGH

¼ cup milk
¼ cup sugar
2 tablespoons shortening

¾ teaspoon salt
¼ cup warm, not hot, water (lukewarm for compressed yeast)
1 package or 1 cake yeast, active dry or compressed
1 egg, beaten
2½ cups enriched flour

Scald milk; stir in sugar, shortening, and salt. Cool to lukewarm. Measure water into a large mixing bowl (warm, not hot, for active dry yeast; lukewarm for compressed yeast). Sprinkle or crumble in yeast; stir until dissolved. Blend in lukewarm milk mixture. Add egg and half the flour. Beat until smooth. Stir in remaining flour. Turn dough out on lightly floured board. Knead until smooth and elastic. Place in greased bowl; grease top. Cover; let rise in a warm place, free from draft, until doubled in bulk, 1¼ hours. Punch down and turn out on lightly floured board. Then shape as follows:

APRICOT JELLY TWIST

Roll dough into rectangle about 16 x 8 inches. Spoon apricot jelly filling down center third of rectangle. Cut 15 1-inch slits in dough along each side of filling. Fold strips at an angle across filling alternating from side to side. Place on greased baking sheet. Cover; let rise in a warm place, free from draft, until doubled in bulk, about 1 hour. Bake at 350° for 35 minutes. Spoon frosting over top.

Apricot Jelly Filling:

Combine in a saucepan 1 cup chopped dried apricots, ⅔ cup apple jelly, ½ cup chopped nuts and 1½ teaspoons lemon juice. Cook until mixture is heated through and of spreading consistency.

Confectioners' Sugar Frosting:

Combine ½ cup sifted confectioners' sugar with 2 teaspoons milk and ¼ teaspoon vanilla. Beat until smooth.

For melt-in-your-mouth goodness, it's hard to beat tender flaky biscuits. This biscuit recipe is "never fail," light, airy, and so good – especially when served with lots of butter.

HOT BISCUITS

2 cups flour, sifted
3 teaspoons baking powder
1 teaspoon salt
⅓ cup shortening
¾ cup milk

Sift flour, baking powder, and salt together; cut in shortening until mixture resembles coarse cornmeal. Add all of milk and mix to smooth dough. Turn out on lightly floured board. Knead lightly. Roll or pat ½" thick. Cut with biscuit cutter. Place on ungreased cookie sheet. Bake in very hot oven (450°) for 12 to 15 minutes. With this as a basic recipe, you may do many variations:

Cheese Biscuits:

Add ½ grated sharp cheese to dry ingredients.

Pineapple Fingers:

Add 1 cup diced candied pineapple. Cut in finger shape and brush with melted butter and sprinkle with granulated sugar.

Rich Tea Biscuits:

Increase the shortening to ½ cup and add 1 egg, beaten.

Herb Biscuits:

Add ½ teaspoon of dried herbs for each cup of flour. I add poultry seasoning or sage for party biscuits.

Cinnamon Pinwheels:

These are nice to keep in your refrigerator and bake as you need them. Roll biscuit into an oblong sheet. Brush with melted butter and sprinkle heavily with cinnamon mixture made by combining 1 cup sugar with 1½ tablespoons of cinnamon. Roll tight as a jelly roll, wrap in wax paper, and chill. Slice thin and bake at 350° until brown.

Onion Biscuits:

Add to recipe ½ cup French-fried onions, chopped fine. Really good with chicken and for brunches or parties with a slice of ham between.

SESAME ROLLS

1 *package oven-ready biscuits*
Milk
1½ *cups crisp rice cereal, coarsely crushed*
2 *tablespoons sesame seed, caraway seed, or celery seed*
2 *teaspoons salt*

Cut biscuits in half, roll each part into pencil-thin sticks (about 4 inches long). Brush with milk. Mix cereal crumbs, seed, and salt. Roll sticks in mixture. Bake on greased baking sheet at 450° about 10 minutes or until lightly browned. *Yield: 20 rolls.*

ORANGE CRUNCHY ROLLS

Place brown-and-serve rolls on a well-buttered baking sheet and brush with melted butter or margarine. Make a topping mixture of:

2 *tablespoons grated orange peel*
1 *cup granulated sugar*
Enough orange juice to moisten

Turn each roll around and around in the mixture until well coated; then replace on the baking sheet and bake as directed on the package.

HIGH-AS-THE-SKY BISCUITS

½ teaspoon soda
2½ teaspoons baking powder
1 teaspoon salt
3 cups flour
6 tablespoons butter
1 cup plus 1 tablespoon buttermilk

Sift the dry ingredients together, cut in the butter, and add the buttermilk gradually. Knead on pastry board and roll out one-half inch thick. Cut with biscuit cutter and bake on buttered cookie sheet in a 450° oven for 12 minutes. *Makes about 18.*

These are made regularly at Easter time on the Copper Kettle Show.

HOT CROSS BUNS

1 cup milk
⅓ cup butter or margarine
½ cup sugar
1½ teaspoons salt
¼ cup warm (not hot) water
2 packages active dry yeast
5 cups sifted, all-purpose flour, about
2 eggs, beaten
Melted shortening
1 cup golden raisins
Confectioners' icing

Scald milk in a saucepan. Add butter, sugar, and salt; stir until sugar dissolves. Cool to lukewarm. Measure warm water into a large bowl. Sprinkle in yeast and stir until dissolved. Add lukewarm milk mixture. Add 2½ cups of the flour; beat until smooth. Stir in eggs. Add 2½ cups more flour or enough to make a soft dough; mix well. Knead about 10 minutes. Place dough in a greased bowl; brush with shortening. Cover; let rise in a warm place until doubled in bulk, about 2 hours. Punch down. Turn out on floured board; knead in raisins. Pinch off pieces of dough and shape into 1½-inch balls. Place on greased pans, 1 inch apart. If desired, brush with egg yolk diluted with a little water. Cover and let rise until doubled in bulk, about 1 hour. Bake in moderately hot oven, 375°, for 30 minutes. Cool. Make crosses on buns with confectioners' icing. *Makes about 24 buns.*

MERRY CHRISTMAS WREATH

1 package active dry yeast or
1 cake compressed yeast
¼ cup water
1 cup milk (scalded)
¼ cup sugar
¼ cup shortening
1 teaspoon salt
1 well-beaten egg
3½ cups sifted enriched flour

Soften active yeast in warm water, compressed yeast in lukewarm water. Combine milk, sugar, shortening, salt. Cool to lukewarm. Add yeast and egg. Gradually stir in flour to form soft dough. Beat vigorously. Cover, let rise in warm place till double, about 2 hours. Grease 10-inch ring mold; spread bottom with sugar.

Fruit Topping:

Melt 2 tablespoons butter, add 2 tablespoons light corn syrup and ½ cup brown sugar. Place halved candied cherries, cut-side up, and almonds on sugar mixture. Shape dough in small balls; roll in melted butter; place 2 rows deep in pan. Let double. Bake in hot oven (400°) for 25 minutes. Loosen; turn out quickly. Serve with whipped butter.

These are quick, easy, and delicious. You'll be surprised anything so easy can be so good!

QUICK BISMARKS

1 package refrigerated biscuits
Jam or jelly

Flatten each biscuit to ¼ inch. Place 1 teaspoon jam or jelly on *half* the biscuits; cover with remaining biscuits; seal edges well. Fry in deep hot fat (375°), 3 minutes on each side. Drain on paper towels. Dust with confectioners' sugar, if you like. Serve warm. Delicious breakfast or dessert treats.
Makes 5.

TOAST CUPS

Trim crusts from thin slices of white bread. Brush thoroughly with melted butter. Press firmly but gently into muffin tins. Brush again with butter. The more butter you use the crisper and more delicious the cups will be. Toast in moderate oven, 375°, for approximately 12 minutes. Reduce heat and continue baking at 275° until golden brown and crisp. Sometimes I bake them for 1½ hours. These make an excellent base for creamed dishes.

For delicious sweet rolls, try this one – it's a Country House favorite. Ruth Aspgren, our cook, turns these out by the dozens. Our staff requests seconds and thirds. For dinner parties, we like to make them in miniature-sized muffin tins. You'll like them made plain as in Parker House rolls, rich with butter, or gooey with brown sugar, butter, and pecan topping.

SWEET ROLL DOUGH

Measure into mixing bowl ½ cup warm water (not hot – 110° to 115°). Add, stirring to dissolve, 2 packages active dry yeast. Stir in 1½ cups lukewarm milk, ½ cup sugar, 2 teaspoons salt, 2 eggs, 1 stick butter, and half of 6 cups sifted flour.

Mix with spoon until smooth. Add enough remaining flour to handle easily; mix with hand. Turn onto lightly floured board; knead until smooth and elastic (about 5 minutes). Round up in greased bowl, greased side up. Cover with damp cloth. Let rise in warm place

(85°) until double (about 1½ hours). Punch down; let rise again until almost double (about 30 minutes). Divide dough for desired rolls and coffee cakes.

Pecan Rolls:

Divide dough into four pieces. Roll into an oblong, approximately 8 x 12 inches. Spread with softened butter and sprinkle with ⅓ cup sugar and one tablespoon cinnamon. Roll up tightly, beginning at wide side. Seal well by pinching edges of roll together. Cut roll into 1-inch slices. Place a little apart in greased 13 x 9-inch pan or 18 muffin cups. To make the pecan rolls – generously butter the muffin tins, place 1 tablespoon light brown sugar, 1 tablespoon melted butter, ¼ teaspoon water, and 3 or 4 whole pecans in muffin tins, add the sliced rolled dough. Cover and let rise until double in bulk (35 to 40 minutes). Bake in oven 375° for 12 to 15 minutes. Turn out immediately on serving tray.

I've been making these for years. If you want to rate high with youngsters and oldsters alike – do try a Christmas tree.

Tom, my younger son, has always made them for his teachers at the holiday time. Miss Jeannetta Sloan, principal of the charming Glencairn School, East Lansing, still talks about the elegant Christmas-tree bread we made for her one Christmas time. They're fun!

CHRISTMAS-TREE BREAD

Use ½ sweet-roll dough. After dough rises, divide dough in 2 (1 for each tree). Form each into 17 1½-inch balls. Arrange on slightly greased baking sheet in a 5, 4, 3, 2, 1 pattern and with 2 balls rolled together for the trunk. Let rise until double (20 to 30 minutes). Bake until golden brown in 350° (moderate oven). Decorate with quick white icing, candied fruits, and decorating candies (including silver *dragées*).

Quick White Icing:

For rolls and coffee cakes.

Sift a little confectioners' sugar into bowl, moisten with cream or milk to spreading consistency. Add flavoring. Spread over slightly warm breads.

A man isn't poor if he can still laugh
—Raymond Hitchcock

Doughnuts, Coffee Cakes, and Muffins

The American people will always love doughnuts, with their big, round, fat hole-in-the-middle goodness in every bite.

OLD-FASHIONED DOUGHNUTS

4½ cups sifted all-purpose flour
4 teaspoons baking powder
¼ teaspoon nutmeg
½ teaspoon salt
¼ cup shortening
1 cup sugar
2 eggs
1 cup sour cream (dairy)
Fat or cooking oil

Sift together flour and next 3 ingredients. Cream shortening; add and blend in sugar a little at a time. Add eggs, one at a time, blending well after each addition. Add sour cream and sifted dry ingredients alternately; stir just until well blended after each addition.

Chill about ½ hour. Roll out dough, about ¼ inch thick, on a lightly floured board. Cut out doughnuts with a floured doughnut cutter. Melt fat or pour cooking oil into a deep-fat fryer or kettle to a depth of 3 to 4 inches; heat to 375°. Fry doughnuts until brown, about 3 minutes; turn once. Drain on absorbent paper. Serve plain, or sprinkle with confectioners' sugar, if desired.
Makes 2 dozen.

RAISED DOUGHNUTS

Dissolve 1 cake compressed yeast (or 1 package dry granular yeast) in ¼ cup lukewarm water. Combine ½ cup boiling water, 2 tablespoons shortening, ¼ cup sugar, 1½ teaspoons salt. Cool to lukewarm by adding ½ cup fresh milk or diluted evaporated milk. Blend in 1 egg, 1 teaspoon nutmeg, and dissolved yeast. Mix well. Add 3¾ cups sifted enriched flour. Mix to a soft dough. Place dough in greased bowl, cover, and refrigerate 2 to 3 hours or overnight. Roll out on floured board or pastry cloth to ¼-inch thickness. Cut into 1 x 3-inch strips or cut rounds with doughnut cutter. Let rise in warm place (85° to 90°) until double in bulk, about 40 minutes. Fry in hot fat (375°) about 2 minutes on each side. Drain on absorbent paper; sprinkle with sugar.

Glaze for Doughnuts:

Add ⅓ cup boiling water gradually to 1 cup confectioners' sugar. Dip warm doughnuts into glaze. Cover with nuts if desired.

The old stand-by of the Channel 6 Copper Kettle viewers.

POTATO DOUGHNUTS

1 *cup unseasoned mashed potatoes*
3 *eggs*
¾ *cup sugar*
3 *tablespoons soft shortening*
2¾ *cups sifted flour*
4 *teaspoons baking powder*
1 *teaspoon salt*
¼ *teaspoon nutmeg*
1 *teaspoon mace*

Beat eggs well. Beat in sugar and shortening. Sift dry ingredients together and stir in. Stir in potatoes. Chill dough 2 hours. Turn onto generously floured board. Roll ⅓ inch thick. Let rest 20 minutes. Cut with doughnut cutter. Fry in hot fat (370° to 380°) until brown. Drain on absorbent paper. Serve plain, sugared, or glazed.
Makes 3 dozen 2½-inch doughnuts.

MINIATURE ORANGE DOUGHNUTS

4 *cups sifted all-purpose flour*
2 *teaspoons baking powder*
1 *teaspoon soda*
1 *teaspoon salt*
2 *eggs*
1¼ *cups sugar*
1 *tablespoon grated orange rind*
2 *tablespoons melted butter*
1 *can (6 ounces) undiluted frozen orange juice*
¼ *cup sour milk*
Fat for deep frying

Sift together flour, baking powder, soda, and salt. Beat eggs until light. Add sugar gradually, beating constantly. Blend in orange rind, butter, defrosted orange juice, and sour milk. Stir in sifted dry ingredients. Chill. Use ⅓ of dough at a time and roll out on lightly floured board to ¼-inch thickness. Cut doughnuts with frozen-juice can. Use thimble to cut centers. Fry in hot deep fat (375°) until well browned on both sides. Drain on absorbent paper. Frost doughnuts with powdered-sugar frosting and sprinkle with grated rind.
Makes 4 dozen.

The talented and charming Mrs. Kay Collins and her wonderful mother, Mrs. Keller, were guests on the Copper Kettle Show the day after Christmas. They made these melt-in-your-mouth, light, airy, and delicious doughnuts. This is a recipe you will want to try. Our thanks to Mrs. Collins and Mrs. Keller.

HUNGARIAN DOUGHNUTS

3 *egg yolks*
1 *cake yeast*

1 cup milk
⅛ pound melted butter
1 tablespoon sugar
¼ teaspoon salt
2 cups flour
Fat for frying

Mix yeast and sugar in lukewarm milk. Let stand until other ingredients are mixed. Mix yolks with melted butter and yeast mixture. Beat well. Place flour in bowl, make a nest, and add yeast and egg mixture. Beat with egg beater, then use a wooden spoon. Beat well. Let stand for about 1 hour to 1½ hours. Let rise. Flour the board. Place dough on board and stretch dough with your hands to ½ inch thick. Cut out with round cookie cutter. Fry in deep fat until golden brown. Make a small gash with a sharp knife and fill with 1 teaspoon of currant jelly. Sprinkle generously with superfine granulated sugar.

Coffee cake hot from the oven, a cup of steaming coffee, and the sharing of conversation with a neighbor or friend—the perfect setting for moments of relaxation in the middle of a busy day.

Here is a delicious but rich coffee cake. This coffee cake was served at the Jewish Smorgasbord. Mrs. Harold A. Shnider made it on the Copper Kettle Show. It was so good, I begged for the recipe—and here it is. Try it. You'll love it!

SOUR-CREAM COFFEE CAKE

Mix in bowl:

1 package yeast
1 teaspoon sugar
¼ cup lukewarm water

Cover and let stand. Melt ¼ pound butter or margarine. In mixing bowl:

3 cups flour
½ cup sugar
Pinch of salt
3 egg yolks

Melted butter
Yeast mixture
½ pint sour cream

Mix on No. 3 speed of electric mixer and put in well-greased bowl, grease top of dough, and let rise in warm place until double in size. On a floured board work dough and make three little balls. Roll out thin and fill with favorite filling.

Fillings:

Cinnamon and sugar
Sliced apples with cinnamon and sugar
Fruits

You can roll this up like a loaf or a ring. Place in desired greased tin and allow to rise for ½ hour. Bake at 350° for 25 minutes.

Serve plain or frost and decorate with confectioners' frosting.

Makes 3 coffee cakes. Courtesy: Mrs. Harold A. Shnider, Sisterterhood Shaarey Zedek, Lansing, Michigan.

Don't miss making the butter-ball coffee cake. The quick ease of making it will simply amaze you.

BUTTER-BALL COFFEE CAKE

2 *cans refrigerated biscuits*
¼ *cup butter, melted*
¾ *cup sugar*
1 *tablespoon cinnamon*
¼ *cup chopped nuts*

Heat oven to 375° (quick moderate). Grease a 9-inch round layer pan. Separate biscuits and dip in melted butter, then coat each entirely with a mixture of the sugar and cinnamon.

Place 15 biscuits around the outer part of the pan, overlapping to make a circle. Overlap remaining 5 biscuits to fill center. Pour remaining butter over. Sprinkle with chopped nuts. Bake 25 to 30 minutes. Allow to stand 5 minutes before serving. The rich, buttery biscuits break apart easily.

Don't be afraid to try this. It's lots of fun and quite spectacular.

SWEDISH TEA RING

Dissolve 2 packages yeast in ⅓ cup lukewarm water. Scald 1 cup milk, add ¼ cup or ½ stick butter and cool to lukewarm. Add ⅓ cup sugar, 1½ teaspoons salt, yeast, and 2 well-beaten eggs.

Gradually stir in 4¾ cups flour. Turn out and knead until smooth. Work into a ball. Cover and let rise until double, 2 to 2½ hours.

Divide into 2 balls. Roll out 8 inches wide, and 23 inches long.

Brush with melted butter and sprinkle with sugar and cinnamon. You may use one cup coarsely ground nuts and fruits. Roll up starting at long side.

Grease cookie sheet. Form roll into ring. With scissors cut diagonally toward center at 1-inch intervals. Brush top delicately with cream and bake at 375°, 25 to 30 minutes. Do not let brown. Drizzle the following glaze over warm coffee ring:

1½ cups confectioners' sugar
2 tablespoons butter
3 tablespoons cream
Dash vanilla
Sprinkle with fruits and nuts

This recipe makes 2 rings.

These pretty date coffee rings are such fun you'll want to bake two —one for the first round of coffee, another for seconds. Simply stuff refrigerator biscuits with fresh California dates, then bake in a luscious glaze of maple syrup, brown sugar, and almonds.

DATE COFFEE RINGS

½ cup butter or margarine
6 tablespoons maple syrup
½ cup brown sugar (packed)

1 teaspoon cinnamon
¾ cup thinly sliced almonds
20 fresh California dates
2 cans refrigerator biscuits

Melt butter; set half aside. Divide rest between 2 8-inch ring molds, coating sides well. Put 2 tablespoons maple syrup in bottom of each mold. Mix brown sugar, cinnamon, and almonds. Set aside half of this mixture. Sprinkle rest in molds over syrup. Pit dates and place in center of each biscuit. Drizzle with a little syrup and a sprinkle of sugar mixture.

Gently stretch biscuit to enclose date and form a ball. Dip in melted butter and place in molds over sugar mixture. Sprinkle rest of sugar evenly on top. Bake in 400° (hot) oven 20 to 25 minutes. Invert over serving plate and let stand a few minutes before lifting pan off rolls. Serve warm.
Makes 2 coffee rings.

HOLIDAY COFFEE CAKE

Mix together thoroughly:

¾ cup sugar
¼ cup soft shortening
1 egg
Stir in ½ cup milk

Sift together and stir in:

2 cups sifted flour
2 teaspoons baking powder
½ teaspoon salt

Spread batter in greased and floured 9-inch square pan. Sprinkle top with ⅓ cup moist, cut-up, candied fruit, ½ teaspoon cinnamon mixed into 3 tablespoons sugar. Bake at 375° for 25 to 35 minutes or until wooden pick thrust into center of cake comes out clean. Serve warm, fresh from the oven.
Amount: 9 3-inch squares.

Variations of Holiday Coffee Cake Recipe:

Streusel-Filled Coffee Cake:

Follow holiday coffee cake recipe—except spread only half the batter in pan. Sprinkle with half the streusel mixture (below). Add the remaining batter, and sprinkle remaining streusel over top.
Mix together:

½ *cup brown sugar*
2 *tablespoons flour*
2 *teaspoons cinnamon*
2 *tablespoons butter, melted*
½ *cup chopped nuts*

Blueberry Buckle:

Follow holiday coffee cake recipe—carefully blend in at the last 2 cups well-drained blueberries. Sprinkle top with crumb mixture:
Mix together:

½ *cup sugar*
½ *teaspoon cinnamon*
¼ *cup soft butter*

Bake 45 to 50 minutes.

SOUR-CREAM COFFEE CAKE

¼ *pound butter*
1 *cup sugar*
2 *eggs*
1 *cup sour cream*
1 *teaspoon vanilla*
2 *cups flour*
1 *teaspoon baking powder*
1 *teaspoon baking soda*
¼ *teaspoon salt*

Topping:

¼ *cup granulated sugar*
1 *teaspoon cinnamon*
1 *cup chopped walnuts*

Cream butter. Add sugar and eggs and beat. Add sour cream and vanilla. Add sifted dry ingredients. Put half of batter in a greased tube pan. Sprinkle with ¾ of the topping. Add the rest of the batter and sprinkle with the rest of the topping. Bake at 350° for 45 minutes. Don't take from oven before the 45 minutes are up. Do not open oven door during baking.

This coffee cake is mouth watering – rich, but fun to make; and so good!

COFFEE CAKE

Mix together:

½ *pound butter*
2 *eggs*
1 *cup sour cream*
½ *cup sugar*

Dissolve 2 packages yeast in:

½ *cup lukewarm milk plus*
½ *teaspoon sugar*

Add 4½ cups sifted flour alternately with milk-and-yeast mixture. Mix thoroughly and place in greased bowl. Cover with wax paper and refrigerate. Divide dough into 4 or 5 parts. Roll out on floured board and spread with filling. Roll up, seal, and place on greased baking sheet. Cover and let rise about 1½ hours. Bake at 350°, 20 to 30 minutes. Dribble glaze of confectioners' sugar and milk on warm coffee cake.

Filling:

Blend in bowl with mixer:

- *1 5-ounce jar pineapple cream cheese*
- *2 small packages cream cheese*
- *2 tablespoons sugar*
- *2 egg yolks*

APPLE COFFEE CAKE

- *5 tablespoons shortening*
- *6 tablespoons sugar*
- *1 egg*
- *½ cup milk*
- *1½ cups sifted flour*
- *1½ teaspoons baking powder*
- *½ teaspoon salt*
- *2 medium apples, sliced*
- *2 tablespoons sugar*
- *¼ teaspoon mace or cinnamon*

Grease 8-inch pan. Cream shortening and sugar. Add unbeaten egg. Mix thoroughly. Add milk. Fold in sifted dry ingredients. Spread evenly in pan. Place apple slices on top of batter, pressing narrow edge into batter. Sprinkle with 2 tablespoons sugar mixed with ¼ teaspoon mace or cinnamon. Bake in moderately hot oven (400°) for 20 to 25 minutes.
6 servings.

As the name implies, it is a delight. Be sure and serve piping hot right out of the oven.

PINEAPPLE DELIGHT COFFEE CAKE

Columbus discovered America in 1492, the pineapple in 1493; and thanks to modern conveniences, we can enjoy pineapple coffee cake in 1963. Reminiscent of the coffee cake served at "Ye Ole Coffee Shoppe," this modern version is as easy to make with biscuit mix as it is delightful to eat.

In the West Indies, where the pineapple was discovered, it became a symbol of friendship when hung by the door of a native hut. This custom spread throughout Europe along with the popularity of this sweet fruit, and today the custom takes the form of pineapple coffee cake served at a hospitable *kaffee klatsch!* Why not bake two – they keep beautifully for later use.

¼ *cup sugar*
1 *egg*
¾ *cup milk*
2 *tablespoons vegetable oil*
2 *cups Bisquick*
2 *tablespoons melted butter*
¼ *cup brown sugar*
1 *cup crushed pineapple, drained*

Heat oven to 400° (moderately hot). Blend sugar, egg, milk, and vegetable oil with Bisquick. Beat vigorously 30 seconds. Spread in greased layer pan, 9 x 1½ inches, or square pan, 8 x 8 x 2 inches. Spread with 2 tablespoons of melted butter, and sprinkle with brown sugar. Arrange crushed pineapple over the top. Bake 25 to 30 minutes. Cut into wedge-shaped pieces or into squares and serve hot.

GLAZED COFFEE RING

2 *packages ready-to-bake buttermilk biscuits (16 biscuits)*
¼ *cup butter or margarine*
½ *cup firmly packed brown sugar*
1 *teaspoon cinnamon*
Whole pecan meats
½ *cup light corn syrup (about)*

Remove biscuits from packages. Melt butter or margarine and blend in brown sugar and cinnamon. Spread one side of each biscuit with this mixture. Scatter whole pecan meats in bottom of 8-inch ring mold. Add corn syrup to a depth of a quarter of an inch. Stand biscuits on end in ring mold, with spread surface of one biscuit next to plain side of the following biscuit. Bake in hot oven (425°) 15 to 18 minutes. Turn out upside down on serving plate.
Makes 6 to 8 servings.

Happiness is a wine of the rarest vintage, and seems insipid to a vulgar taste.

These are oh, so good. The coating of cinnamon, butter, and sugar gives the finishing touch. I always serve these with sauerkraut and roast pork.

CINNAMON-COATED CUPCAKES

Mix thoroughly:

> ⅓ *cup soft shortening (part butter)*
> ½ *cup sugar*
> 1 *egg*

Sift together:

> 1½ *cups sifted flour*
> 1½ *teaspoons baking powder*
> ½ *teaspoon salt*
> ¼ *teaspoon nutmeg*

Stir in alternately with:

> ½ *cup milk*

Fill greased muffin cups ⅔ full. Bake 20 to 25 minutes in 350° oven until golden brown. Immediately roll in 6 tablespoons melted butter. Then in mixture of ½ cup sugar and 1 teaspoon cinnamon. Serve hot.
Amount: 12 medium muffins.

A standard muffin recipe serves the same purpose as your roll or biscuit recipes.

COPPER KETTLE MUFFINS

2 cups sifted flour
4 teaspoons baking powder
½ teaspoon salt
2 tablespoons sugar
2 eggs, well beaten
1 cup milk
4 tablespoons melted butter

Mix and sift dry ingredients. Mix the egg and milk and stir into the dry ingredients. Stir in the melted butter. Bake in greased muffin tins, ¾ full, at 425° for 20 to 25 minutes.
This will make 12 medium muffins or 24 small ones.

Variations for Muffins:

Blueberry Muffins:

Fold in carefully 1 cup blueberries, fresh or frozen. If frozen, be sure they are thoroughly defrosted and drained.

Orange Coconut Muffins:

Fold in 2 tablespoons grated orange peeling plus ½ cup coconut; ½ cup toasted chopped almonds are nice, too, with the orange.

Guava Jelly Muffins:

Put ¼ teaspoon of Guava jelly on top of each small muffin.

Children love these!

ORANGE MUFFINS

Make your favorite muffins from a package of corn-meal muffin mix,. according to directions on package. Grease muffin tins; fill ⅓ full; place a cube of sugar in center, which has been dipped in orange juice. Fill to ¾ full and bake at 400° for 8 to 10 minutes. Serve hot with lots of butter.

These are good served with whipped butter.

GINGER MUFFINS

½ cup shortening
½ cup sugar
1 egg
1 cup molasses
3 cups sifted enriched flour
1½ teaspoons soda
½ teaspoon salt
1 teaspoon cinnamon
1 teaspoon ginger
½ teaspoon cloves
1 cup hot water

Cream together shortening and sugar. Beat in the egg, then the molasses. Sift together dry ingredients; stir into molasses mixture. Gradually add hot water, beating till smooth. Line muffin pans with paper bake cups; fill ⅔ full. Bake in moderate oven (375°) 20 to 25 minutes or till done.
Makes 2 dozen.

BANANA SURPRISE MUFFINS

1¾ cups sifted cake flour
2 teaspoons baking powder
¼ teaspoon baking soda
¾ teaspoon salt
⅓ cup sugar
1 egg, well beaten
⅓ cup melted shortening
1 cup mashed ripe bananas
Strawberry jam

Sift together flour, baking powder, soda, salt, and sugar into mixing bowl. Mix together egg, shortening, and bananas. Add to dry ingredients, mixing only enough to dampen all flour. Turn into well-greased small muffin pans. Drop about a teaspoonful of jam on top of each muffin. Bake in a moderately hot oven (400°) for about 20 minutes.
16 *small muffins.*

This potato muffin recipe was given to me by a friend in Chicago. These muffins are served daily in one of the popular downtown Chicago restaurants. They are different – but oh, so good! Be sure you serve them warm. They fairly melt in your mouth. Please try them!

POTATO MUFFINS

1 *yeast cake dissolved in 2 tablespoons warm water*
½ *cup mashed potatoes*
½ *cup hot water*
½ *cup sugar*

Combine and let rise until light and bubbly or spongelike. Add:

2 *beaten eggs*
½ *cup butter*
A pinch of salt
3 *cups flour*

Roll out and cut with small round cookie cutter. Place on greased cookie sheet. Let rise 30 minutes and bake in low oven 325°-350° about 20 minutes. Brush with melted butter and sprinkle with confectioners' sugar.

I wholeheartedly recommend any recipe that calls for sour cream. This one is especially good. The muffins are light and airy.

SOUR-CREAM MUFFINS

2 *tablespoons butter or margarine*
¼ *cup sugar*
2 *eggs*
2 *cups flour*
4 *teaspoons baking powder*
¼ *teaspoon salt*
¼ *teaspoon soda*
1 *cup sour cream (commercial cultured type)*

Use an electric mixer for speed. Cream together the butter and sugar until the mixture resembles whipped cream. Beat eggs until light, and mix in. Sift flour, measure, sift again with baking powder and salt.

Dissolve soda in the sour cream and add to the creamed mixture alternately with the dry ingredients, beating until very fluffy. Spoon into well-greased small muffin cups. Bake in a hot oven (425°) for 15 minutes.

Makes 24 small muffins.

The happiest people are those who are too busy to notice.

Pancakes

Pancakes are so versatile, they can be used as a canapé, main dish, or dessert in this modern cookery age.

COUNTRY HOUSE PANCAKES

These little prize-winning pancakes are the best I've ever eaten – that is, if you like a small thin pancake, which I do!

Be sure you heat the butter and syrup. I serve a variety of syrups with pancakes. Blueberry and old-fashioned maple syrup top my list, however.

1 *cup milk*
2 *tablespoons sugar*
¾ *teaspoon salt*
¼ *cup shortening*
1 *package active dry yeast*
¼ *cup warm, not hot, water*
1 *egg, beaten*
1 *cup sifted flour*

Scald milk; stir in sugar, salt, and shortening. Cool to lukewarm. Sprinkle yeast into warm (not hot) water. Stir until dissolved. Stir in lukewarm milk mixture. Add egg and flour. Beat until smooth,

about 1 minute. Cover and let rise in warm place, free from draft, until doubled in bulk (40-50 minutes). Stir down batter. For each pancake pour one tablespoon batter onto moderately hot, slightly greased griddle. (For larger pancackes use two tablespoons of batter.) Bake over low to medium heat until bubbles appear over surface and edges seem dry. Turn only once. Stack on warm plate. Serve with butter and syrup. Stir down batter occasionally as it is used.
Makes 18-20 or 6-8 servings of 3 pancakes each.

TOLLHOUSE PANCAKES

1¼ cups buttermilk
½ teaspoon soda
2 beaten egg yolks
1 cup sifted enriched flour
2 teaspoons sugar
¾ teaspoon baking powder
¼ teaspoon salt
2 tablespoons soft butter
2 stiffly beaten egg whites
1 recipe chicken filling and mushroom sauce
2 tablespoons grated Parmesan cheese

Beat buttermilk and soda into egg yolks with rotary beater, or use your electric mixer at low speed. Sift together flour, sugar, baking powder, and salt; add to egg yolk mixture along with butter; beat till just smooth. Fold in egg whites. Heat griddle or heavy frying pan. Coat lightly with shortening or salad oil. Drop batter from ⅓ cup measure onto griddle to make 5-inch pancakes. When cakes are full of bubbles, and edges are cooked well, turn cakes and cook on other side. (To keep first pancakes warm, place towel-covered baking sheet in very slow oven.) Put a tablespoon of chicken filling on each pancake; roll. Place cakes, edges down, in 11½ x 7½ x 1½-inch baking dish. Top with mushroom sauce; sprinkle with Parmesan cheese. Broil till golden.
Serves 4.

Chicken Filling and Mushroom Sauce:

3 *tablespoons butter*
3 *tablespoons enriched flour*
½ *teaspoon salt*
1⅓ *cups chicken broth*
1 *cup ½-inch cubes cooked chicken*
⅓ *cup sliced mushrooms*
3 *tablespoons light cream*

Chicken Filling:

Melt butter; blend in flour and salt; gradually stir in broth; cook till thick, stirring constantly. Reserve half of this sauce for mushroom sauce. To other half, add chicken; heat through.

Mushroom Sauce:

Stir mushrooms and cream into reserved sauce; heat.

Ideal for a quick, delicious luncheon dish.

ROLLED HAMBURGER PANCAKES

1 *cup ground beef*
2 *cups prepared pancake mix*
Prepared mustard

Lightly brown the meat in heavy skillet. Drain. Prepare pancake batter according to package directions. Stir in meat. Bake pancakes on hot griddle, making cakes about 6 inches in diameter. Brush pancakes with prepared mustard, and roll up. Place on lightly greased oven-proof platter, and keep warm in slow oven (250°) until serving time. Serve with tomato sauce.
Makes 4 to 6 servings.

Tomato Sauce:

1 *can cream of tomato soup*
¼ *cup grated Cheddar cheese*
½ *teaspoon Worcestershire sauce*

1 *teaspoon catsup*
½ *cup sliced ripe olives*
Cream

Heat soup and cheese, stirring constantly until cheese melts. Add Worcestershire sauce, catsup, and ripe olives. Heat thoroughly. Thin with a little cream, if necessary.

Fresh corn off the cob is a late August must.

FRESH CORN FRITTERS

1 *pint grated fresh corn*
½ *cup milk (from the corn and milk added to make the ½ cup)*
2 *eggs, separated*
½ *cup flour*
1 *teaspoon salt*
1 *teaspoon baking powder*
1 *tablespoon melted butter*

The corn is grated off the uncooked cob and mixed with the milk and egg yolks. The flour, salt, and baking powder are mixed together and added and then the melted butter. The egg whites are beaten stiff and folded in last. Drop them on a greased hot griddle or frying pan and cook like pancakes. Serve with melted butter, syrup, and lots of crisp bacon.
Serves 6.

Nothing great was ever achieved without enthusiasm — Emerson

The German pancake, often referred to as "indescribably delicious" served with maple syrup, lemon, and butter must be seen and eaten to be appreciated. This recipe has been one of the specialties served at Pandl's Inn, Whitefish Bay, Wisconsin, for over 45 years. We have made it with great success on the Copper Kettle Show. It's fun to watch it rise. Be sure you serve it at once!

We thank Mrs. Gary R. Hultgren, 2654 Melville Drive, East Lansing, Michigan.

PANDL'S FAMOUS GERMAN PANCAKE

½ cup all-purpose flour
½ cup milk
4 large eggs
Pinch of salt

Mix flour, milk, and salt until smooth. Crack in eggs and mix smooth. Pour into heavy frying pan which has been greased with 1 pat butter, equal amount shortening. (Frying pan with sloping sides is best.) Fry until golden brown, turn with spatula. Make 4 criss-cross cuts (2 each way) with spatula. Bake in hot oven, 425°, for 12 minutes. Pancake will not begin to rise for about 7 or 8 minutes.

Don't let these little fudge pancakes frighten you. They are different—but delicious. I dare you to try them. They are amazing!

FUDGE PANCAKES

1½ cups sifted flour
2 teaspoons baking powder
1 tablespoon sugar
3 tablespoons butter
1 teaspoon salt
2 tablespoons cocoa
2 eggs, separated
2 tablespoons milk
¾ cup milk
Powdered sugar

Sift the flour and baking powder together. Cream 1 tablespoon of the butter; add the sugar, salt, cocoa, and the well-beaten egg yolks. Stir in the 2 tablespoons of milk, and mix very well. Stir in the dry

ingredients and add the ¾ cup of milk. Beat the egg whites until stiff, and fold into the mixture. Melt the other 2 tablespoons of butter in a preheated skillet, and drop small amounts (about the size of a silver dollar) of the batter from the tip of a spoon. Cook slowly, and turn to brown both sides. Coat the cakes with powdered sugar, and serve.
Serves 6.

STAN BRAUER'S 1861 HOUSE POTATO PANCAKES

Stan Brauer and his wonderful Pop, Max R. Brauer, made these on the Copper Kettle Show one day. We had hundreds of requests for the recipe. Finally Stan and Pop agreed to share the old German recipe with all the Copper Kettle viewers. We love them for it, too. They are delicious. Stan insists you serve Michigan applesauce with his pancakes. I agree.

Grate 8 large potatoes and 1 large onion on fine grater. Drain in colander 5 minutes. Remove from colander and place in mixing bowl. Add 6 large eggs, 1 teaspoon salt, dash of pepper, ¼ cup parsley flakes, and enough flour to hold mixture together. (Too much flour makes batter heavy.) Mix well. Heat frying pan, using enough grease to cover bottom. Spoon pancake mixture into hot pan. Flip pancake when outer edge turns light brown. Takes about 7 minutes. They should be served with sour cream (on the side) or fresh Michigan applesauce.
This makes 15-17 servings.

Oven-baked pancakes are such fun to make. Easy, and a real time saver!

OVEN-BAKED PANCAKES WITH SAUSAGE

1 *package (½ pound) brown-and-serve sausage*
2 *eggs*
1 *cup milk*
1¼ *cups sifted flour*
3 *teaspoons baking powder*

1 *tablespoon sugar*
½ *teaspoon salt*
2 *tablespoons melted shortening*

Beat the eggs with rotary beater until light and fluffy. Combine with the milk. Sift together the flour, baking powder, sugar, and salt. Add dry ingredients and shortening to the milk mixture. Beat until batter is smooth. Pour into baking dish rubbed with shortening. Arrange sausage links on the batter. Bake in a very hot oven (450°) for 15 minutes. Cut into 6 squares and serve with butter and syrup.

Blueberry pancakes are my favorites. Don't allow the season to go by without making them. The Michigan-grown blueberries are wonderful, sweet, juicy, and delectable.

BLUEBERRY PANCAKES

1¼ *cups sifted all-purpose flour*
3 *teaspoons baking powder*
1 *tablespoon sugar*
½ *teaspoon salt*
1 *beaten egg*
1 *cup milk*
2 *tablespoons salad oil or melted shortening or bacon fat*

Sift together flour, baking powder, sugar, and salt. Combine egg, milk, and salad oil; add to dry ingredients, stirring just till flour is moistened. (Batter will be lumpy.)

Bake on hot griddle. Gently sprinkle a few of these choice berries atop the pancake before turning.

Be sure the butter and syrup are hot!

Makes about 12 dollar-size or eight 4-inch pancakes.

True luxury lies not in richness and ornateness; but in the absence of vulgarity

Desserts

"'Tis the Dessert That Graces All the Feast"
In our sweet-talk section, we run the gamut in long-time favorites from big bubbly apple dumplings, velvety chocolate cake, to Cherries Jubilee.

Glamorous or simple, the success of your meal or party depends upon the dessert you serve. One well-known French chef said, "Last impressions linger with the guests."

Ice Cream Desserts

A classy climax for any meal! It's a breeze to make and all done ahead of time.

CHOCOLATE ICE-CREAM SOPHISTICATE

½ cup chopped blanched almonds
2 tablespoons butter
½ square unsweetened chocolate
¼ cup sifted powdered sugar
1 quart vanilla or chocolate ice cream
1 cup whipping cream, whipped

Lightly brown almonds in butter over very low heat. Add chocolate and stir until melted. Remove from heat and blend in powdered sugar. Break ice cream into chunks and let soften slightly. Fold in whipped cream, and lightly stir in chocolate mixture to give marbled effect. Spoon into 1½-quart ring mold and freeze. To serve, unmold on chilled platter, and fill center with cocoa-dusted pears or coconut snowballs.

Coconut Snowballs:

Cut cake into small cubes and frost with powdered sugar icing. Coat heavily with flaked coconut.

A beautiful dessert to serve any time of the year. We used to make this often when we were living in Coral Gables, Florida. We snipped fresh gardenias from the bushes in the yard, placing them on the silver platter around the Party Dessert.

SUMMERTIME FROZEN PARTY DESSERT

Use a large angel-food cake pan. Fill within 2½ to 3 inches from top with sherbet balls. You may use lime, red raspberry, orange, or any combination of the sherbets you desire. Approximately 2 quarts sherbet will be needed. Soften 1½ to 2 quarts vanilla ice cream or a combination of pistachio and vanilla in a large dish. Add to the ice cream ½ cup shredded German sweet chocolate and ½ cup toasted almonds. Pour the softened ice cream around sherbet, and quickly place back in the freezing compartment of refrigerator. You may have to leave sherbet balls in the freezer while preparing the ice cream. Place in freezer until frozen firm. When ready to serve, loosen around edges of pan with warm knife. Turn out on pretty serving platter and quickly cover sides and top with green whipped cream. It is well to return to freezer for a short time before serving. This is a very easy dessert to make if you have a freezer available. Delicious served with fresh strawberries or red raspberries.
Serves 12-14.

Note: To make mint ice cream use softened vanilla ice cream and add a dash of green food coloring and mint extract to taste (just a dash!). This may be used as the ice cream to be poured around sherbet balls.

Cherries Jubilee are for the discriminating. Everyone should make them at least once. For a dramatic effect, prepare in chafing dish at table. Superb over vanilla ice cream.

BLACK CHERRIES JUBILEE

1 *cup black cherry juice*
1 *tablespoon cornstarch*
¼ *cup sugar*
½ *cup black cherries*
1 *tablespoon butter*
2 *tablespoons kirsch*
2 *tablespoons brandy*

Bring juice to a boil. Mix cornstarch, sugar, and a little of the juice and add to the boiling mixture. Boil 1 minute. Add the cherries. Remove from heat; add the butter, kirsch, and brandy. Serve hot over vanilla ice cream. If you wish to ignite it, pour good cognac over and light.
6 servings.

BING CHERRIES JUBILEE

Pour the juice from a pint jar of pitted Bing cherries into the top pan, or blazer, of a chafing dish. Place the pan directly over the flame and bring the juice to a boil. Thicken it with ½ teaspoon arrowroot dissolved in a little cold water and then add the cherries. Stir the cherries in the sauce until they are heated through. Pour over the cherries 2 ounces kirsch and blaze. Serve the flaming cherries and sauce alone or with vanilla ice cream.

BIMINI PARFAIT

This dessert was inspired by the tiny island of Bimini, a brief plane hop to the east of Miami, Florida. Fill dessert glasses about one-third with vanilla ice cream. Add a layer of coffee caramel sauce, then a layer of fudge sauce. Fill with ice cream. Add more fudge sauce. Top with whipped cream and powdered instant coffee.

Coffee Caramel Sauce:

¾ cup brown sugar, firmly packed
1 cup sugar
⅔ cup light corn syrup
¼ cup butter or margarine
Few grains salt
⅓ cup cream (heavy or light)
½ teaspoon vanilla
½ cup strong coffee

Combine brown sugar, granulated sugar, corn syrup, butter, and salt in saucepan. Cook, stirring, until sugar dissolves. Cook without stirring to 236° (soft-ball stage). Cool slightly. Stir in cream, vanilla, and coffee. Mix well.
Makes about 2 cups.

Strawberry Melba requires fresh strawberries and frozen red raspberries.

This dessert is downright rich, luscious, and pretty. I scoop mounds of French vanilla ice cream into pretty glass dishes; then ladle generous amounts of strawberry melba over it. Oh! it's good!

STRAWBERRY MELBA

1 pint strawberries
½ cup sugar
1 cup whipped cream
1 quart vanilla ice cream

Mash berries, add sugar. Fold into whipped cream. Top ice cream with strawberry sauce.

Melba Sauce:

2 *teaspoons cornstarch*
2 *tablespoons sugar*
¼ *cup light corn syrup*
1 *cup frozen raspberries*
1 *pint crushed fresh strawberries*
1 *tablespoon lemon juice*

Mix cornstarch, sugar, and syrup. Add raspberries and cook till clear and slightly thickened. Cool. Strain to remove seeds, mix with strawberries and lemon juice. Ladle melba sauce over strawberry sauce.
Makes 6 servings.

Lemon sherbet in a graham-cracker crust.

FROZEN LEMON SHERBET

3 *egg yolks*
½ *cup sugar*
¼ *cup lemon juice*
2 *teaspoons grated lemon peel*
⅛ *teaspoon salt*
1 *cup heavy cream, whipped*
3 *stiffly-beaten egg whites*
½ *cup graham-cracker crumbs*

Beat egg yolks until thick and lemon-colored; gradually beat in sugar. Add lemon juice and peel and salt. Fold in whipped cream and stiffly-beaten egg whites. Cover bottom of refrigerator tray with ¼ cup crumbs. Pour in sherbet mixture. Top with remaining crumbs. Freeze firm.
Makes 2 quarts.

Ice-cream pies can be made days ahead. Keep several in the freezer at all times. Mix and match flavors, too!

DELICIOUS ICE-CREAM PIE

Make your favorite pie crust, bake. Cool. Fill with your choice of ice cream, return to freezer, then top with a high meringue, return

to freezer and just before you wish to serve your
place it under broiler for about 30 to 60 seconds. Watch
and serve immediately. I like a double fudge sauce or frozen strawberries on top of pie. Rich but delicious!

Meringue:

4 *egg whites*
8 *tablespoons sugar*
⅛ *teaspoon cream of tartar*

Beat egg whites with cream of tartar until stiff, add sugar gradually and continue beating until the mixture is fine grained and will hold its shape. For less meringue, use only 2 egg whites plus 4 tablespoons sugar. I like a meringue on an ice cream pie to be about five inches high.

Double Fudge Sauce:

1½ *cups sugar*
1 *cup sifted cocoa*
⅓ *cup water*
¼ *cup corn syrup*
1 *cup evaporated milk*
1½ *teaspoons vanilla*

Mix sugar and cocoa in a heavy 1½-quart saucepan. Stir in the water and syrup. Cook and stir until mixture comes to a full, all-over boil. Then stir and boil 3 minutes, or until mixture thickens. Remove from heat and stir in the evaporated milk and vanilla. Chill. Serve warm or cold over ice cream, cake, or pudding.
Makes 2½ cups.

If you have not been one of those fortunate individuals to have an old-fashioned ice cream freezer handed down to you from past generations, don't delay in dashing to the nearest hardware to purchase one. Every family should have the experience, (even if it's only one time), the joy, the laughter, and fun of making a freezer of ice cream — especially on the 4th of July.

Making homemade ice cream takes time and patience but is well worth the effort. It's one of the little traditions which will long remain in the hearts and minds of the youngsters—our whole family enjoys it—even we oldsters!

I insist upon the old-style freezer, too. The kind you have to turn, turn, and turn—slowly, ever so slowly—the result—smooth, creamy ice cream!

HOMEMADE VANILLA ICE CREAM

1 *quart milk*
5 *eggs*
2½ *or* 3 *teaspoons vanilla*
1 *quart cream (I use whipping cream)*
2½ *cups sugar*

Scald milk in top of double boiler. In large bowl beat eggs until light and fluffy. Add sugar and beat thoroughly. Gradually add scalded milk. Place all three ingredients in large pan and return to range, moderate temperature, for 2 or 3 minutes. Remove from heat. Chill thoroughly. Add cream and vanilla. Place the above ingredients in freezer, place ice and salt around container* and turn freezer handle until you are unable to turn any longer. Be sure to turn slowly the first ten minutes. This method will produce a smoother textured ice cream.

When you can no longer turn the handle, carefully remove lid from container to test the firmness of ice cream. Be sure you have a spoon ready for sampling. If ice cream is firm, remove the paddle or leave it in container until you are ready to serve ice cream. Children love to lick the paddle.

Wonderful with fresh strawberries or plain. We like it just as it comes out of the freezer container.

*Use 1 cup rock salt to 8 cups chipped ice.

ICE-CREAM SNOWBALLS

Roll scoops of ice cream in coconut, nuts, or cookie crumbs. Place in ice-cream tray and freeze. These are delicious served with hot fudge sauce.

Hot Fudge Sauce:

½ cup butter
2¼ cups confectioners' sugar
⅔ cup evaporated milk
6 squares bitter chocolate

Mix butter and sugar in top of double boiler; add evaporated milk and chocolate and cook over hot water for 30 minutes. Do not stir while cooking. Remove from heat and beat. You may store in refrigerator and reheat as needed. If you wish to have a thinner sauce, add cream, but do not add water.

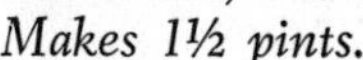
Makes 1½ pints.

Fruit Desserts

This recipe is over 100 years old. When you need a quick one, reach for old-fashioned apple roll. You'll use it regularly, I know!

OLD-FASHIONED APPLE ROLL

1 *cup white sugar*
1 *cup water*

Mix and boil 5 minutes.

Chop 2 cups apples (peeled)
⅓ *cup sugar*
1 *teaspoon cinnamon*

Biscuit dough:

1 *cup flour (sifted)*
2 *teaspoons baking powder*
½ *teaspoon salt*
2 *tablespoons butter*
⅓ *cup milk*

Roll dough out. Spread dough with butter, apples, and cinnamon. Roll up. Cut in slices 1½ inch in thickness. Place close together in pan about 8x8x2 inches. Pour syrup over sliced pin wheels. Bake 25 minutes at 400°. Delicious served warm with cream or vanilla ice cream.

QUICKIE HOT DESSERT

Sprinkle canned cling peach halves with sugar, cinnamon, and slivers of orange rind. Dot with butter and bake in a hot oven about 10 minutes. Dollop with whipped cream if desired.

By any name this dessert is good eating — call it blueberry "slump" or blueberry "dumplings," or a "grunt" as on Cape Cod. Doubly delicious with rich cream.

BLUEBERRY DUMPLINGS

2½ cups fresh blueberries
⅓ cup sugar
Dash salt
1 cup water
1 tablespoon lemon juice
1 cup all-purpose flour
2 tablespoons sugar
2 teaspoons baking powder
¼ teaspoon salt
1 tablespoon butter
½ cup milk

Bring first 4 ingredients to boiling. Cover; simmer 5 minutes. Add lemon juice. Sift together dry ingredients; cut in butter till like coarse meal. Add milk all at once; stir only till flour is dampened. Drop batter from tip of tablespoon into bubbling sauce, making 6 dumplings. Don't let them overlap. Cover tightly; cook over low heat 10 minutes without peeking. Serve hot.

Here are some tips for you:

While the blueberry sauce is cooking, there's just time to stir up the dumplings. Dovetailing like this makes this a quick, easy dessert. Dip the spoon into the bubbling sauce each time before you dip into the batter. Then dumplings will slide off the spoon easily. No peeking while dumplings cook. Now lift lid. Blueberry slump is light as a cloud! Serve hot with the luscious sauce spooned over. Pass cream.

BAKED PEACHES

Peel, cut in halves, and remove stones from peaches. Place in shallow baking pan. Fill each cavity with chopped nuts, fruits, macaroon crumbs or 1 teaspoon sugar, ½ teaspoon butter, few drops lemon juice, and a slight grating of nutmeg. Bake 20 minutes at 350°. If desired, baste with sherry. Serve warm with hard sauce or chilled with whipped cream.

The use of water chestnuts is simply unlimited!

FRUIT SAUCE WITH WATER CHESTNUTS

2 *tablespoons butter*
1 *can (5 ounces) water chestnuts, sliced*
1 *can (approximately 20 ounces) pineapple juice*
1 *can (6 ounces) frozen tangerine-juice concentrate*
2 *sticks cinnamon*
½ *cup sugar*
¼ *cup cornstarch*
¼ *teaspoon ginger*
⅛ *teaspoon salt*
2 *tablespoons lemon juice*
2 *teaspoons grated lemon rind*

Heat 1 tablespoon butter in a skillet; add the water chestnuts. Stir until butter is absorbed and water chestnuts lightly browned. Remove from heat. In a large saucepan mix the pineapple juice with enough water to make 3 cups. Add the tangerine juice and cinnamon sticks. Bring to a boil, reduce heat, and simmer for 5 minutes. Meanwhile, mix the sugar, cornstarch, ginger, and salt in a bowl. Blend thoroughly. Stir until smooth. Return to fruit juices and cook, stirring, until clear and thickened. Remove from heat. Add the lemon juice, lemon rind, and 1 tablespoon butter. Cool to room temperature. When cool, remove cinnamon sticks, and chill. Just before serving, add the water chestnuts. This sauce keeps well for about a week. Serve with a combination of fresh fruits.
Yield: 3 cups.

Mixes are handy. Try these little upside-downies. They are mouthwatering when served warm. Add a dash of cinnamon to the whipped cream.

PEACH UPSIDE-DOWNIES

Prepare 1 package yellow cake mix (1-layer size) according to package directions. Spoon 1 teaspoon soft butter, 1 teaspoon brown sugar, and 1 peach half or 2 or 3 peach slices into each muffin cup or custard cup. Spoon cake batter over peaches.

Bake as directed for cupcakes on cake-mix package. Remove from cups. Serve warm with whipped cream.
Makes 7 or 8.

Wonderful for summertime treat.

FROZEN BANANA POPPETTES

4 or 5 medium bananas, fully ripe
8 or 10 skewers (wooden)
1 6-ounce package (1 cup) semi-sweet chocolate pieces
1 tablespoon shortening
Flaked coconut, assorted sprinkles, chopped nuts

Peel bananas, halve crosswise; insert skewers in cut ends. Wrap in foil; freeze. Melt chocolate pieces and shortening over hot (not boiling) water; blend until smooth. With spatula or table knife, quickly spread melted chocolate on frozen bananas; immediately roll in coconut, sprinkles, or nuts. Serve, or rewrap in foil and return to freezer until ready to serve.
Yields 8 to 10.

Variation:

Substitute 1 6-ounce package (1 cup) butterscotch pieces for chocolate pieces.

When you have a beautiful, tall, stately, fresh pineapple, make an ambrosia. It's always a popular dessert. This is my favorite recipe.

AMBROSIA

1 ripe pineapple
6 oranges
2 cups freshly grated coconut

Peel and prepare the pineapple, and slice in thin slices. Peel the oranges and cut into sections. Place in layers in a bowl, with ½ cup of powdered sugar. Cover with the fresh coconut and chill. If you like, you may pour over ⅓ cup sherry or ¼ cup apricot brandy. It is a wonderful sweet ending to any kind of meal.

CRÈME DE MENTHE

Plump cooked prunes served ice cold with a tablespoon of crème de menthe over each serving taste amazingly good.

I like crème de menthe in the summertime. Dress up your desserts with it, especially fruit or ice cream. For company, pile ice cream on top of any fresh fruit, and pour lighted crème de menthe over.

Try this for St. Valentine's Day. It's quick and good.

CHERRY QUICK

1 *No. 303 can sour pitted cherries*
2 *tablespoons cornstarch*
1 *cup sugar*
1 *cup flour*
½ *teaspoon baking powder*
¼ *cup margarine or butter*
1 *egg*

Combine cherries, cornstarch, and ½ cup of sugar in top of double boiler; cook until thickened; cool. Combine flour, ½ cup of sugar, baking powder, and margarine until crumbly; stir in egg. Flour hands and pat flour mixture into a 9-inch pie plate; add cherry filling. Bake at 350° for 30 minutes.

They come out of the oven bubbling in their own juice.

BIG APPLE DUMPLINGS

1¼ *cups sugar*
2 *cups water*
½ *teaspoon cinnamon*
¼ *cup butter or margarine*
6 *apples, pared and cored*

2 tablespoons chopped raisins
2 tablespoons chopped walnut meats
1 tablespoon honey
2 cups flour
1 teaspoon salt
⅔ cup shortening
⅓ cup light cream

Combine sugar, water, and cinnamon. Cook 5 minutes. Add butter. Pare and core apples. Fill with mixture of raisins, nuts, and honey. Sift flour and salt into mixing bowl. Cut in shortening. Add cream, a tablespoon at a time, mix and press together. Roll ¼ inch thick. Cut in squares. Place apple in each square; sprinkle with additional sugar and spices. Dot with butter, fold corners, and pinch edges. Place in greased baking pan. Pour sauce over. Bake at 375° for 35 minutes.

FRESH APPLE COBBLER WITH HOT RUM SAUCE

2½ cups sliced cooked apples
1 cup sugar
½ cup butter
1 teaspoon cinnamon
Pie crust

Hot Rum Sauce:

2 cups juice from cooked apples
2 cups sugar
4 tablespoons Cuban rum

Stir sugar into apples. Fill a greased deep-dish pie pan or casserole ⅔ full. Dot with butter and sprinkle cinnamon over the surface. Roll pastry out very thin, cut into strips and crisscross over surface. Bake in 450° oven until apples are glazed. Simmer juice and sugar until thick or consistency of light syrup. When ready to serve, add ½ tablespoon rum to each 2 tablespoons hot apple syrup and pour over each serving of hot cobbler.

Children like this.

PEACHES OVER PUDDING FLAMBÉ

Fill serving dishes half full of your favorite pudding and top with a cling peach half. Saturate a sugar lump with lemon extract, place in the peach center, then set the sugar ablaze. For the full drama of your flaming dessert, turn out the lights just as you bring it into the dining room. This is a real event.

Don't miss this one during the peach season.

FRESH PEACH COBBLER

3 cups sliced fresh peaches
1 cup sugar
¼ teaspoon almond extract
1 tablespoon lemon juice
1 teaspoon grated lemon peel
1½ cups sifted enriched flour
3 teaspoons baking powder
1 tablespoon sugar
½ teaspoon salt
⅓ cup shortening
½ cup milk
1 well-beaten egg
2 tablespoons sugar

Arrange peaches in greased 8 x 8 x 2-inch pan. Sprinkle with mixture of 1 cup sugar, almond extract, lemon juice, and lemon peel. Heat in oven while preparing shortcake. Sift together flour, baking powder, 1 tablespoon sugar, and salt. Cut in shortening until mixture is like coarse crumbs. Add milk and egg at once, stir until flour is just moistened. Spread dough over hot peaches. Sprinkle with 2 tablespoons sugar. Bake in hot oven (400°) 35 to 40 minutes. *Makes 8 servings.*

PEACHES IN CHAMPAGNE

8 beautifully ripened peaches, peeled and halved
⅓ cup brandy
1 bottle chilled champagne

Peaches can be peeled more easily without removing any of the fruit if they are plunged into boiling water for a few seconds as you would do for removing the skins of tomatoes. Peel peaches, halve, and remove stones. Place the halves in your most beautiful bowl. Sprinkle with brandy, cover, and place in refrigerator to chill for ½ hour or more. When ready to serve, cover with chilled champagne; the remainder is intended for the wine glasses. Serve with a deep-bowled serving spoon which will dip up fragrant liquid with each serving of peaches.
Makes 8 servings.

PARTY PEACHES

There's a party flair to a dessert of warm peaches with brandy sauce. Simply heat canned cling peach halves in a saucepan or oven. Top with a sauce made by whipping ½ cup powdered sugar into ½ cup heavy cream. Fold in 2 tablespoons brandy and serve over hot peaches.

PEACHES FLAMBÉES

Pour the juice from a pint jar of halved peaches into the top pan, or blazer, of a chafing dish. Place the pan directly over the flame and bring the juice to a boil. Thicken it with ½ teaspoon arrowroot dissolved in a little cold water and put in the peach halves. Baste the peaches with the sauce until they are heated through. Pour over the fruit 2 ounces bourbon and set ablaze. Or flame the peaches with *eau de vie de framboise,* a raspberry brandy, or with any of the brandies distilled from fruit.

For a change in pace, give Miss Hèléne a try. Pear Hèléne is a marvelous addition to any meal, be it simple or elegant.

PEAR HÈLÉNE

4 *medium-sized pears*
1 *cup water*
½ *cup sugar*
1 *quart vanilla ice cream*

Pare, halve and core pears. Combine water and sugar in saucepan; bring to boiling, stirring constantly until sugar dissolves; boil 5 minutes. Simmer pears in syrup in covered pan until tender (about 10-15 minutes). Chill pears in syrup. To serve, spoon ice cream into serving dish; top with pear half; pour on glossy chocolate sauce.
Serves 8.

Glossy Chocolate Sauce:

Combine 1 package semi-sweet chocolate pieces, 2 tablespoons butter and 3 tablespoons water in top of double boiler. Cook over hot water, stirring frequently, until smooth and well blended; stir in ¼ teaspoon vanilla.
Serve warm or cool.
Makes 1 cup.

Pies

The word "pie" definitely signifies a sweet pastry. Since this dessert is typically American, it certainly rates special attention. We have listed what we think are a few "attention-getters." Try 'em. They're all good.

Of all the pastry recipes I've used through the years, this one is the best. Practice makes perfect. Keep trying until you have attained just the "right feel" of the dough. You can't fail with this one.

MY FAVORITE PASTRY

2 cups sifted enriched flour
Scant cup shortening (not quite a full cup)
1 teaspoon salt
6 to 8 tablespoons cold water

Sift the flour and salt together. Cut in the shortening quickly and lightly with a pastry blender. Stir in the cold water as lightly as possible to form a smooth ball. Roll out on a lightly floured board. This will make 1 2-crust pie, or 12 individual tart shells. Remember to handle as little as possible so the pastry will be light and flaky.

SMORGASBORD APPLE PIE

Combine:

¾ cup light brown sugar
¼ cup white sugar
½ teaspoon cinnamon
1 tablespoon lemon juice
6 cups sliced Spy apples (6-8 medium apples)
3 tablespoons butter

Place in unbaked 9-inch shell and dot with 3 tablespoons butter. Add top crust and bake at 425° for 10 minutes. Reduce to 350° and continue baking 40 more minutes.

Apple cobbler has a new topping. Cream cheese is delightful used in this pastry.

APPLE COBBLER WITH CREAM-CHEESE PASTRY

- 4 *tart apples, pared, cored, and sliced*
- ½ *cup sugar*
- 1 *teaspoon cinnamon*
- 1 *recipe cream-cheese pastry*

Arrange apple slices in buttered 1½-quart casserole. Sprinkle on combined sugar and cinnamon. Cut thin slices from ball of chilled cream-cheese dough. Place over fruit. Bake at 425° for 35 to 40 minutes or until pastry is browned. Yield: 6 servings.

Cream Cheese Pastry:

- ½ *cup chilled salted butter*
- ¼ *pound chilled cream cheese*
- 1 *cup sifted flour*

Cut butter and cream cheese into flour until pieces are size of peas and each piece is well coated with flour. Work with hands to form a small ball of dough. Chill several hours.

Oh, I love blueberry pie.

BLUEBERRY PIE

- 4 *cups blueberries*
- 1 *cup sugar*
- 2 *to* 3 *tablespoons cornstarch*
- ⅛ *teaspoon salt*
- ¼ *teaspoon nutmeg*
- ¼ *teaspoon cinnamon*
- 2 *tablespoons lemon juice*
- ¼ *teaspoon grated lemon peel*
- 1 *recipe plain pastry*

Combine blueberries, sugar, cornstarch, salt, spices, lemon juice, and peel. Fill 9-inch pastry-lined pie pan. Adjust top crust. Bake in hot oven (450°) 10 minutes, then moderate oven (350°) 30 minutes.

Light enough for the angels.

LEMON ANGEL PIE

4 egg whites
1 cup sugar
¼ teaspoon cream of tartar

Beat egg whites and cream of tartar to a peak. Slowly add sugar, and beat until glossy. Grease pie pan with shortening. Spread meringue well out to the edges of pie pan. Bake 250° for 20 minutes, then increase heat to 300° for 40 minutes. When cold spread with ½ pint whipped cream.

Filling:

4 egg yolks
⅓ cup sugar
¼ teaspoon salt
3 tablespoons lemon juice
1 teaspoon grated lemon rind

Cook slowly in double boiler. Cool and put on top of cream. Put additional whipped cream on top of filling. Place in refrigerator. Should stand in refrigerator at least two hours before serving, and may be made several hours ahead.

Marvelous flavor.

CREAMY COFFEE CHIFFON PIE

1 envelope unflavored gelatin
1 cup strong coffee, divided
1 cup sugar, divided
½ teaspoon salt
1 cup heavy cream, divided
3 eggs, separated
1 teaspoon vanilla

¼ teaspoon cream of tartar
1 9-inch baked pie shell
Flaked coconut

Soften gelatin in ¼ cup cold coffee. Combine ½ cup sugar, salt, remaining coffee, and ½ cup cream in saucepan. Stir over low heat until scalding point is reached. Beat egg yolks and add hot mixture slowly. Return to saucepan and stir over low heat until just boiling. Stir in softened gelatin. Chill until partially set, then beat until smooth. Add vanilla. Whip remaining cream and fold in. Beat egg whites until they form soft peaks. Add cream of tartar, then remaining sugar slowly, beating well after each addition. Fold coffee mixture carefully into meringue. Spoon into pie shell. Garnish with toasted flaked coconut and swirls of sweetened whipped cream.

Can you imagine a "sesame-seed pie" — I love it!

OPEN-SESAME PIE

4 tablespoons sesame seeds
1 cup sifted flour
½ teaspoon salt
⅓ cup shortening
3 to 4 tablespoons cold water

Toast seeds in pan for 2 minutes at 450°. Make pie crust, mixing seeds with sifted flour. Roll out and fit loosely into 9-inch pie pan. Bake at 450° for 10-12 minutes. Cool.

Date Chiffon Filling:

Soften one envelope of gelatin in ¼ cup cold water. Beat together 1 cup milk, 2 egg yolks, ¼ cup sugar, and ¼ teaspoon salt in top of double boiler, until well blended. Cook over hot water, stirring constantly until mixture will just coat a metal spoon. Add softened gelatin, stir until dissolved. Chill, stirring occasionally, until thickened and partially set. Stir in 1 teaspoon vanilla and 1 cup pitted, chopped dates. Fold in ¾ cup whipping cream beaten very thick. Beat 2 egg whites till slight mounds form, add 2 tablespoons sugar gradually, beating until glossy peaks are formed. Fold gently into the date mix. Spoon into cooled shell. Chill until firm (about 1 hour). Sprinkle lightly with nutmeg.

You can't miss this — it's great. Thanks, Golly dear. Golly is Mrs. Jack Miner, of Chesterfield, Mo.

GOLLY'S OZARK PIE

Cream together:

1 egg
¾ cup sugar

Add:

¼ cup flour
1 teaspoon baking powder
½ cup nuts
½ cup apples (cut up)
1 teaspoon vanilla
Pinch of salt

Bake in greased 9-inch pie pan 30 minutes at 375°. Serve with ice cream.

Maine or Michigan — it's tops!

MAINE CUSTARD PIE

Beat 1 egg white, add ½ cup sugar, ¼ teaspoon salt, 1 teaspoon vanilla.
Drop in egg yolk and 2 large or 3 small whole eggs. Blend slightly; stir in 2½ cups warm milk. Pour into unbaked pie shell.
Place in 450° oven. Turn down to 425° *immediately*. Bake *exactly* 30 minutes. If there is a soft spot in the center, pay no attention.

If you like peanut butter, this is it!

PEANUT-BUTTER PIE

½ cup peanut butter
1½ cups light corn syrup
4 eggs, beaten
½ cup sugar
½ teaspoon vanilla
¼ teaspoon salt

½ recipe basic pastry
1 cup whipping cream
½ cup chopped peanuts

Place peanut butter in mixing bowl and add syrup slowly, blending the two ingredients. Add the eggs, sugar, vanilla, and salt. Stir until mixture is smooth and creamy.

Line a 9-inch pie pan with the pastry and pour in the peanut butter mixture. Bake in a hot oven 425° for 20 minutes. Then reduce the heat to 350° for 30 minutes more, or until the custard is firm. After it is cooled, top with whipping cream and sprinkle with peanuts.

Just what it says—"utterly deadly," but so good! This pie derives its title from the richness of the filling.

UTTERLY DEADLY SOUTHERN PECAN PIE

4 eggs
1½ cups Southern cane syrup (or corn syrup)
1½ cups pecans, coarsely broken
1 cup white sugar
4 tablespoons butter
1 teaspoon vanilla

Boil sugar and syrup together for 2 to 3 minutes. Beat eggs thoroughly, and slowly pour the hot syrup into the eggs. Add butter, vanilla, and pecan meats. Turn into unbaked pie shell and bake in moderate oven about 45 minutes, or until set.
Serves 6 to 8.

FAVORITE PECAN PIE

3 eggs
⅔ cup sugar
½ teaspoon salt
⅓ cup butter, melted
1 cup dark or light corn syrup
1 cup pecan halves

Mix above ingredients, pour into unbaked pie shell. Bake for 40 to 50 minutes at 375°. Serve warm with ice cream or chill and serve with cinnamon-flavored whipped cream.

This unusual recipe originated in the Florida Keys.

KEY LIME PIE

Beat 3 egg yolks until they are light and lemon-colored and add ½ cup freshly squeezed lime juice and 1 teaspoon grated lime rind. Beat in the contents of a 15-ounce can of sweetened condensed milk and a drop or two of vegetable food coloring to make a natural lime tint. Pour the custard into a baked pie shell with a fluted standing rim. Beat 4 egg whites stiff but not dry and beat into them gradually ½ cup fine granulated sugar and 1 teaspoon lime juice.

Spread the meringue thickly over the filling, bringing it to the crust all around and swirling it into regular peaks.

Bake the pie in a moderate oven (350°) for about 15 minutes, until the meringue is delicately browned. Serve the pie well chilled.

Always just right during the holidays.

PUMPKIN CHIFFON PIE

3 beaten egg yolks
¾ cup brown sugar
1½ cups pumpkin
½ cup milk
½ teaspoon salt
1 teaspoon cinnamon
½ teaspoon ginger
½ teaspoon nutmeg

1 tablespoon unflavored gelatin
¼ cup cold water
3 stiffly beaten egg whites
¼ cup granulated sugar

Combine yolks, brown sugar, pumpkin, milk, salt, and spices. Cook in double boiler till thick, stirring constantly. Soften gelatin in cold water, stir into mixture. Chill until partially set. Beat egg whites, gradually add granulated sugar, beat stiff, fold into gelatin mixture. Pour into pie shell and chill until set. Garnish with whipped cream.

It's de luxe, all right, and nice party fare.

DE LUXE CHOCOLATE PEPPERMINT CREAM PIE

⅔ cup butter
1 cup sugar
3 eggs, beaten until light
2 ounces (2 squares) unsweetened chocolate
2 ounces semi-sweet chocolate
¼ teaspoon peppermint extract
1 9-inch graham-cracker crust
1 cup heavy cream (whipped)
2 tablespoons confectioners' sugar
4 sticks peppermint candy, crushed

Cream butter. Add sugar gradually. Continue creaming until mixture is light and fluffy. Add eggs and blend into creamed mixture. Melt chocolate. Cool and add to creamed mixture. Add peppermint extract. Turn mixture into graham-cracker pie shell. Chill 3 to 4 hours. Spread with whipped cream to which confectioners' sugar has been added. Sprinkle crushed peppermint candy on top of whipped cream. *6 to 8 servings.*

Extra work is involved in preparing the coconut, but you'll not regret it.

FRESH COCONUT-CREAM PIE

⅓ cup sifted flour
⅔ cup sugar

¼ teaspoon salt
2 cups scalded milk
1½ cups shredded fresh coconut
3 eggs separated
2 tablespoon butter
½ teaspoon vanilla
1 baked 9-inch pie shell
6 tablespoons sugar

Mix flour, ⅔ cup sugar, and salt in saucepan. Gradually stir in milk. Cook over moderate heat, stirring constantly, until mixture thickens and boils. Cook 2 minutes longer. Remove from heat. Add 1 cup coconut. Beat egg yolks slightly. Stir a little hot mixture into egg yolks, then stir egg yolks into hot mixture. Cook 1 minute. Remove from heat. Add butter and vanilla. Cool slightly. Pour into baked pie shell.

Beat egg whites until they stand in soft mounds. Gradually beat in 6 tablespoons sugar, continuing to beat until egg whites stand in stiff peaks. Spread meringue over pie, making sure it comes to edge of crust. Sprinkle with remaining ½ cup coconut. Place in moderate oven (350°) to brown lightly, about 12 minutes.

SOUR-CREAM PIE

3 eggs, beaten
1½ tablespoons all-purpose flour
1 cup sugar
½ teaspoon salt
2½ teaspoons cinnamon
½ teaspoon cloves
1⅓ cups thick sour cream
1 cup seedless raisins

Beat eggs until light and fluffy. Mix flour, sugar, salt, and spices together and add to egg mixture, blending well. Fold in the cream and raisins. Pour into unbaked pastry-lined pie plate. Bake at 350° for approximately 45 minutes. *Serves 6.*

Different twist to a "nutty pie."

PEANUT PIE

1 *cup coarsely chopped salted peanuts*
1½ *cups white corn syrup*
4 *eggs, slightly beaten*
1 *teaspoon vanilla*
Dash of nutmeg
1 *unbaked pie shell*

Spread peanuts in the bottom of the unbaked pie shell. Mix thoroughly the corn syrup, slightly beaten eggs, and vanilla. Pour over the peanuts in the pie shell, add a dash of nutmeg if desired. Bake in moderate oven (350°) for 45 minutes.

Everyone has asked for Rum Pie. Here is a choice one. The flavor will linger forever... I promise!

RUM CREAM PIE

6 *egg yolks*
1 *cup sugar*

Beat eggs until light. Add sugar slowly to yolks.

1 *tablespoon gelatin*
½ *cup cold water*

Soak gelatin in cold water, put gelatin and water over low heat and let come to a boil. Pour it over the sugar and egg mixture, stirring briskly.

1 *pint heavy cream*
½ *cup Jamaica rum*

Whip cream until it is stiff. Fold into above mixture. Add rum, stir well, cool but do not let set. Pour into a crumb shell or a cooked pastry shell, mound generously with sweetened whipped cream and shaved bittersweet chocolate. Use a deep spring form pan for this rather than a regular pie tin as this makes a very thick pie. If you don't have a spring form pan, use a large 10-inch pie dish.

CRANBERRY CLARET PIE

Combine 2¼ cups sugar, 1 tablespoon flour, ¼ teaspoon salt, and ½ teaspoon mace. Add ¼ cup water and ¼ cup claret wine. Stir over low heat until sugar dissolves. Add 4 cups fresh cranberries; cook slowly until all the skins pop open. Add 1 tablespoon grated lemon peel. Pour into pastry-lined 9-inch pie pan. Dot with 2 tablespoons butter. Top with crisscross strips of pastry or pastry cutouts. Bake at 425° for 30 minutes.

Famous at the Hollywood Brown Derby.

BLACK BOTTOM PIE

Crust:

Roll fourteen gingersnaps fine and mix well with 5 tablespoons melted butter. Press firmly into a 9-inch pie pan. Bake in slow oven 300° for 5 minutes. Cool.

Filling:

Add 1½ tablespoons of cornstarch, mixed well with ½ cup sugar, to 4 beaten egg yolks. Add 2 cups scalded milk slowly and cook in a double boiler for twenty minutes. Remove one cup of the custard and add 1½ squares chocolate and one teaspoon vanilla. Pour into crust. Blend 1 tablespoon gelatin soaked in 4 tablespoons cold water with the remaining custard. Fold in meringue (4 egg whites, ½ teaspoon cream of tartar, a pinch of salt, and ½ cup sugar). Add 2 teaspoons light Cuban rum (more if desired). Pour on top of chocolate layer. When set, cover with whipped cream sweetened with 1 tablespoon powdered sugar. Sprinkle with shaved chocolate. Be generous with chocolate, too!

FRENCH DATE PIE

Pastry for 1 9-inch crust
1 *cup fresh California dates*
3 *eggs*
½ *teaspoon cornstarch*

Dash of salt
½ teaspoon freshly grated nutmeg
¾ cup brown sugar (packed)
1 cup all-purpose cream
1 teaspoon vanilla

Line pie plate with pastry; flute or crimp edges. Pit and slice dates into thin strips. Beat eggs enough to mix thoroughly. Blend cornstarch, salt, and nutmeg into brown sugar. Stir into eggs, then blend in cream and vanilla. Pour into pastry shell. Bake at 450° (hot oven) for 10 minutes. Reduce heat to 350° (moderate oven). Bake 20 to 25 minutes longer, until firm around edges when tested with a knife — but still a little quivery in the center. Cool completely before cutting.

The all-time American favorite.

LEMON MERINGUE PIE

4 tablespoons cornstarch
4 tablespoons flour
½ teaspoon salt
1½ cups sugar
1½ cups boiling water
2 tablespoons butter
Few gratings lemon rind
½ cup lemon juice
4 egg yolks, slightly beaten
Baked pie shell
Meringue made with 4 whites

Mix cornstarch, flour, salt, and sugar in top of double boiler. Add boiling water and cook over direct heat, stirring constantly, until mixture boils. Set over hot water, cover, and cook 20 minutes. Add butter, lemon rind, and juice. Stir in egg yolks. Cook and stir until thick. Cool. Fill pie shell.

Meringue:

Beat egg whites until frothy. Add ¼ teaspoon cream of tartar and continue to beat until egg whites are stiff enough to hold a peak. Gradually beat in sugar, using 2 tablespoons sugar for each egg white, and beat until meringue is stiff and glossy.

Putting Meringue on Pies or Tarts:

Pile meringue lightly on cooled pie, making sure it touches edges of pastry to prevent it from shrinking. With tablespoon or spatula swirl large graceful curls and bake at 425° until delicately brown, about 5 to 6 minutes.

Not the usual apple pie — still an all-time favorite!

UPSIDE-DOWN APPLE PIE

Pastry:

½ *cup shortening*
1 *egg*
1½ *tablespoons lemon juice*
1½ *cups all-purpose flour*
¼ *teaspoon salt*

Cut chilled shortening into flour. Add lemon juice to egg and beat slightly. Add to flour mixture, and mix. Press into shape in wax paper. Chill before rolling.

⅓ *cup melted butter or margarine*
½ *cup walnut halves*
½ *cup light brown sugar*
2½ *cups canned apple slices*
½ *cup granulated sugar*

1½ tablespoons all-purpose flour
½ teaspoon cinnamon
½ teaspoon nutmeg
½ teaspoon salt

Place melted butter in bottom of pie tin. Place walnut halves (flat side up) in melted butter. Pat brown sugar over nut meats. Roll pastry and fit into pie pan on top of nut mixture. Combine apples, sugar, flour, spices, and salt. Place in shell. Cover with pastry and seal edges. Bake in a 375° oven 40 minutes. Cool 5 minutes. Loosen edge of pie with spatula. Invert on serving plate. Serve warm, topped with whipped cream or ice cream.

AUTUMN PUMPKIN PIE

Make pastry for one-crust pie. Line pie pan. Build up high fluted edge.

Filling:

Beat together with rotary beater:

2 *cups mashed cooked pumpkin (may be canned)*
½ teaspoon salt
1¾ cups milk (½ cream)
3 *eggs*
⅔ cup brown sugar (packed)
3 *tablespoons granulated sugar*
1¼ teaspoons cinnamon
½ teaspoon ginger
½ teaspoon nutmeg
¼ teaspoon cloves

Pour into pastry-lined pie pan. (For crispness, have bottom pastry a little thicker than ⅛".) Bake at 425° just until a silver knife inserted 1" from side of filling comes out clean, 45 to 55 minutes. The center may still look soft but will set later. Serve slightly warm or cold.
If served cold, spread with whipped cream and sprinkle black walnuts on top – wonderful!

Michigan apples used this way are wonderful.

SOUR-CREAM APPLE PIE

1 *cup sour cream*
2 *tablespoons enriched flour*
¾ *cup sugar*
¼ *teaspoon salt*
1 *teaspoon vanilla*
1 *egg*
1 *recipe plain pastry*
3 *cups tart Michigan apples, diced*

Beat together cream, sugar, flour, salt, vanilla, and egg. Add apples. Pour into 9-inch unbaked pie shell and bake at 400° for 25 minutes. Mix ½ cup brown sugar, ⅓ cup flour, and ¼ cup butter. Sprinkle on top and bake 20 minutes more.

I make one a year!

CONCORD GRAPE PIE

Stem 4 cups Concord grapes and slip the pulp out of the skins. Reserve the skins. Cook the pulp until the seeds loosen and press it through a sieve to remove the seeds. Combine the pulp and skins with ¾ cup sugar, 1½ tablespoons lemon juice, and 1 tablespoon each grated orange rind and quick-cooking tapioca or 2 tablespoons flour. Blend the filling thoroughly, let it stand for 5 minutes, and pour it into a 9-inch pie pan lined with pastry. Cover with a lattice topping. Bake in hot oven 450° for 10 minutes, lower heat to moderate 375° and bake for 20 minutes longer.

Beautiful warm spring days reveal this gorgeous long-stalked plant. It tastes good and makes one's mouth pucker.

RHUBARB PIE

3 *tablespoons flour*
1 *cup sugar*
1 *egg*
3 *cups cut-up fresh rhubarb*
Pastry

Combine flour and sugar. Add egg and beat well. Stir in rhubarb and arrange mixture in pastry-lined pie plate. Cover with slashed-top crust or lattice strips and flute edges. Bake at 400° for 30 to 40 minutes, or until browned.

Springtime Fruit Pie:

Follow directions for recipe above and use 1 cup each fresh strawberries and fresh, canned, or frozen pineapple chunks in place of 2 cups of the rhubarb. Reduce sugar to ¾ cup and add 1 teaspoon grated lemon or orange rind. Two tablespoons quick-cooking tapioca may be used in place of flour.

FRESH PEACH PIE

4 *cups sliced fresh peaches (about 6 medium-sized)*
1 *tablespoon lemon juice*
1 *to 1½ cups sugar*
¼ *teaspoon salt*
2 *tablespoons flour*
1 *tablespoon margarine or butter*

Place peaches in a bowl. Add lemon juice, sugar (only 1 cup for peaches of "eating ripeness"), salt, and flour. Blend. Place in pan lined with pie crust. Dot with margarine. Cover with top crust. Bake in a hot oven (425°) about 35 minutes. *Yield: 9-inch pie.*

The unusual tang of this light and airy dessert is especially welcome after a rich and elegant dinner.

COINTREAU PARFAIT PIE

1 *package lemon- or orange-flavored gelatin*
1 *cup hot water*
⅓ *cup Cointreau*
1 *pint vanilla ice cream*
1 *baked 8-inch pie shell*

Dissolve gelatin in hot water in 2-quart saucepan. Add Cointreau. Add ice cream by spoonfuls, stirring until melted. Then chill until thickened, but not set (15 to 25 minutes). Pour into baked pie shell

and chill again until set. Garnish thickly with whipped cream and shaved chocolate, toasted almonds or coconut, or strawberries soaked in Cointreau.
Makes 8-inch pie.

Mr. Gross was triumphant when he returned from one of his trips to Arizona with this recipe. He had found it in scenic Scotsdale at the Lu-La Belle Restaurant and persuaded the manager to divulge the secret of this wonderful pie. I know you'll be delightful with it.

GRASSHOPPER PIE

Crust:

1¼ *cups crushed chocolate cookie wafers*
⅓ *cup melted butter*

Pat into 9″ pie pan and chill.

Filling:

⅔ *cup milk, scalded*
24 *marshmallows*

Add to milk and melt slowly in double boiler, stirring often. Cool to room temperature.

2 *ounces green crème de menthe*
1 *ounce white crème de cacao*

Whip and fold ½ pint whipping cream into above. Pour into chocolate crust and freeze. Serve with whipped cream if you wish.

SOUR-CREAM PEACH PIE

1 *unbaked pie crust*
5 *fresh peaches, peeled and sliced*
¾ *cup brown sugar*
1 *tablespoon cornstarch*
½ *teaspoon cinnamon*

¼ teaspoon nutmeg
Salt
1⅓ cups sour cream

Combine peaches, brown sugar, cornstarch, cinnamon, nutmeg, salt, and sour cream. Pour into unbaked pastry shell. Bake 25 minutes at 400°. Delicious served warm.

DEEP-DISH BERRY PIE

4 cups fresh blueberries, blackberries, raspberries, or boysenberries
¾ cup sugar
1½ teaspoons tapioca or flour
⅛ teaspoon salt
Grated rind of ½ lemon
1 tablespoon lemon juice
1 tablespoon butter
Pastry for one crust

Combine fruit, sugar, tapioca or flour, salt, rind and juice and turn mixture into an oblong baking dish. Dot with butter. Roll pastry into a rectangle ⅛ inch thick and about 1½ inches larger than dish. Arrange pastry lightly over berries and trim edges, leaving ½ inch overhanging. Moisten rim of dish, turn overhanging edge of pastry under and press it onto rim. Flute or crimp edge with tines of a fork. Cut slits in pastry for steam to escape and bake at 400° for 30 to 45 minutes, or until browned. Serve with cheese, hard sauce, or whipped cream. If canned berries are used, drain them well. Use only ¼ cup sugar.

Prize of the harvest season—sweet, tart, juicy.

UNCOOKED STRAWBERRY PIE

1 *quart large firm berries*
3 *tablespoons cornstarch*
½ *cup water*
1 *tablespoon lemon juice*
¼ *teaspoon salt*
1 *cup sugar*
1 *baked pie shell*
⅔ *cup whipped cream (optional)*

Wash and hull berries. Mix half of them with cornstarch and water. Crush. Add lemon juice, salt, and sugar. Cook, stirring constantly, until mixture thickens (about 5 minutes). Cool. Pour rest of berries into pie crust; cover with cooked mixture. Cool. Spread with whipped cream, if desired. Refrigerate until ready to use.

FRENCH APPLE PIE

Pie Dough:

2⅓ *cups flour*
1 *teaspoon salt*
¾ *cup shortening*
5 *tablespoons water*

Cut flour, salt, and shortening with pastry blender until well blended. Add just enough water to hold dough together. Line pie plate with pastry.

Filling:

5 *apples*
1 *cup sugar*
1 *teaspoon cinnamon*
⅛ *teaspoon salt*
½ *cup soft butter or margarine*

Peel apples, and slice very thin. Place slices in unbaked shell. Mix together the sugar, cinnamon, and salt; rub into this mixture the half cup of butter, spread over apples, bake 25 minutes at 400°; then decrease heat to 300° and bake until apples are done. Serve with either cream or whipped cream.

BLUEBERRY TARTS

Make tart shells with favorite pastry. Wash and drain blueberries. Make sugar glaze:

½ *cup sugar*
1 *tablespoon cornstarch*
¾ *cup water*
2 *tablespoons lemon juice*
1 *heaping teaspoon butter*

Cook first three ingredients. Let thicken; add butter and lemon juice. Cool slightly. Fill tart shells with blueberries and spoon glaze over berries. Chill. Top with pie crust designs or whipped cream. This glaze can be used with other fruits as well.

Good, oh, so good chocolate pie—our favorite at the WJIM Country House.

COUNTRY HOUSE CHOCOLATE PIE

Heat 2 cups milk in saucepan, add 2 squares baking chocolate, cook 5 minutes, stirring constantly. Blend together 1 cup granulated sugar, 3 tablespoons flour, ½ teaspoon salt, slowly add to milk and chocolate mixture. Blend well. Add 2 eggs, beating constantly over low temperature (about 5 minutes). Remove, add generous tablespoon butter and 1 teaspoon vanilla flavoring. Rum flavoring may be added rather than vanilla. For banana chocolate pie, slice 2 medium-sized bananas on bottom of baked pastry shell. Pour chocolate mixture over bananas, cool, cover with sweetened whipped cream. Grated sweet chocolate sprinkled on whipped cream is a nice garnish. Rich—but delicious!

Cherry pie, cherry tarts—number one in popularity always.

ALMOND-CRUST CHERRY CREAM PIE

Make your favorite pastry and add to it ½ cup slivered almonds, finely chopped.

1⅓ *cups (15-ounce can) sweetened condensed milk*
⅓ *cup lemon juice*

1 teaspoon vanilla
½ teaspoon almond extract
½ cup whipping cream, whipped

Prick sides of pie crust only. Bake as directed for baked pie shell. Cool. Combine sweetened condensed milk (you *must* use condensed milk!), lemon juice, vanilla, and almond extract. Stir until mixture thickens. Fold in whipped cream and spoon into cooled shell. Top with cherry glaze or use your favorite brand of prepared cherry pie filling. Chill 2 to 3 hours.

Cherry Glaze:

2 cups (1-pound can) pitted sour cherries, drained
⅔ cup cherry juice
¼ cup sugar
1 tablespoon cornstarch
2 to 3 drops red food coloring, if desired

Set aside drained cherries. Blend cherry juice with sugar and cornstarch. Cook over low heat, stirring constantly, until mixture is thickened and clear. Add cherries and food coloring; spread over cream filling. Chill.

NUTMEG CHERRY PIE

¾ cup sugar
¼ teaspoon salt
½ teaspoon ground nutmeg
3 tablespoons cornstarch
1 cup cherry juice (drained from canned cherries)
1 tablespoon fresh lemon juice
3 cups drained sour cherries
2 tablespoons butter or margarine
¼ teaspoon almond extract
2 teaspoons unflavored gelatine
3 tablespoons cherry juice
9-inch baked pie shell
¾ cup heavy cream, whipped
1 tablespoon sugar
Grated nutmeg for garnish

Combine first 4 ingredients in a saucepan, add cherry juice, and cook until thickened, stirring constantly. Add lemon juice, cherries, butter or margarine and heat. Add almond extract. Soften gelatin in 3 tablespoons cherry juice in a custard cup. Place in a pan of hot water to dissolve. Add to cherry mixture. Cool. Pour into a cold baked pie shell. Sweeten whipped cream with 1 tablespoon sugar and use to garnish top of pie. Sprinkle with additional nutmeg, if desired. *Yield: 6 servings.*

CHERRY TARTS

Make tarts from favorite pie-crust recipe.

For filling:

2 *cups cherries and juice*
1½ *teaspoons cornstarch (more or less, depending on thickness you like)*
½ *teaspoon salt*
½ *cup sugar*
½ *cup water*
½ *teaspoon almond extract*
2 *tablespoons butter*

Combine cherries and ½ cup sugar. Mix the water and cornstarch together. When cherries, sugar, salt are to boiling point, add cornstarch mixture and let boil until mixture is clear, about 5 minutes. Remove from fire, add flavoring and butter. Fill tart shells. Cool. Add whipped cream or other designs cut from pastry and place on top of tarts.

Sauces for Desserts

"At every meal, just before the dishes are brought to the table, there is always a last touch. Perhaps it's a bit of flavor added to the sauce, perhaps it's a deft tossing together of the salad, or a sprinkling of color. Often these ministrations are inspired strokes of genius that turn mediocrities into masterpieces. They are like the secrets of a smartly groomed woman. Her basic costume naturally is faultless, but it is the faint dab of perfume that touches off or dramatizes the whole ensemble."

Louis P. De Gouy

VANILLA SUGAR

Split a vanilla bean down the center. Place in a tightly covered container with 2½ pounds of sugar. Store for at least two weeks. When you open the container you will be delighted by the unbelievably wonderful flavor and aroma of the sugar. Use Vanilla Sugar in baked goods, custards, over cereals, pancakes, waffles, fruit compotes, and numerous other dishes.

VANILLA DESSERT SAUCES

Chocolate Sauce:

2 *squares unsweetened chocolate*
1 *tablespoon butter or margarine*
¼ *cup white corn syrup*
⅛ *teaspoon salt*
1 *cup vanilla sugar*
½ *cup boiling water*

Melt chocolate and butter or margarine over hot water. Blend in corn syrup, salt, and vanilla sugar. Stir in boiling water. Boil 3 minutes over medium heat. Cool.
Yield: approximately 1⅔ cups.

Vanilla Sauce:

½ cup vanilla sugar
1 tablespoon cornstarch
⅛ teaspoon salt
1 cup water
2 tablespoons butter or margarine

Combine first 3 ingredients in a saucepan. Stir in water. Cook over medium heat until thickened, about 5 minutes. Add butter or margarine. Cool. Serve over cake, ice cream, or use for making parfaits. *Yield: 1 cup.*

BUTTERSCOTCH SUNDAE SAUCE

1⅓ cups firmly packed light brown sugar
⅓ cup cream
¼ cup butter
Few grains salt
1½ teaspoons vanilla

Combine brown sugar, cream, butter, and salt in saucepan. Cook over low heat, stirring constantly, until sauce boils, and continue boiling for 1 minute. Remove from heat and stir in vanilla. Cool to lukewarm before serving. This sauce may be stored in a covered jar in the refrigerator. Before serving, heat and thin with a little cream, if necessary.

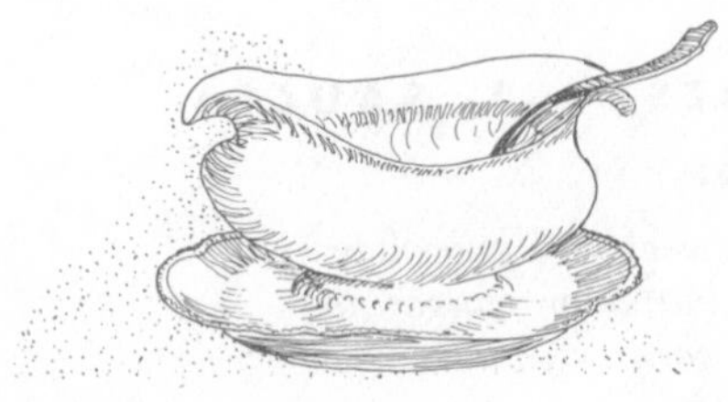

BING CHERRY SAUCE

1 No. 303 can Bing cherries, drained, pitted, and halved
1 cup liquid from canned cherries
2 teaspoons cornstarch
1 tablespoon butter

Combine liquid and cornstarch in saucepan. Mix well. Cook over medium heat, stirring constantly, until sauce thickens. Remove from heat and add cherry halves and butter. Chill before serving.

Don't forget mince pie . . . but don't cook the brandy. You'll lose the flavor.

BRANDY SAUCE

- 1 *cup sugar*
- 1 *tablespoon cornstarch*
- ¼ *teaspoon salt*
- 1 *tablespoon butter*
- 1 *cup boiling water*
- ¼ *cup or more brandy*

Mix together dry ingredients. Add butter and boiling water. Mix well and cook 6 minutes or until clear.

Add brandy after you remove saucepan from fire.

Serve quite warm over any little plain cake or pudding.

COUNTRY HOUSE CHOCOLATE SAUCE

Mrs. Charlotte Gross gave me this recipe some years ago. It's the only sauce we use in the Country House dining room.

The flavor and texture improve with long and slow cooking, and the sauce can be stored in refrigerator indefinitely. When hot chocolate sauce is needed, just reheat in double boiler. For cold sauce, allow to stand at room temperature for 45 minutes. Ideal for ice cream, cream puffs, cakes, and frozen-pie topping.

- 1 *1-pound package of baking or cooking chocolate*
- ¼ *cup warm water*
- 4 *cups granulated sugar*
- 1 *quart coffee cream or 1 pint whipping cream and 1 pint milk*

Place water, chocolate, and sugar in double boiler. Cook until chocolate is thoroughly melted. Add cream. Blend well. Cook for at least 3 hours over hot water, not boiling. I prefer 5 to 6 hours cooking time. Stir often. This is a great sauce.

Country House Desserts

PINEAPPLE-CHERRY SQUARES

1½ cups fine vanilla-wafer crumbs
1 can (1⅓ to 1½ cups) flaked or shredded coconut
½ cup butter or margarine
1½ cups sifted confectioners' sugar
2 eggs
1 9-ounce can (1 cup) crushed pineapple, drained
1 cup broken California walnuts
¾ cup chopped maraschino cherries, well drained
1 cup heavy cream, whipped

Place half of crumbs in bottom of 9x9x2-inch pan; sprinkle with half the coconut. Cream butter; gradually add confectioners' sugar, creaming till light. Add eggs, one at a time, beating well after each. Spread mixture over coconut. Fold pineapple, nuts, and cherries into whipped cream; spread over mixture in pan. Sprinkle with remaining coconut and crumbs. Chill about 4 hours. Cut in squares. Trim with pineapple and maraschino cherries.
9 servings.

An old stand-by.

BAKED LEMON PUDDING

3 tablespoons shortening
1⅛ cups sugar
Juice of 1½ lemons
Grated rind of one lemon
1½ cups milk
3 tablespoons flour
3 eggs

Cream shortening, add sugar gradually, and cream well. Add well-beaten egg yolks, flour, lemon juice and rind, mix thoroughly. Add milk and then fold in stiffly beaten whites. Pour in greased baking dish set in pan of hot water. Bake in moderate oven (350°) about 45 minutes. A delicate crust will form on top. No sauce needed. May serve with whipped cream.

I have been making baked fudge for years. It's a very old recipe—a favorite of my two sons, Bob and Tom. Be sure you serve it warm.

BAKED FUDGE PUDDING

4 *eggs, well beaten*
2 *cups of sugar*
¼ *cup flour*
¼ *cup cocoa*
1 *cup melted butter or margarine*
1 *cup broken pecan meats*
1 *teaspoon vanilla*
¼ *teaspoon salt*

Beat eggs and sift dry ingredients. Combine and beat until well blended. Mix in butter and remaining ingredients. Pour into pan and set in hot water. Bake very slowly (like custard) in oven, 300°, from 40 to 60 minutes. Serve with whipped cream or ice cream. Very good!

CHOCOLATE FUDGE PUDDING

¼ *cup butter*
1 *cup sugar*
1 *teaspoon vanilla*
1 *ounce unsweetened chocolate, melted*
1½ *cups sifted flour*
½ *teaspoon salt*
3 *teaspoons baking powder*
¾ *cup milk*
½ *cup chopped nuts*

Cream butter and sugar. Add vanilla and chocolate and mix until well blended. Sift flour, salt, and baking powder together. Add all of flour, then all of milk to the chocolate mixture. Add chopped nuts and mix well. Pour batter into greased 9-inch square pan. Top with:

Topping Mixture:

1 cup granulated sugar
1 cup brown sugar
¼ cup cocoa
½ teaspoon salt
2 cups boiling water

Mix together the granulated sugar, brown sugar, cocoa, and salt. Sprinkle over cake batter. Pour boiling water over the batter. Do *not* stir. Bake in moderate oven (350°) for 40 to 45 minutes. This will separate into two layers, crust on top and chocolate fudge on the bottom. Serve crust-side down with the chocolate sauce on top. Garnish with whipped cream. *8-10 servings.*

Definitely not a dessert of the past!

FLOATING ISLAND

Soft Custard:

4 eggs or 3 eggs and 2 yolks, slightly beaten
⅔ cup sugar
1 teaspoon flour
2½ cups milk, scalded
½ teaspoon salt
2 teaspoons vanilla or other flavoring

Mix eggs, sugar, and flour. Pour milk into egg mixture, blend well. Cook, stirring constantly, in double boiler or over *low* heat until mixture coats spoon. Remove from heat immediately. Cool slightly. Stir in salt and flavoring. Chill. Serve with meringue topping.
4 to 5 servings.

Meringues:

2 egg whites
⅛ teaspoon cream of tartar
⅛ teaspoon salt
½ teaspoon vanilla or lemon extract
¼ cup sugar

Sprinkle cream of tartar and salt over egg whites. Beat whites to a coarse foam. Add flavoring and the sugar in 1-tablespoon portions beating after each addition. Continue beating until shiny and stiff. Serve in "islands" on Soft Custard or bake for serving.

To Bake: Drop by spoonfuls making 4 to 5 "islands" on ½ inch of hot water in a shallow baking pan. Bake in a moderate oven (350° F.) until delicately browned, 15 to 18 minutes. Transfer, draining off all of the water, to top of chilled Soft Custard.

From the collection of recipes belonging to my good friend, Mrs. Elizabeth Thorpe, Shreveport, Louisiana.

DELMONICO PUDDING

Shake one envelope plain gelatine over 3 cups cold milk. Let stand one hour. Add 4 egg yolks that have been well beaten and to this add ¾ cup white granulated sugar. Place all the above ingredients in top of double boiler and cook until the mixture coats a spoon. Take off range and cool mixture. Beat the 4 egg whites until they are very stiff and fold gently into the cooled custard. Rinse mold or angel food cake pan with cold water. Place 8 to 10 coconut macaroons, which have been broken in small pieces, and ½ cup chopped maraschino cherries in bottom of mold. Pour the custard mixture into the mold and place in refrigerator overnight or for several hours before serving. This dessert needs no garnish. It's delicious.

To unmold, invert pan, loosen with spatula, and place on your prettiest cake plate.

It's definitely not what the name implies; it's really something! Thanks to my friend, Mary Jane Middlebrook, Jackson, Michigan.

NOTHING DESSERT

Melt over low flame ½ pound marshmallows with ½ cup milk. Cook just until marshmallows are melted and completely blended with the milk. Cool. Then fold in a round flat tin of crushed pineapple, well drained (you can use any fresh fruit). Add ½ pint whipping cream (whipped to a very stiff stage). Combine all ingredients. Pour into a loaf pan or any dish. Sprinkle crushed (6 or 8) graham crackers over top, then few chopped walnuts. Chill thoroughly before serving. Very good.

For an old-fashioned taste treat!

TAPIOCA CREAM PUDDING

⅓ *cup sugar*
2 *cups milk*
3 *tablespoons quick-cooking tapioca*
Dash salt
1 *slightly beaten egg yolk*
1 *teaspoon vanilla*
1 *egg white*

Reserve 2 tablespoons of sugar. Combine remaining sugar with the milk, tapioca, and salt. Let stand 5 minutes. Add egg yolk. Bring mixture quickly to boiling over medium heat, stirring constantly. Remove from heat (mixture will be thin); add vanilla. Beat egg white to soft peaks. Slowly add reserved 2 tablespoons sugar, beating to stiff peaks. Gradually stir in the hot mixture. Chill. Spoon into sherbets.
Makes 5 or 6 servings.

Exciting and different.

CHOCOLATE DUMPLINGS

Chocolate Sauce:

¾ *cup brown sugar*
¼ *cup cocoa*

1 *tablespoon cornstarch*
⅛ *teaspoon salt*
2 *cups water*
2 *tablespoons butter or margarine*

Combine brown sugar, cocoa, cornstarch, and salt in heavy frying pan. Stir in water. Cook until mixture begins to boil and thicken slightly, stirring constantly. Add butter or margarine and mix well. Remove from heat while making chocolate dumplings.

Dumplings:

1 *cup sifted flour*
2 *teaspoons baking powder*
½ *teaspoon salt*
½ *cup sugar*
2 *tablespoons cocoa*
3 *tablespoons shortening*
1 *egg*
⅓ *cup milk*
1 *teaspoon vanilla*

Sift together flour, baking powder, salt, sugar, and cocoa. Add shortening, egg, milk, and vanilla. Stir to blend ingredients, then beat thoroughly for 1 minute. Return frying pan to heat and bring chocolate sauce to boil. Drop dumplings by spoonfuls on chocolate sauce. Reduce heat, cover and simmer gently 20 minutes. Serve warm with cream, if desired.
6 to 8 servings.

One associates French crêpes with the more exclusive eating establishments rather than with the average American kitchen, especially when he thinks of crêpes suzettes as a de luxe dessert whereas in reality these pancakes are economical. Don't be afraid to try them!

CRÊPES SUZETTES

Ingredients for pancakes:

4 *rounded tablespoons of all-purpose flour*
1 *egg*
1 *egg yolk*
Pinch of salt
2 *tablespoons cool melted butter*
1 *cup milk*

Ingredients for sauce:

2 *large oranges*
2 *ounces sweet butter*
¾ *cup granulated sugar*
¾ *cup light rum*
Pinch of salt
¼ *cup cognac*

Put the flour into a small bowl, add a pinch of salt, egg, egg yolk, and 4 tablespoons of the milk. Beat until very smooth with a small wire whisk. Then stir in the cool melted butter and the rest of the milk. Allow to stand in the refrigerator for at least 1 hour. Heat a heavy omelet pan and wipe it out with a little salt butter. Pour a very thin coating of this batter to cover the bottom of the omelet pan. Brown on one side, turn over, and brown the other side. Use up all the batter this way. (If the batter should be too thick, a little more milk can be added.) Fold the pancakes in three and reheat them in the following sauce: Put into a large flat copper skillet the butter, sugar, the juice of one orange, the finely shredded rind of one orange, and the rum. Simmer very slowly until the orange rind is quite translucent. If too thick, add a little more orange juice. Add cognac. Ignite the cognac and pour over hot pancakes. Serve at once while still flaming.

Yields 9-10 Crêpes Suzettes.

CRÈME DE VIN BLANC

Wellington Edness, the competent and indispensable houseman of the Grosses, and I served this delightful dessert at one of the imaginatively prepared dinners Mr. and Mrs. Harold Gross gave for their party-loving friends. The flavor and texture of the dessert puzzled them. We've kept it a secret until now.

¾ *cup granulated sugar*
7 *egg yolks*
1 *whole egg*
1 *cup white wine*
1 *lemon*

Grate lemon rind into sugar. Mix all ingredients together and pour in double boiler and heat slowly, stirring constantly. Pour in dessert glasses and chill.

Be sure to add fresh strawberries dripping with sherry, either on top or bottom, or both. Wonderful!

CHOCOLATE ANGEL FOOD DESSERT

Slice an angel food cake crosswise 1 inch from top. Scoop out inside ½ inch from sides. Fill with chocolate whipped cream, replace top and frost with same.

3 *cups cream, whipped*
6 *tablespoons cocoa*
6 *tablespoons sugar*
½ *cup toasted almonds, chopped*

Use ½ of mixture for filling and the rest for spreading. Reserve enough nuts to sprinkle on frosting.

All cooks should try a Charlotte Russe at least once.

CHARLOTTE RUSSE

¾ *tablespoons gelatin*
¼ *cup cold water*
⅓ *cup scalded milk*
⅓ *cup powdered sugar*

½ teaspoon maple flavoring
2 tablespoons strong coffee
1 cup heavy cream
Lady fingers
Flavored custard

Soak gelatin in cold water. Dissolve it in scalded milk. Beat in powdered sugar. Cool these ingredients. Flavor them with maple flavoring and coffee. Whip heavy cream until stiff. Fold it lightly into the chilled ingredients. Line a mold with lady fingers. Pour the pudding into it. Chill it thoroughly. Unmold it and serve it with boiled custard flavored with rum. To make about 2½ cups boiled custard, beat slightly 3 or 4 egg yolks, add ¼ cup sugar, ⅛ teaspoon salt, scald 2 cups milk, and stir in slowly. Place custard over slow fire. Stir constantly. Take care that it does not boil. Strain and cool and add rum flavoring, vanilla, or a little grated lemon rind.

MACAROON CHARLOTTE RUSSE WITH BUTTERSCOTCH SAUCE

1 pint whipping cream
½ tablespoon almond extract
½ tablespoon vanilla
½ pound macaroons — crumbled
5 ounces egg whites
1/16 teaspoon salt

Ladyfingers

Whip cream and blend in flavorings. Beat egg whites and salt and fold with macaroons into cream mixture. Arrange ladyfingers as desired in glasses in which the Charlotte Russe is to be served and fill with creamy mixture. (Sponge cake may be used in place of ladyfingers if cut in the same shape.) Place in refrigerator until ready to serve. Serve with butterscotch sauce.

Butterscotch Sauce:

1 *pound brown sugar*
1 *can evaporated milk (14½-ounce size)*
4 *tablespoons butter*

Put all ingredients in a double boiler and cook until it coats the spoon. This sauce is very necessary as its richness complements the Charlotte Russe.
Serves 15.

Yes, they're good.

CRÈME CARAMEL

½ *cup sugar*
3 *eggs*
⅓ *cup sugar*
¼ *teaspoon salt*
2 *cups milk*
½ *teaspoon vanilla*

Carmelize ½ cup sugar by melting over medium heat, stirring constantly when sugar begins to melt. When sauce is golden brown, pour a little into each of 6 custard cups. Move cups about so that caramel will coat sides. When caramel is hard, fill cups with custard.

Beat eggs, sugar, and salt slightly to mix. Scald milk (crinkly film forms on top) and stir milk into egg mixture. Add vanilla and pour into caramel custard cups. Set cups in pan of hot water 1″ deep and bake 45 to 50 minutes at 350 degrees, until silver knife comes out clean. Remove from heat and chill. When unmolded, caramel runs down sides forming a sauce.

Ideal party dessert.

MERINGUE SHELLS

Beat 4 egg whites until foamy. Add gradually 1 cup sugar, a tablespoon at a time, beating thoroughly after each addition. Continue beating until meringue forms sharp peaks when beater is raised.

Add 1 tablespoon lemon juice and continue beating until meringue again forms sharp peaks.

Shape into nests or rounds with spoon or pastry bag on unglazed paper or greased baking sheet.

Bake in a very slow oven (250°), 1 hour and 20 minutes until shells are thoroughly dried and the tops are cream colored.

Remove from paper carefully as soon as baked. Cool completely before serving. Fill shells with sweetened fruit, topped with flavored whipped cream. Top with whipped cream, sauce, or fruit.
12 medium-sized shells.

Everyone asks for these – even weight watchers. Here are our favorites from the Copper Kettle recipe file.

CREAM PUFFS

½ cup butter
1 cup boiling water
1 cup sifted flour
¼ teaspoon salt
4 eggs, unbeaten

Combine butter and water in saucepan and bring to boil. Add flour and salt and stir constantly until mixture leaves sides of pan in smooth compact mass. Remove from heat and cool slightly. Add eggs, one at a time, beating thoroughly after each addition. Beat steadily until mixture is smooth and satiny. Shape with a pastry bag or drop from tablespoon 2 inches apart on ungreased cooky sheet, 15½ x 12 inches. Bake in hot oven (450°) 10 to 15 minutes, then reduce heat to moderate (350°) and bake about 25 minutes longer. When cool, cut slit in side of each puff and fill with whipped cream or cream filling. Top with chocolate glaze.

French Cream Filling:

Combine ⅓ cup enriched flour, ½ cup sugar, and ⅛ teaspoon salt in top of double boiler. Blend in 2 cups milk gradually. Cook over boiling water until thickened, stirring constantly. Blend a little hot filling into 3 slightly beaten egg yolks, then return to hot mixture. Cook about 2 minutes longer, stirring constantly. Remove from heat. Add 2 tablespoons butter and 1 teaspoon vanilla. Cover. Cool. Fold in 1 cup whipped cream.

Chocolate Glaze:

2 *tablespoons butter*
2 *squares unsweetened chocolate*
3 *tablespoons hot milk*
1 *cup confectioners' sugar*
Dash of salt

Heat butter and chocolate in double boiler until melted. Combine milk, confectioners' sugar, and salt. Add to chocolate mixture gradually, stirring until smooth.

CHOCOLATE ÉCLAIRS

Use cream puff recipe.

Onto ungreased baking sheet, drop dough by rounded tablespoonfuls, about 6 inches apart, in rows an inch apart.

Shape each ball of dough into 4 x 1-inch rectangle. Bake éclairs about 45 minutes or until golden and puffed. Remove from oven immediately. Cut small slit in side of each; return to oven for 10 minutes longer. Then remove and cool on cake racks. Split éclairs almost all the way around; then fill with French Cream Filling. (If you're in a hurry, packaged chocolate pudding will do.) Top with chocolate glaze. If filled éclairs are not served at once, be sure to refrigerate them until served.

Today should always be our most wonderful day – Thomas Dreier

Cakes and Frostings

Cakes are a symbol of home life – from the beautiful cake blazing with candles to the humble loaf cake. Cakes play an important role in the most significant moments in our lives.

Cake and frostings in some form have been known since earliest times. The use of sweetened dough is referred to in ancient writings. In England, as elsewhere, nearly every religious occasion was celebrated with a cake of one sort or another, and to this day there is something serious about an English cake which our own more frivolous sweets lack. "Black as the devil, heavy as sin, sweet as young love," is the way an Englishman has described the ceremonial cakes of his country; solid, romantic, and frequently good, but with quite a different kind of goodness from our own more casual sort.

Mrs. Marge Priebe, Mrs. America of 1959, is not only a beautiful and charming woman, but also a superb cook. She graciously shared her favorite recipe with us the day she was our guest on the Copper Kettle Show. Being a busy homemaker, she especially likes these little French cupcakes since they can be made ahead and stored in the refrigerator until serving time. Here is her recipe.

MARG'S FRENCH CUPCAKES

3 *squares chocolate*
2 *cups powdered sugar*
1 *cup butter*

3 *eggs, separated*
½ *cup English walnuts*
1 *teaspoon vanilla*

Melt chocolate, cream butter, and powdered sugar. Add yolks and melted chocolate. Mix thoroughly, add nuts and vanilla, fold in stiffly beaten egg whites, and pour in paper cups which have been sprinkled with graham cracker crumbs.

Sprinkle a few crumbs over the top. Chill 8 to 12 hours. Serve with whipped cream. Makes 12 to 14 cupcakes. Vanilla-wafer crumbs may be used instead of graham crackers.

BRAZIL-NUT SENSATION

And a sensation it is. Mr. Daniel B. Wallace not only created this Brazil-nut sensation, but he is also sensational as an executive in the advertising field of Wallace-Blakeslee, Inc., Grand Rapids.

Thanks, Dan – it's delicious.

1 *pound or 3 cups Brazil nuts, shelled and chopped*
1 *pound pitted dates, chopped*
¾ *cup sifted flour*
¾ *cup sugar*
½ *teaspoon baking powder*
½ *teaspoon salt*
3 *eggs*
½ *teaspoon vanilla*
1 *cup maraschino cherries, chopped*

Combine Brazil nuts and dates. Mix well. Add flour, sugar, baking powder, and salt. Continue to mix. The mixture is thick and may require mixing by hand. Beat the eggs in a bowl, add the vanilla and chopped maraschino cherries, and combine with other ingredients. Work with hands. Grease loaf pan, line with wax paper. Pack mixture into pan and bake for 1½ hours in oven at 300°. Stores beautifully!

This is one of Natalja Kishenia's prize recipes. She's been making it for many years, having captured it from her native country, Poland, before departing for the United States some ten years ago. She is proud to be a naturalized citizen of the U.S.A. Natalja will make this "lovely thing" only upon request because she says it *is* special. Decorate as she instructs and it makes a beautiful festive cake.

Natalja, dear, we love your homemade bread, rolls, and Obsttorte Mit Gelatine, but most of all we love you for the happy spirit you radiate as you go about your duties of serving guests and making them happy as they dine at the WJIM Country House.

OBSTTORTE MIT GELATINE (Cake with Gelatin)

Cake:

1½ cups sifted cake flour
1½ teaspoons baking powder
¼ teaspoon salt
1 teaspoon grated orange rind
½ cup butter
1 cup sugar
2 eggs, unbeaten
½ cup fresh orange juice – not from can

Sift dry ingredients together. Add orange rind to butter and cream thoroughly. Add sugar gradually and cream until fluffy. Add eggs, one at a time, beating thoroughly after each addition. Add sifted dry ingredients and orange juice alternately in small amounts, beating thoroughly after each addition.

Use deep spring pan. Bake in moderate oven 350° for 30 minutes. *Make 2 9-inch layers.*

Do not remove the cake from pan, let it cool – then decorate.

Decoration:

Spread a thin layer of apricot preserves on top of the cake. Decorate the cake with any design you prefer, using peach halves, pear, strawberries, grapes, and any other fruit you desire.

Gelatin:

Use 4 packages of lemon-flavored gelatin. Mix 4 cups of water and 4 cups of apple juice and let it boil. Add the gelatin and boil for one minute. Let the gelatin thicken a little; then pour it over the cake, to cover the fruit.

Keep the cake in the refrigerator. Serves best next day.

Frank Ives and I had the pleasant association of working together on the Copper Kettle Show for many years at WJIM. Frank was a tremendous assistant in the Copper Kettle Kitchen, both on and off the air, in programming our recipes, meeting guests, and arranging props for commercials. A very eligible bachelor who loved good food, he asked for this cake often. It was one of his favorites.

CHOCOLATE PEANUT-BUTTER CAKE

Prepare one package of chocolate cake mix according to package directions. Beat in three heaping tablespoons creamy peanut butter. Bake in the usual manner. If you are frosting your cake with chocolate icing, add two tablespoons creamy peanut butter to the icing and beat until smooth! This makes a delicious rich cake with a rich frosting.

Children love it, too!

This is another of the popular Country House desserts. We like to serve it at the popular fall football parties held each year at the Country House. The cakes can be made the night before and refrigerated. For a real glamor touch, sprinkle toasted slivered almonds on top.

CHOCOLATE ANGEL LAYERS

Prepare 1 package chocolate angel-cake mix according to directions on package, mixing 1 tablespoon instant coffee with flour mixture. Bake in ungreased tube pan according to package directions. Cut cooled cake crosswise in 3 even layers. Put together with chocomallow frosting between layers and on top and sides. Chill 45 minutes or till frosting is set.

Choco-Mallow Frosting:

I double the recipe for one large angel food cake. In top of double boiler, place 1 6-ounce package semi-sweet chocolate pieces or 6 1-ounce squares semi-sweet chocolate, ¼ pound (16) marshmallows, and ½ cup milk or rich cream. Heat over simmering water till blended, stirring occasionally. Chill. Stir till smooth. Whip 1 cup heavy cream; fold in.
Makes 3 cups.

A good cake for St. Valentine's Day.

CHERRY FUDGE CAKE

- 1⅓ *cups sifted all-purpose flour*
- 1 *cup sugar*
- ⅓ *cup cocoa*
- 1 *teaspoon soda*
- ¾ *teaspoon salt*
- ⅔ *cup soft shortening*
- 1 *egg*
- ½ *cup evaporated milk*
- ¼ *cup water*
- 2 *tablespoons maraschino cherry syrup*
- ½ *cup cut-up maraschino cherries*

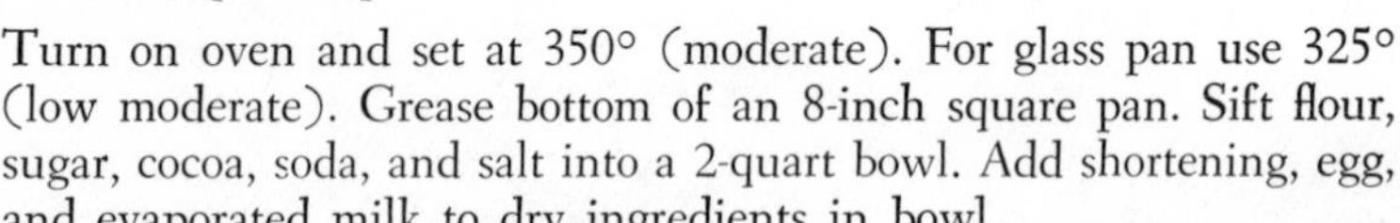

Turn on oven and set at 350° (moderate). For glass pan use 325° (low moderate). Grease bottom of an 8-inch square pan. Sift flour, sugar, cocoa, soda, and salt into a 2-quart bowl. Add shortening, egg, and evaporated milk to dry ingredients in bowl.

Beat hard 2½ minutes with electric beater at medium speed or with mixing spoon. Add water and cherry syrup and beat hard one minute longer. Stir in cut-up cherries. Put into prepared pan. Bake on center rack of oven 50-55 minutes, or until cake pulls from sides of pan. Remove from oven. Let stand in pan 10 minutes before turning out to cool. If desired, cool and frost in pan.

Remember, mixes are good, too. This one is tops.

CHEERY CHERRY CAKE

- 1 *can (20-ounce) frozen cherries, defrosted*
- 1 *cup sugar*

½ *teaspoon red food coloring*
¼ *teaspoon almond extract*
1 *package white cake mix (2-layer size)*

Drain cherries and measure juice. Add water, if necessary, to make ¾ cup liquid. Combine cherry liquid and sugar in saucepan and bring to a boil. Add drained cherries and red food coloring. Remove from heat and add extract. Cool. Prepare cake mix according to directions on package. Pour cake batter into greased and floured 9 x 13-inch pan. Pour cherry mixture over top of batter. Bake in moderate oven (350°) for 50 minutes. When baked, the juice and cherries will be on the bottom. Invert on serving platter. Serve warm with whipped cream or ice cream.
Makes 10 to 12 servings.

If the setting is right, try Baba Au Rhum.

BABA AU RHUM

Sift 2 cups of cake flour with ⅓ teaspoon of salt; make a well in the center and put in 1 yeast cake which has been crumbled into ¼ cup of lukewarm milk; then, using a fork, cover the yeast mixture with a little of the flour and let it stand for 5 or 6 minutes. Now add 4 well-beaten eggs, and using a wooden spoon, work all thoroughly together, adding a little more milk if too stiff. Knead for about 5 minutes; cover the bowl, and let stand in a warm place for 30 minutes. Then add 6 tablespoons of melted butter, alternately with 1½ tablespoons of sugar, and work for another 4 minutes mixing in ⅔ cup of plumped and dried seedless raisins. Butter a tube mold; half fill it with the dough, and let rise again until doubled in bulk, or up to the top of the mold. Bake in a moderate oven (350°) about 35 to 40 minutes. Remove at once from the oven and cool on a cake rack.

Buttered Rum Sauce:

Boil together for 2 or 3 minutes ½ cup of cold water and 1¼ cups of sugar. Add a dash of salt, cool to lukewarm; then stir in ½ cup of good rum and 1 tablespoon butter and pour over the cake.

Small cakes definitely have their place!

FUDGE CUPCAKES

½ cup shortening
1 cup sugar
1 egg
1 teaspoon vanilla
1½ cups sifted all-purpose flour
½ cup cocoa
1 teaspoon soda
½ teaspoon salt
½ cup buttermilk or sour milk
½ cup boiling water

Cream shortening, sugar, egg, and vanilla; add sifted dry ingredients alternately with buttermilk. Stir in boiling water. Blend well. Fill greased muffin cups ⅔ full, bake at 375° for 25 minutes. Frost with white frosting.
Yield: 1½ dozen.

PEACH SHORTCAKE

It's June-in-January when you bring this sunny peach shortcake to your table. Bake your flakiest baking-powder biscuits, sprinkling each with a sugar-cinnamon mixture before baking. While slightly warm, split biscuits and fill with sweetened whipped cream and juicy canned cling peach slices.

The dessert may be upside-down but the taste is right-side-up when you bake date-apple gingerbread.

DATE-APPLE CAKE

Arrange 2 cups thinly sliced apples and ½ cup sliced fresh California dates in bottom of 9-inch square pan. Combine ¼ cup melted butter, ½ cup brown sugar, and ¼ cup *each* flour and chopped pecans. Add dash of nutmeg or cinnamon. Spread evenly over dates and apples. Cover with prepared packaged gingerbread mix and bake in moderate oven about 45 minutes. Cool about 10 minutes before inverting onto serving plate.

A year-round favorite—both in the North and deep South. This is an original pound-cake recipe.

POUND CAKE

1 *pound butter (no substitute)*
10 *large or 12 medium-sized eggs*
3 *tablespoons brandy or any flavoring you prefer*
1 *pound granulated sugar*
1 *pound (4 full cups) sifted cake flour*

Cream butter and work in flour until the mixture is mealy (use electric mixer). Beat egg yolks and sugar until fluffy. Add flavoring. Add first mixture gradually, beating thoroughly (electric mixer). Fold in stiffly beaten egg whites. Beat a few strokes (by hand). Pour into 10-inch angel-food cake pan with sides and bottom lined with two layers of brown paper (clean grocery bags). Do not grease this paper. (Extend paper an inch above cake pan.) Put circle of brown paper, which has been cut 2 inches larger than top of cake pan on top of pan. Prevents excessive browning. Bake at 300° for 2 hours or more. Test with fine wire to see if done. Cool in cake pan. Don't remove paper until ready to serve.

Cut in thin slices. Best when left to ripen in cool place for 2 or 3 days before serving. May have to use 325° depending on range. Lift paper from cake and watch closely during baking time.

This is delightful.

STRAWBERRY WHIRL BAKED ALASKA

4 *egg whites*
⅔ *cup sugar*
½ *teaspoon cream of tartar*
1 *8-inch square layer sponge or white cake*
2 *pints strawberry ice cream*

Beat egg whites with sugar and cream of tartar until very stiff and glossy. Place cake layer on wooden board or heat-proof platter. Cover cake layer with strawberry ice cream. Cover with meringue.

Brown in very hot oven (450°) about 3 minutes or until delicately brown. Serve at once.

This can be done with one layer cake or two layer cakes. For two layer cakes, place ice cream between layers and place meringue on top and sides of cake.
Makes 8 to 10 servings.

Your recipe file box will definitely be earmarked as not up to date if it doesn't include a basic butter-cake recipe. This one is good!

BUTTER CAKE

2 round, 8-inch cake pans. Preheated 350° oven.

¾ cup (1½ sticks) butter
1¼ cups sugar
2 eggs
¾ teaspoon vanilla
⅛ teaspoon almond extract
2½ cups sifted cake flour
2½ teaspoons baking powder
½ teaspoon salt
¾ cup milk

Butter and flour cake pans; set aside. Cream butter and sugar. Add eggs and beat until fluffy. Blend in vanilla and almond extract. Sift dry ingredients, add to the creamed mixture alternately with the milk, beginning and ending with dry ingredients, pour into prepared pans. Bake 30-35 minutes. Cool 10 minutes. Remove from pans onto cake rack and cool completely. Frost and fill with creamy butter frosting.

Creamy Butter Frosting:

½ cup (1 stick) butter
4 cups (1-pound box) sifted confectioners' sugar
¼ cup cream
¼ teaspoon almond extract
¼ teaspoon vanilla
1 egg

Cream butter until fluffy; gradually add half the confectioners' sugar, beating until smooth. Blend in cream, flavorings, and egg. Gradually add remaining confectioners' sugar; beat until smooth and creamy.

Sufficient to frost and fill a 2 layer 8-inch cake.

OLD-FASHIONED WHITE CAKE

This is a wonderful recipe—if you like a rather moist and heavy cake.

Upon returning home from the studio one evening—just in time for dinner—I met the delicious aroma of this old-fashioned white cake. My young son, Tom, who was then around ten years old, had just taken it from the oven—his first attempt in the masterful skill of cake-baking. He was mighty proud and so was I! Incidentally, he mixes the cake by hand using a bowl and the wooden spoon. He says the cake tastes better mixed by hand.

We love the recipe and hope you will, too!

1¼ *cups flour (sifted)*
½ *teaspoon salt*
½ *cup milk*
⅓ *cup shortening*
1 *teaspoon vanilla*
¾ *cup sugar*
1 *egg*
2 *teaspoons baking powder*

Mix all together, stir well, and bake at 375° in an 8-inch pan for 30 minutes.

This cake is of a heavy and moist variety but very good. Frost with your favorite frosting. We like chocolate butter frosting!

Chocolate Butter Frosting:

1 *pound confectioners' sugar*
½ *cup cocoa*
⅛ *teaspoon salt*
¼ *pound soft butter or margarine*
1 *teaspoon vanilla extract*
5-7 *tablespoons milk*

Mix sugar, cocoa, and salt together. Cream part of sugar mixture with butter or margarine. Blend extract, 3 tablespoons milk, and remaining sugar mixture into creamed mixture. Gradually stir remaining milk into frosting until desired spreading consistency is reached. *Yields frosting for 2-layer 9-inch cake.*

If you like the little black seeds – we mean poppy seeds – this is the cake for you. Different and unusual.

POPPY-SEED CAKE

Cake:

- ⅓ *cup poppy seeds*
- ¾ *cup milk*
- ¾ *cup shortening*
- 1¼ *cups sugar*
- 1 *teaspoon vanilla*
- ⅛ *teaspoon almond extract*
- 2 *cups sifted cake flour*
- 2 *teaspoons baking powder*
- ½ *teaspoon salt*
- 4 *egg whites*

Soak poppy seeds in milk for about two hours. Cream shortening; add sugar and continue creaming until light and fluffy. Add extracts. Sift flour, baking powder, and salt together. Add alternately with the milk and poppy seeds to the creamed shortening and sugar mixture. Beat egg whites to soft-peak stage and fold into batter. Pour batter into 2 greased 9-inch layer cake pans. Bake in moderate oven, 350°, 30 to 35 minutes. When cool, spread filling between layers. Powdered sugar or whipped cream may be used as topping.

Filling:

- 2 *cups milk*
- 1 *cup sugar*
- 1½ *tablespoons cornstarch*
- ¼ *teaspoon salt*
- 4 *egg yolks*
- ¾ *cup chopped nuts*

Scald milk in double boiler. Mix sugar, cornstarch, and salt together. Add to scalded milk, stirring constantly until thick. Beat egg yolks; add some of cooked mixture to egg yolks, then combine both mixtures and cook for 2 to 3 minutes longer. Cool. Add chopped nuts.

FIESTA BANANA CAKE

½ cup butter or vegetable shortening
1⅓ cups sugar
2 eggs
1 teaspoon vanilla
1 cup mashed ripe bananas
2 cups sifted flour
1 teaspoon baking powder
1 teaspoon soda
¾ teaspoon salt
½ cup sour milk

Beat shortening and add sugar, then eggs and vanilla. Add mashed bananas, then sifted flour and salt alternately with sour milk. (If butter, margarine or lard is used, use ½ cup sour milk minus 2 tablespoons.) Last of all add baking powder and baking soda. Bake at 375° for about 25 minutes in 3 well-greased, floured baking pans. When thoroughly cool, put together with about a pint and a half of whipped cream, sweetened and flavored, and garnish with slices of maraschino cherries arranged as petals of flowers. Keep refrigerated.

The most completely lost of all days is that on which one has not laughed
Chamfort

If you're a lover of prunes, may we recommend this recipe.

PRUNE CAKE

3 eggs
1½ cups sugar
1 cup shortening (melted)
1 teaspoon soda
1 cup buttermilk
1 teaspoon cinnamon
1 teaspoon nutmeg
1 teaspoon allspice
1 teaspoon baking powder
2 cups flour
1 cup chopped prunes (stewed and stoned)

Beat eggs and sugar together. Add melted shortening, buttermilk, and dry ingredients sifted together. Stir in prunes. Bake in 3 layers in 350° oven for 30 minutes. Put together with whipped cream to which has been added a few drops of vanilla and sugar.

A chocolate-roll dessert belongs in a class all its own. In my opinion, it is simply wonderful.

CHOCOLATE ROLL

4 eggs
½ cup sifted cake flour
½ teaspoon baking powder
¼ teaspoon salt
2 squares unsweetened chocolate
¾ cup sifted granulated sugar
1 teaspoon vanilla extract
2 tablespoons granulated sugar
¼ teaspoon baking soda
3 tablespoons cold water
Confectioners' sugar
1 cup heavy cream
¼ teaspoon almond extract or peppermint extract

Set out eggs 1 hour ahead. Heat oven to 375°. Grease jelly roll pan, then line with waxed paper, grease again. Sift flour, baking powder, and salt. Melt chocolate.

Break eggs into large electric-mixer bowl; sift ¾ cup sugar over them, then beat at high speed until very thick and light. Fold flour mixture and vanilla, all at once, into egg mixture. To melted chocolate, add 2 tablespoons sugar, soda, and cold water; stir until thick and light; quickly fold into batter. Turn into pan. Bake 15 to 20 minutes or till cake springs back at gentle touch.

Sift a thick layer of confectioners' sugar over clean dish towel on flat surface. Invert baked cake onto towel, peel off paper, and cut away crisp edges of cake. Cool exactly 5 minutes.

Roll up cake, rolling towel up in it. Place on wire rack to finish cooling for about 1 hour.

Just before serving, unroll cake so it will be on the towel. Quickly spread whipped cream or any desired filling to within one inch of edges. Roll cake, lifting the towel higher and higher with one hand while guiding roll with other hand. Finish the roll with open end on underside. Cut into crosswise slices.

Serve plain or top with ice cream.

The top of roll can be dusted with cocoa or confectioners' sugar. The slices can be covered with a chocolate sauce.

Makes 8 servings.

My dear friend, Martha Phillips, served this delicious orange loaf cake when we visited her and her family in their charming Florida home several years ago. She is a marvelous cook.

DELICIOUS LOAF CAKE

Grease and line with paper a 9 x 5 x 3″ loaf pan. Sift together into bowl:

2¼ *cups cake flour (sifted)*
1 *cup sugar*
2 *teaspoons baking powder*
1 *teaspoon salt*

Add:

½ *cup soft shortening (half butter)*
1 *teaspoon vanilla*
6 *egg yolks (¾ cup), unbeaten*
½ *cup milk*

Beat 2 minutes. Add another ¼ cup milk. Beat 2 minutes more.

Spoon batter into prepared pan. Bake in 350° oven (moderate) for 60-70 minutes. Cool and finish with orange glaze.

Orange Glaze:

It soaks into the warm cake, making it moist and giving it an orange flavor. Mix:

½ cup orange juice
½ teaspoon grated orange rind
1 cup sifted confectioners' sugar

Warm glaze slightly, stirring occasionally. When cake is baked, remove from pan and punch holes on top surface with a fork. Pour the warm glaze, a little at a time, over the top.

This cake freezes beautifully.

This is a very different and unusual cake. It's delicious. It came from one of our loyal Copper Kettle viewers.

APPLE CAKE AND SAUCE

2 cups diced apples
1 cup granulated sugar
1 egg
1 cup sifted all-purpose flour
1½ teaspoons soda
½ cup chopped nuts

Mix sugar and apples, stir and let stand until sugar is dissolved, about 45 minutes. Add the egg and beat well. Sift dry ingredients together and stir into apple mixture. Add nuts. Pour into 8 x 8-inch pan and bake 40 minutes at 375°. Immediately cover with sauce.

Sauce:

⅓ cup brown sugar
⅓ cup granulated sugar
2 tablespoons flour
1 cup water
¼ cup butter or margarine
1 teaspoon vanilla

Mix together the sugars and flour, add to melted butter and water. Then add vanilla. Bring to boil and pour over cake. Frosting will harden on cake.

One of the best.

APPLE-SAUCE LOAF CAKE

½ cup shortening
1 cup sugar
1 egg
1 cup unsweetened applesauce
1¾ cups sifted flour
1 teaspoon baking soda
1½ teaspoons cinnamon
1 teaspoon allspice
1 teaspoon nutmeg
¼ teaspoon cloves
½ teaspoon salt

Cream shortening and sugar until light and fluffy. Add egg and beat well. Add apple sauce. Mix and sift remaining ingredients and stir in. Bake in greased and floured loaf pan (8 x 5 x 3 inches or 11 x 4½ x 2½ inches) for 60 to 75 minutes. Cool on cake rack. Frost top with lemon butter frosting. Decorate with whole walnut meats.

Butter Frosting:

⅓ cup butter
4 cups sifted confectioners' sugar
1 egg yolk
1½ teaspoons vanilla
About 2 tablespoons light cream

Cream butter; gradually add about half the sugar, blending well. Beat in egg yolk and vanilla. Gradually blend in remaining sugar. Add enough cream to make of spreading consistency.

Lemon Butter Frosting:

Add ½ teaspoon grated lemon peel to butter in butter frosting. Stir in lemon juice instead of cream to make of spreading consistency.

It's rightfully named—it's fit for a king.

KING CAKE

1 *standard recipe for 8-or 9-inch double-crust pie*
½ *cup white sugar*
½ *cup flour (sifted)*
2 *eggs, separated*
1 *teaspoon vanilla*
1 *jar raspberry jam*
Nut meats

Preparing the cake mixture is a little tricky. Measure the ½ cup sugar and add the 2 egg yolks and vanilla. Mix thoroughly until sugar is dissolved, then stir in flour. Fold in the beaten egg whites and set aside until pastry is mixed and pan lined. The few lumps in the cake mix do not harm the cake.

Line a 9 x 12-inch cake pan halfway up the sides of the pan and flute edges. Spread the raspberry jam (it must be raspberry) over the pie crust. On top of this spread the cake mixture. Sprinkle with nut meats and cover with lattice of pastry strips, starting at the corners of the pan. Bake in moderate oven 350-375° for about 35 minutes.

As soon as the pan is removed from oven, sprinkle cake generously with powdered sugar and cut in squares.

Many stories have been told about the popular Queen Elizabeth cake. The one story I know to be true is that it's marvelous!

QUEEN ELIZABETH CAKE

Pour one cup boiling water over one cup chopped dates and add one teaspoon baking soda. Let stand while mixing cake ingredients.

1 *cup sugar*
1 *egg, beaten*
1½ *cups sifted enriched flour*

½ *teaspoon salt*
¼ *cup butter*
1 *teaspoon vanilla flavoring*
1 *teaspoon baking powder*
½ *cup chopped nuts*

Cream the ¼ cup butter and 1 cup sugar until light and fluffy. Add egg, blend well. Add 1½ cups sifted flour, 1 teaspoon baking powder, ½ teaspoon salt, and vanilla. Add cooled date mixture and stir well. Put in greased 8-inch square pan, bake 35 to 40 minutes at 350°. Remove from oven, add topping, broil 2 minutes, cool and serve.

Topping:

5 *tablespoons brown sugar*
5 *tablespoons cream*
5 *tablespoons butter*
¾ *cup chopped nuts or coconut (if desired)*

Combine brown sugar, cream, butter. Boil together 3 minutes and spread on cake. Sprinkle with nuts and coconut. Run under broiler for 2 minutes.

The best little cakes you'll ever make.

WONDERFUL CUPCAKES

Put together and cool:

1½ *cups boiling water*
1 *cup chopped dates*
1 *teaspoon soda*

Batter:

1 *cup sugar*
¾ *cup shortening*
2 *eggs, beaten*
1½ *cups plus 2 tablespoons flour*
¾ *teaspoon soda*
¼ *teaspoon salt*
1 *teaspoon vanilla*

After you have mixed this, add the water, dates, and soda mixture and pour into tins.

Topping:

Sprinkle ½ package chocolate chips, ½ cup chopped nuts, and ¼ cup white sugar on the cupcakes. Bake at 375° approximately 30 minutes or until done. Delicious.
Yields 18.

We all long for the first fresh luscious strawberries.

STRAWBERRY SHORTCAKE SQUARES

2 cups sifted enriched flour
2 tablespoons sugar
3 teaspoons baking powder
½ teaspoon salt
½ cup butter or margarine
1 beaten egg
⅔ cup light cream
Soft butter or margarine
3 to 4 cups sugared sliced strawberries
1 cup heavy cream, whipped

Sift together dry ingredients; cut in butter till mixture is like coarse crumbs. Combine egg and light cream; add all at once to dry ingredients, stirring only to moisten. Spread dough in greased 8 x 8 x 2-inch pan. For evenly shaped cake, slightly build up dough on sides. Bake in very hot oven (450°) 15 to 18 minutes or till done. Cool 5 minutes, then remove from pan. With serrated knife, cut in 6 rectangles; split each in 2 layers. Butter bottom layers. Fill and top with strawberries and whipped cream. Serve warm. *Makes 6 servings.*

DATE LOAF CAKE

2 cups sifted enriched flour
¼ teaspoon salt
1 cup brown sugar

½ teaspoon baking soda
1 teaspoon vanilla
½ cup chopped walnuts
1 teaspoon baking powder
¾ cup shortening
2 eggs, beaten
½ cup milk
1 pound pitted dates, chopped

Line the bottom of a 5 x 9-inch loaf pan with waxed paper. Sift flour, baking powder, and salt together. Cream shortening with sugar until light and fluffy. Add the beaten eggs; dissolve the baking soda in milk and add with vanilla to creamed mixture. Add chopped dates and nuts to flour mixture. Stir flour mixture into creamed mixture. Mix well. Pour into loaf pan and bake in a moderate oven (350°) 50 to 60 minutes. Serve with a butter-cream frosting or whipped cream, if desired.

Frosting:

Cream ¼ cup butter or shortening, ¼ teaspoon salt. Blend in 3 cups sifted confectioners' sugar alternately with 4 to 6 tablespoons scalded cream. Add 1 teaspoon vanilla. Beat until creamy.

This is a beautiful, elegant cake. At Easter time we receive hundreds of requests for this receipe.

EASTER CAKE

¾ cup margarine
1½ cups sugar
1½ teaspoons vanilla
4 teaspoons baking powder
2¾ cups sifted flour
¼ teaspoon salt
1 cup plus 2 tablespoons milk
½ cup egg whites (about 4)
3-4 drops yellow food color

Grease 1 13 x 9 x 2-inch cake pan or 2 9-inch layer pans. Line with waxed paper. Cream margarine till soft. Add sugar gradually, creaming till light and fluffy. Stir in vanilla. Sift together flour, baking powder, and salt. Add flour ¼ at a time, alternately with milk. Blend smooth after each addition. Beat egg whites stiff but not dry. Fold gently into batter. Pour ⅔ of batter into pan. To remaining ⅓ of batter, add yellow coloring. Drop yellow on white batter and stir 3 or 4 times to make marbled effect. Bake in moderate oven (375°) 30 to 35 minutes. Let cool in pan 10 minutes. Turn out of pan. When thoroughly cool, frost with jonquil frosting and decorate with coconut and small candy Easter eggs.

Jonquil Frosting:

½ *cup margarine*
2 *egg yolks*
1 *teaspoon grated lemon rind*
2 *tablespoons lemon juice*
¼ *teaspoon salt*
4 *cups confectioners' sugar, (sifted)*
2 *tablespoons water*
½ *teaspoon yellow food color*
2 *cups coconut*
18-20 *small candy Easter eggs*

Stir margarine until soft. Beat in egg yolks, rind, lemon juice, and salt. Gradually stir in confectioners' sugar, mixing smooth after each addition. Add little water at a time as needed to make frosting fluffy and of good spreading consistency. Frost sides of cake first, then top, press coconut into frosting on sides of cake. Sprinkle circles of coconut on top of cake so each serving will have an "Easter nest." Arrange 3 small colored candy Easter eggs in each circle of coconut.

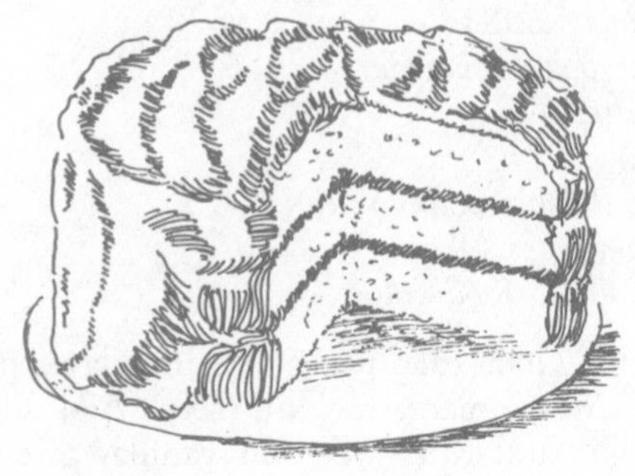

DUTCH APPLE CAKE

1½ cups sifted pastry flour
1 egg
3 teaspoons baking powder
½ cup milk
½ teaspoon salt
2 tablespoons melted butter
3 tablespoons sugar
3 apples
2 tablespoons sugar
¼ teaspoon cinnamon

Sift together flour, baking powder, salt, and 3 tablespoons sugar. Add egg, well beaten, milk, and butter. Beat well, and spread in a greased pan, having mixture about an inch deep. Core, pare, and quarter apples, cut quarters in thick slices, and arrange in rows on top of cake. Sprinkle with 2 tablespoons sugar and cinnamon, and bake in hot oven half an hour. Serve with hard or soft sauce.

Hard Sauce:

¼ cup butter
1 teaspoon milk
1 cup powdered sugar
1 teaspoon vanilla, or
¼ teaspoon nutmeg

Cream butter, add sugar and milk gradually, and beat until very light. Add flavoring and chill before serving.

Soft Sauce:

To hard sauce, add 2 tablespoons hot milk, a few drops at a time; beat well and do not chill.

APPLESAUCE SPICE CUPCAKES

½ cup butter
1 cup sugar
1 egg, beaten

¾ cup thick apple sauce
1¾ cups sifted cake flour
1½ teaspoons baking powder
½ teaspoon soda
¼ teaspoon salt
½ teaspoon cloves
1 teaspoon cinnamon
¾ cup raisins, chopped
½ cup chopped walnuts
8 to 10 glacé cherries

Cream butter and add sugar; beat until light and fluffy. Stir in egg and ¼ cup of applesauce and beat well. Sift flour, soda, salt, baking powder, and spices together. Add alternately with remaining applesauce and mix until smooth. Fold in raisins and nuts. Fill 2-inch greased muffin pans ⅔ full. Bake in moderate oven (350°) 20 minutes. Frost with thin confectioners' frosting flavored with lemon. Decorate with bits of glacé cherry. *Yield: 4 dozen.*

Lemon Confectioners' Frosting:

2 cups confectioners' sugar
2 teaspoons grated lemon peel
⅛ teaspoon salt
3 tablespoons lemon juice
¼ cup milk

Combine confectioners' sugar, lemon peel, and salt. Add lemon juice and milk, and mix until smooth and of spreading consistency. *Yields about 1 cup.*

If you want to boost your ego as a gourmet pastry cook, try making this delicious German sweet-chocolate cake. I'll admit it takes time – but it's worth it. It's glamorous looking and elegant. This cake is featured regularly on the luncheon menu at the WJIM Country House, Lansing.

GERMAN SWEET-CHOCOLATE CAKE

1 package German sweet chocolate
½ cup boiling water
1 cup butter, margarine, or other shortening

- 2 *cups sugar*
- 4 *egg yolks, unbeaten*
- 1 *teaspoon vanilla*
- 2½ *cups sifted cake flour*
- 1 *teaspoon baking soda*
- ½ *teaspoon salt*
- 1 *cup buttermilk*
- 4 *egg whites, stiffly beaten*

Melt chocolate in ½ cup of boiling water. Cool. Cream butter and sugar until light and fluffy. Add egg yolks, one at a time, beating after each. Add vanilla and chocolate; mix until blended. Sift flour with soda and salt.

Add sifted dry ingredients alternately with buttermilk to chocolate mixture, beating after each addition until batter is smooth. Fold in stiffly beaten egg whites. Pour batter into 3 8- or 9-inch layer pans, lined on bottoms with paper.

Bake in moderate oven (350°) for 30 to 40 minutes. Cool. Frost top and between the layers with coconut-pecan frosting.

Coconut-Pecan Frosting:

- 1 *cup evaporated milk*
- 1 *cup sugar*
- 3 *egg yolks*
- ¼ *pound butter or margarine*
- 1 *teaspoon vanilla*
- 1⅓ *cups (about) flaked coconut*
- 1 *cup chopped pecans*

Combine milk, sugar, egg yolks, butter or margarine, and vanilla in a saucepan. Cook over medium heat, stirring constantly until mixture thickens, about 12 minutes. Remove from heat. Add coconut and pecans. Beat until cool and of spreading consistency. *Makes enough frosting to cover tops of three 8- or 9-inch layers, about 2½ cups.*

The first Christmas we made this elegant white fruit cake on the air, we received over 6,000 requests for the receipe. It's our favorite. Try it, you'll love it, too!

WHITE FRUIT CAKE

¼ *cup fruit juice (any kind will do) or brandy or rum*
½ *pound candied citron, chopped*
½ *pound whole candied cherries*
¾ *pound orange and lemon peel, chopped*
2 *pounds white raisins*
¾ *pound candied pineapple, chopped or sliced*
1 *pound butter*
1 *pound sugar (2 cups)*
10 *eggs*
1 *pound flour, sifted (4 cups)*
1½ *pounds whole pecans*

Prepare the fruit and soak in the fruit juice or brandy or rum while preparing the rest of the batter. Cream the butter and add the sugar gradually. Then add one egg at a time, beating well after each addition. Add flour and mix well, then the nuts and fruit. Pour into three 9¼ x 3¼ x 2¾-inch loaf pans which have been buttered, lined with waxed paper, and buttered over the waxed paper. Bake in a 275-300° oven for 2 to 2¾ hours. Remove from pan immediately, cool on cake racks. Wrap in foil or a tea towel which has been soaked in fruit juices or brandy or rum. Place in covered container. *Yields 8 pounds.*

COPPER KETTLE'S FAVORITE CHOCOLATE BUTTERMILK CAKE

Melts in your mouth. Don't forget to garnish with pistachio nuts.

1 *cup (2 sticks) butter*
2¼ *cups sugar*
2 *eggs*
1 *teaspoon vanilla*
½ *cup cocoa*
3 *cups sifted cake flour*
2 *teaspoons baking soda*
1 *teaspoon salt*
2 *cups buttermilk*

Butter 3 round, 9-inch cake pans, line bottoms with waxed paper, and butter again. Cream butter and sugar until light and fluffy. Add eggs one at a time, beating well after each addition. Add vanilla. Sift together cocoa, flour, baking soda, and salt; add to creamed mixture alternately with buttermilk, beginning and ending with dry ingredients. Pour into cake pans. Bake 25 to 30 minutes in preheated 350° oven. Let stand in pans 5 minutes. Remove from pans onto wire rack. Cool completely before frosting with browned butter icing.

Browned Butter Icing:

½ *cup (1 stick) butter*
1 *teaspoon vanilla*
¼ *teaspoon salt*
6 *cups sifted confectioners' sugar*
⅓ *to* ½ *cup cream*

In saucepan brown butter lightly over low heat, stirring constantly. Remove from heat; pour into mixing bowl. Add vanilla, salt, and half of confectioners' sugar; beat well. Add remainder of sugar alternately with cream, beating until smooth and of spreading consistency. Spread between layers and on tops and sides of chocolate buttermilk cake. This cake is delicious garnished with chopped pistachio nuts.

Always a favorite whenever you serve it. Please serve it warm with whipped cream.

PINEAPPLE UPSIDE-DOWN CAKE

Topping:

¼ *cup butter*
¾ *cup brown sugar*
9 *slices pineapple (1 No. 2 can)*
9 *maraschino cherries*

Melt butter in 9-inch square pan and sprinkle brown sugar over it. Place slices of pineapple in pan and put a cherry in center of each slice.

Cake:

½ cup butter
1 cup sugar
2 eggs, beaten until light
2 cups cake flour
3 teaspoons baking powder
¼ teaspoon salt
⅔ cup milk
1 teaspoon vanilla

Cream butter and sugar until light and fluffy. Add eggs and beat well. Add sifted dry ingredients alternately with milk and mix well. Add vanilla. Pour cake batter over fruit. Bake in moderate oven (350°) 30 to 35 minutes. Turn onto large plate and cut cake so there is a whole slice of pineapple for each serving.

Garnish with whipped cream and a maraschino cherry.

FROSTED GINGERBREAD SQUARES

1 package gingerbread mix
1 cup dairy sour cream
¼ cup brown sugar (packed)
⅓ cup chopped, lightly toasted blanched almonds

Prepare and bake gingerbread by packaged directions, in 8-inch square pan. Remove from oven and let stand 10 minutes. Mix sour cream and 3 tablespoons brown sugar. Spread over gingerbread. Sprinkle with almonds and rest of brown sugar. Bake in moderate oven 10 minutes. Serve warm or cold.

Absolutely nothing, and I mean nothing, can compare with a snowy-white fresh coconut cake.

FRESH COCONUT CAKE

2 cups sifted cake flour
1 teaspoon baking powder
¾ teaspoon soda
¼ teaspoon salt
½ cup shortening

2 cups shredded fresh coconut
1 cup sugar
1½ teaspoons vanilla
2 eggs, unbeaten
1 cup buttermilk or sour milk
Lemon filling, boiled
Frosting or favorite white frosting

Sift together flour, baking powder, soda, and salt. Stir shortening to soften, then add sugar slowly and cream together until light and fluffy. Add vanilla. Add eggs, one at a time, beating well after each addition. Add sifted dry ingredients alternately with milk, mixing until smooth after each addition.

Turn into 2 9-inch round layer pans which have been greased and floured lightly. Bake in a moderate oven (350°) for 25 minutes. Remove from pans and cool on racks. Spread lemon filling between layers. Frost with boiled frosting or favorite white frosting and sprinkle generously with coconut.

Lemon Filling:

¾ cup sugar
2 tablespoons cornstarch
Dash of salt
1 slightly beaten egg yolk
¾ cup water

Blend, and cook over low heat or over boiling water until thick, stirring. Add 3 tablespoons lemon juice, 1 teaspoon grated lemon rind, and 1 tablespoon butter. Cool slightly.

Favorite White Frosting:

2 egg whites
Dash of salt

Whip the egg whites until they are firm and will stand in little soft peaks. In a separate pan combine 1 cup sugar, 7 tablespoons water, 2 tablespoons corn syrup, and boil gently until mixture spins a thread (hold spoon over pan and allow some of the mixture to drip from spoon). If it spins a tiny thread, it's ready to remove. Pour syrup over whipped egg whites (beating on high speed all the while you are pouring). Beat until desired spreading consistency. Add 2 teaspoons vanilla flavoring and spread on your favorite cake. It's a delicious icing, and holds up nicely for several days.

Boiled Frosting:

2 *cups sugar*
¾ *cup water*
1 *tablespoon light corn syrup, or*
¼ *teaspoon cream of tartar*
Dash salt
2 *stiff-beaten egg whites*
1 *teaspoon vanilla*

Cook first 4 ingredients over low heat, stirring till sugar dissolves. Cover pan 2 to 3 minutes to dissolve sugar crystals on sides of pan. Uncover; cook to soft-ball stage (236°).

Gradually add hot syrup to egg whites, beating constantly. Add vanilla; beat till frosting is of spreading consistency. Frosts tops and sides of 2 8- or 9-inch layers.

Popular at the Homestead, Glen Arbor, Michigan. Boys and girls at the Leelanau schools love it, too!

LAZY-DAISY CAKE

1 *cup flour*
1½ *teaspoons baking powder*
½ *teaspoon salt*
2 *eggs*
1 *cup sugar*
½ *cup milk*
1 *teaspoon vanilla*
2 *tablespoons butter*

Beat eggs and sugar gradually, beat until fluffy. Sift flour, salt, and baking powder together. Add to egg mixture. Beat thoroughly. Heat milk and butter to boiling point. Add to batter. Add vanilla, beat slightly. Pour into greased 8 x 8-inch cake pan. Bake in moderate oven 350° for about 30 minutes. When done, spread immediately with topping and place under broiler until browned.

Topping:

5 *tablespoons sugar*
3 *tablespoons cream*
3 *tablespoons butter*
½ *cup coconut*
½ *cup pecans*

Mix all ingredients and beat just enough so it is of the right consistency to spread.

This is a delicious cake—one you will cherish.

CHOCOLATE CREAM CAKE

6 *tablespoons butter*
1½ *cups sugar*
2 *eggs, beaten*
3 *1-ounce squares unsweetened chocolate*
¾ *cup boiling water*
1½ *teaspoons soda*
2¼ *cups sifted cake flour*
1½ *teaspoons baking powder*
¼ *teaspoon salt*
¾ *cup dairy sour cream*
1 *teaspoon vanilla*

Cream butter; gradually add sugar and continue creaming until fluffy. Add beaten eggs. Melt chocolate with water; cool. Add sifted dry ingredients alternately with sour cream, mixing well after each addition. Stir in chocolate mixture and vanilla. Pour batter into 3 buttered and floured 8-inch cake pans. Bake at 350° preheated oven for 25-30 minutes. Frost with chocolate butter frosting.

Chocolate Butter Frosting:

⅓ cup butter
4 cups sifted confectioners' sugar
1 egg yolk
1½ teaspoons vanilla
About 2 tablespoons light cream
2 1-ounce squares unsweetened chocolate, melted and cooled

Cream butter; gradually add about *half* the sugar, blending well. Beat in egg yolk, vanilla, and chocolate. Gradually blend in remaining sugar. Add enough cream to make of spreading consistency. *Frosts 2 8-or-9-inch layers.* Double recipe for above cake.

Sponge cake — light, airy, and simply delightful. Frost or use with fresh fruits.

SPONGE CAKE

1½ cups granulated sugar
½ cup water
6 eggs, beaten separately
1 cup sifted cake flour
½ teaspoon cream of tartar
¼ teaspoon salt
1 teaspoon flavoring

Place sugar and water in saucepan, boil until the thread measures 5 or 6 inches long. Pour gradually into well-beaten egg whites to which the salt and cream of tartar have been added. Then fold in very well-beaten egg yolks, the flavoring, and, lastly, the sifted flour. Bake 1 hour at 325° in ungreased angel-food pan. Invert until cool.

GINGER

Ginger is regarded as the mystery plant by the Sherlock Holmeses of the botanical world, for none of them can tell for a certainty just where this important spice plant had its origin. Some say Asia, some say Brazil; but however indefinite its background, its popularity as a seasoner has been known from ancient times. *To ginger* means "to put spirit into" and that is exactly what the ginger root does to anything with which it comes in contact, be it candy or preserves. Wise old kings of the Orient nibbled ginger properly boiled in honey. Great-grandmama kept a little stone jar of candied ginger on the pantry shelf. Today we are losing track of the fine practice of "gingering" our food.

Add a few snips of candied or preserved ginger to a fruit cocktail or to a salad and, zingo! every taste bud snaps to strict attention. Like that little cup of black coffee, the morning eye-opener, ginger has the power to waken you. Put the bite of ginger into a soufflé, either the ground ginger or preserved, and the dish begins to sing.

The aroma of gingerbread filling the house makes any heart feel light, gay, and happy.

BANANA GINGERBREAD SHORTCAKE

2 *cups sifted enriched flour*
1 *teaspoon baking powder*
1 *teaspoon soda*
1 *teaspoon ginger*
2 *teaspoons cinnamon*
1 *cup molasses*
½ *cup shortening*
½ *cup sour milk or buttermilk*
1 *egg*
2 *bananas*
1 *cup heavy cream*

Grease 2 8-inch layer pans. Sift together the dry ingredients. Mix the molasses and shortening and heat to boiling. Add the milk and egg to the dry ingredients and quickly stir in the hot molasses mixture. Pour into pans and bake in a moderate oven (375°) 20-25 minutes. Cool, place sliced bananas between and on top of layers. Cover with whipped cream and banana slices. 6-8 *servings.*

Our cheese cake is one of the most popular desserts served at the Country House. We have made hundreds of them over the years—especially when the first Michigan strawberries appear in our markets. Big, bright-red, luscious berries on top the cake are as pretty as a picture. However, they are served each year at the colorful and fabulous traditional Country House Football Parties when WJIM Channel 6 plays host to its many outstanding clients, time buyers, account executives, media directors, and others in the broadcasting industry.

COUNTRY HOUSE CHEESE CAKE

Crust:

1½ *cups fine zweiback crumbs*
3 *tablespoons melted butter*
1 *teaspoon cinnamon*
4 *tablespoons sugar*

Filling:

½ *cup sugar*
2 *tablespoons flour*
¼ *teaspoon salt*
1 *teaspoon vanilla*
2 *8-ounce packages cream cheese*
4 *egg yolks*
1 *cup light cream*
4 *stiffly beaten egg whites*
1 *teaspoon lemon juice*

Blend zweiback crumbs with butter, cinnamon, and 4 tablespoons sugar. Press into bottom and partially up sides of 9-inch spring pan. Blend ½ cup sugar with flour, salt, and cream cheese which has been softened at room temperature. Add vanilla and lemon juice. Stir in egg yolks and mix well. Add cream and blend well. Fold in stiffly beaten egg whites. Pour the mixture on top of the crumbs. Bake in moderate oven 350° about 1¼ hours or until set in the center.

Remove from oven, cool cake a few minutes. Gently spoon sour-cream topping over cake.

Sour-Cream Topping:

1 *pint sour cream*
1 *tablespoon sugar (granulated)*
1 *teaspoon vanilla*

Fold ingredients together, spread on top of cake, and bake at 450° for 5 to 7 minutes. When cool, chill in refrigerator until time to pour strawberry glaze over cake.

Strawberry Glaze:

2 *or* 3 *cups fresh strawberries*
1 *cup water*
1½ *tablespoons cornstarch*
½ *to* ¾ *cup sugar*

Crush 1 cup of the strawberries; add the water, and cook 2 minutes; sieve. Mix cornstarch with sugar (amount of sugar depends on sweetness of berries); stir into hot berry mixture. Bring to boiling, stirring constantly. Cook and stir till thick and clear. (Add a few drops red food coloring, if needed.) Cool at room temperature.

Place remaining strawberries atop cooled cheese cake. If fresh strawberries are not available, I use frozen ones and pipe edges with sweetened whipped cream.

Be sure glaze is thick enough to hold its shape!

Here are a few frostings and toppings we've enjoyed using with success both in our Country House Dining Room and the Copper Kettle Show. Hope you'll like them, too.

HEAVENLY ICING

1 *cup milk*
¼ *cup flour*

Cook until thick, cool. While this is cooling, mix:

1 *cup granulated sugar*
½ *cup all-purpose shortening*
½ *cup butter*

and beat until fluffy, at high speed. Add first mixture (milk and flour) and 1 teaspoon vanilla to second mixture and continue beating until thick.
Makes enough for two layers.

CREAMY ICING

2 tablespoons water
4 tablespoons granulated sugar
2⅓ cups sifted confectioners' sugar
¼ teaspoon salt
1 egg
½ cup vegetable shortening
1 teaspoon vanilla

Boil water and granulated sugar together for a few minutes. Mix confectioners' sugar, salt, and egg. Blend with syrup. Add shortening and vanilla. Beat until creamy.

For creamy chocolate icing stir in 2 squares melted chocolate before icing the cake.

CHOCOLATE SATIN FROSTING

It's a fluffy, light-chocolate frosting when whipped by mixer. For darker, more glossy frosting, beat with spoon.

3½ 1-ounce squares unsweetened chocolate
3 cups sifted confectioners' sugar
4½ tablespoons hot water
1 egg
½ cup soft butter or margarine
1½ teaspoons vanilla

Melt chocolate in mixing bowl over hot water. Remove from heat. With electric mixer blend in sugar and water. Beat in egg, then butter and vanilla. Frosting will be thin at this point, so place bowl in ice water; beat till of spreading consistency.
Frosts tops and sides of two 9-inch layers.

CHOCOLATE CHEESE FLUFF FROSTING

Have 2 3-ounce-packages cream cheese at room temperature. Blend in 1 egg, 1 teaspoon vanilla, and dash of salt; gradually beat in 5 cups sifted confectioners' sugar.

Blend in 3 1-ounce squares unsweetened chocolate, melted and cooled slightly.

Frosts tops and sides of two 9-inch layers.

ANGEL FOOD CAKE TOPPING

1 *egg white*
1 *cup sugar*
1 *10-ounce-package frozen strawberries half-thawed (or red raspberries)*

Combine all ingredients. Beat in electric mixer for at least 30 minutes.

Makes a delicious topping for white cake.

QUICK CARAMEL FROSTING

½ cup butter or margarine
1 cup brown sugar
Few grains salt
5 tablespoons milk
2½ to 2¾ cups sifted confectioners' sugar

Melt butter in saucepan; add brown sugar and salt, cook over low heat 2 minutes, stirring constantly. Add milk and continue stirring until mixture comes to a boil. Remove from heat. Add confectioners' sugar, about ½ of a cup at a time, beating well after each addition until frosting is of smooth-spreading consistency.

Makes about 2 cups or enough to frost tops and sides of 2 9-inch layers.

JELLY FROSTING

Place ¾ cup pure currant or grape jelly in bowl over hot water and melt. Add 2 egg whites, unbeaten, 6 tablespoons granulated sugar, and dash of salt. Beat with egg beater until mixture stands up in peaks; remove from hot water, and continue beating until cool enough to spread on cake.

This is an amazing frosting. Quick, easy, and fun to make – nice on angel food cakes.

EASY CHOCOLATE FROSTING

¾ cup semi-sweet chocolate pieces
⅓ cup evaporated milk
1½ cups sifted powdered sugar

Put chocolate pieces and evaporated milk into a heavy 1-quart saucepan. Melt chocolate over very low heat, stirring all the time. Take off heat. Add powdered sugar and stir until smooth. Spread on cooled cake. If frosting becames too thick to spread easily, add a few drops of evaporated milk.
Makes enough to frost 8-inch cake.

This is a most unusual frosting. It's quick, easy, and good on both light or dark cake.

DELICIOUS FROSTING

4 *tablespoons flour (rounded)*
1 *cup water or milk*

Thicken water and flour on range and let cool till almost cold. Then add with electric beater:

6 *tablespoons soft margarine*
6 *tablespoons shortening*
Almost 1 cup granulated sugar
½ teaspoon vanilla or 1 drop of almond extract or your favorite flavoring

Beat till it looks like whipped cream. Spread on your favorite cake.

The secret of success is constancy to purpose – Disraeli

Candies and Confectioneries

How wonderful they are. Sweets play such a tremendously important and happy role in the lives of American people today. Sweets have been known to tempt men and women since the days of ancient Egypt, since the glory of the Nile and the scarab. Gifts, decoration, food – all these at once are candy. A year-round favorite, it really comes into its own at Christmas, when it seems to be everywhere. It's fun to make candy. I love it! There is a ritual to it, an anticipatory lingering, a fragrance sweet, delicious, pervading. And in the finished product, there is not only pleasure, but the mark of a good cook. Try your luck with some of these recipes. They're all good!

This one I have made for years and it's wonderful!

ALMOND BUTTER CRUNCH

1 *cup butter*
1⅓ *cups sugar*
1 *tablespoon light corn syrup*
3 *tablespoons water*

1 *cup coarsely chopped blanched almonds, toasted*
4 *4½-ounce bars milk chocolate, melted*
1 *cup finely chopped blanched almonds, toasted*

Melt butter in large saucepan. Add sugar, corn syrup, and water. Cook, stirring occasionally, to hard-crack stage (300°).* Quickly stir in coarsely chopped nuts; spread in ungreased 13 x 9½ x 2-inch pan. Cool thoroughly. Turn out on waxed paper; spread top with half the chocolate, sprinkle with *half* the finely chopped nuts. Cover with waxed paper, invert and spread again with chocolate. Sprinkle top with remaining nuts. If necessary, chill to firm chocolate. Break in pieces.

**Watch carefully after temperature reaches 280 degrees.*

This is delicious and well worth the effort it takes to make it. Package it in a pretty box for gift-giving.

BUTTER-NUT CRUNCH

1 *cup sugar*
½ *teaspoon salt*
¼ *cup water*
½ *cup butter*
1½ *cups walnuts, chopped fine*
2 *6-ounce packages semi-sweet chocolate pieces, melted*

Combine sugar, salt, water, and butter; heat to boiling. Cook to light-crack stage (285°). Add ½ cup of the nuts, pour onto well-greased cookie sheet. Cool. Spread half of chocolate mixture over top. Sprinkle with ½ cup walnuts. Cool. Turn and spread remaining chocolate and sprinkle with remaining nuts. Break in pieces to serve. *Makes about 2 dozen pieces.*

Caramelly and crisp—a favorite with the waiting-for-Santa set. And quick as a wink!

PEANUT BUTTER-CEREAL CANDY

3 *cups crisp rice cereal*
1 *cup salted peanuts*
½ *cup sugar*

½ *cup light corn syrup*
½ *cup peanut butter*
½ *teaspoon vanilla*

Mix cereal and peanuts; set aside. Combine sugar and syrup. Cook, stirring constantly, till mixture comes to a full rolling boil. Remove from heat. Stir in peanut butter and vanilla. Immediately pour syrup over cereal mixture, stirring gently to coat. Pat cereal mixture evenly into buttered 8 x 8 x 2-inch pan. Cool; cut in 2-inch bars.

There's a surprise layer of tiny marshmallows—and way to the bottom, a layer of nuts.

MARSHMALLOW-ROAD FUDGE

¾ *cup broken walnuts*
2 *cups sugar*
1 *cup evaporated milk*
¼ *teaspoon salt*
1 *12-ounce package (2 cups) semi-sweet chocolate pieces*
1 *teaspoon vanilla*
2 *cups tiny marshmallows*

Sprinkle walnuts evenly over bottom of buttered 9x9x2-inch pan; set aside. Butter sides of heavy 2-quart saucepan. In it combine sugar, milk, and salt. Heat and stir till sugar is dissolved. Bring to rolling boil and boil 2 minutes (222°), stirring frequently to prevent sticking. Remove from heat; immediately stir in chocolate and vanilla. Beat until chocolate is melted and blended. Cover walnuts with *half* of fudge mixture. Top with tiny marshmallows, pressing them gently into fudge. Spread with remaining fudge. Chill. Cut in squares.

VERSATILE ALMONDS

Slivered blanched almonds sprinkled over cooked vegetables are sure to perk up appetites.

Stir roasted diced almonds into applesauce and add a dash of cinnamon for a crunchy meat accompaniment.

Try toasting and salting whole blanched almonds for delightful nibbling any time of day.

These will surprise you. Try 'em!

PEANUT CLUSTERS

Melt over water:

1 package chocolate chips
Add 1 tablespoon shortening
Stir in 1 cup salted peanuts

Drop by spoonfuls on wax paper or greased cookie sheet. Chill until firm.

If you want to try a Christmas candy that's fun to make, try this one. The recipe was given to me by the women of the Okemos Community Church. It's made in great quantities, packaged gaily, and sold at the church bazaar. Have your own bazaar and try it. You'll need help with the cutting. My dear mother helped me when I made it. It was such fun.

CHRISTMAS HARD CANDY

3½ *cups white sugar*
1 *cup white syrup*
1 *cup water*
1 *teaspoon oil flavoring*

Boil to scant 300°, remove from range, add flavoring and coloring, and pour on well-covered (with powdered sugar) marble slab.

Immediately sprinkle with plenty of powdered sugar and cut as soon as possible in small pieces with scissors.

Total 3 pounds.

Suggested color and flavor combinations:

1. *oil of cloves – blue-green*
2. *oil of anise – violet*
3. *oil of sassafras – yellow*
4. *oil of cinnamon – orange*
5. *oil of wintergreen – green*
6. *oil of peppermint – red*

These oils may be obtained at any drugstore.

Smooth, coffee-flavored candy with crunchy chocolate bits and nuts scattered throughout.

COFFEE DOT FUDGE

3 cups sugar
1 cup milk
½ cup light cream
2 tablespoons instant coffee
1 tablespoon light corn syrup
Dash salt
3 tablespoons butter or margarine
1 teaspoon vanilla
½ 6-ounce package (½ cup) semi-sweet chocolate pieces
½ cup broken pecans

Butter sides of heavy 3-quart saucepan. In it combine sugar, milk, light cream, instant coffee, corn syrup, and salt. Heat over medium heat, stirring constantly, till sugar dissolves and mixture comes to boiling. Then cook to soft-ball stage (234°), stirring only if necessary. Immediately remove from heat; add butter and cool to lukewarm (110°) without stirring. Add vanilla. Beat vigorously till fudge becomes very thick and starts to lose its gloss. At once stir in chocolate pieces and pecans. Quickly spread in buttered shallow pan or small platter. Score in squares while warm and, if desired, top each with a pecan half. Cut when firm.

The ripest peach is highest on the tree
—James Whitcomb Riley

A little sweet, a little salty – with wonderful butter flavor! Here's a come-back-for-more nut confection that's just right for open house. And it's easy as 1-2-3!

ICED ALMONDS

1 cup whole blanched almonds
½ cup sugar
2 tablespoons butter or margarine
½ teaspoon vanilla
¾ teaspoon salt

Heat almonds, sugar, and butter in heavy skillet over medium heat, stirring constantly, till almonds are toasted and sugar is golden brown, about 15 minutes. Stir in vanilla. Spread nuts on a sheet of aluminum foil; sprinkle with salt. Cool. Break into 2- or 3-nut clusters.

This is an old-time favorite given to me by a dear neighbor, Mrs. Russell Goodrich, in Jackson, many years ago. It wouldn't be Christmas at our house without several batches of Aunt Thelma's candy caramels.

GOLDEN CANDY CARAMELS

½ pound butter (2 sticks butter)
1 pound sugar (2 cups)
1 cup light corn syrup
1 can sweetened condensed milk
1 teaspoon vanilla

Melt butter and add rest of ingredients, stirring constantly and cook to 240°. Remove, add 2 cups broken nut meats and vanilla. Pour into pan. Cut into squares. Wrap in wax paper.

Rich, but oh, so good!

NUT PRALINES

3 cups brown sugar (firmly packed)
¼ cup butter

1 cup thick cream
1½ cups nuts
⅛ teaspoon cinnamon
Pinch of salt

Combine sugar, butter, and cream. Blend thoroughly. Place over low heat. Stir till dissolved and boiling. Cook to soft ball stage or 236°. Remove from heat, add nuts, salt, and cinnamon. Beat at once till it holds its form. Drop by spoonfuls on waxed paper or greased cookie sheet.

This is the best peanut brittle I've ever tasted. It is golden in color and flavor. We've made hundreds of batches of it and expect to make hundreds more. It is positively a non-fail peanut-brittle recipe.

PEANUT BRITTLE

Cook 2 cups sugar, 1 cup light corn syrup, and ½ cup water to 280°, medium crack stage. A sample dropped in cold water will clink against the cup. Add 2 cups peanuts. Cook about 3 minutes, or until light golden brown. Add 2 teaspoons soda. Remove at once from heat. Add 1 teaspoon vanilla and 1 teaspoon butter. As soon as foaming has subsided, pour candy into greased shallow pan in a thin layer. When cold, break into pieces.

Some years ago I made several batches of divinity fudge and much to my horror our son Tom, then seven years old, packaged the candy and sold it by the piece to the neighbors. He not only sold all I had made but took orders for some additional ten pounds. Incidentally, I filled the orders.

DIVINITY FUDGE

2 cups sugar
½ cup corn syrup
½ cup water
¾ cup candied cherries
2 egg whites
¾ cup blanched almonds
1 tablespoon almond or lemon extract

Put the sugar, water, and corn syrup into a saucepan. Stir it while it dissolves over the fire, then let it boil without stirring to the light crack stage (265°). While it is cooking, beat the whites of eggs stiff and when the syrup is ready, pour it over them, beating constantly. Beat until creamy, add nuts, cherries, and extract, and pour into buttered tins.

Every holiday candy dish must have brandy-nut balls in it!

BRANDY-NUT BALLS

1 *pound butter or margarine*
1 *egg yolk*
¼ *cup sugar*
2 *tablespoons brandy*
1 *teaspoon vanilla extract*
1 *cup grated or ground walnuts*
6 *cups sifted cake flour*
Whole cloves
Confectioners' sugar

Work butter until soft and very creamy, using an electric beater, if possible. Beat in egg yolk well, then add sugar, brandy, and vanilla. Next beat in grated walnuts and flour thoroughly. Dough will be heavy, slightly moist, but not sticky.

Start oven at 325°. Shape little balls of dough about size of a walnut, stick a clove on top, and bake on an ungreased cookie sheet 15 to 20 minutes. Cool before removing from sheet. Cookies may be rolled in confectioners' sugar if desired.

Makes 7 to 8 dozen.

EASTER NESTS

1 package quick-fudge mix
2 tablespoons butter
3½ tablespoons water
1 can shredded coconut
Jelly beans

Make quick fudge following direction on package, using double boiler. When glossy, stir in shredded coconut. Remove top of double boiler from heat and drop fudge by spoonfuls on wax paper. Shape with teaspoon, while still warm, to resemble a nest. Place 3 or 4 jelly beans in each nest. If fudge gets too thick, reheat over boiling water.

We have made this in our family for years. Even though my sons are now teen-agers, they still ask for their favorite vanilla taffy. Saturday night was always "taffy night!"

VANILLA TAFFY

2 cups sugar
¼ cup white corn syrup
⅔ cup water
1 tablespoon cider vinegar
1 tablespoon butter or margarine
1 teaspoon pure vanilla extract

Combine first 5 ingredients in a 5-quart saucepan. Mix well and cook slowly until sugar is dissolved, stirring constantly.

Increase heat to medium and boil, without stirring, until syrup separates into threads which are hard but not brittle, when a little is dropped in cold water (270°).

Pour onto buttered, large, shallow pan or platter. Sprinkle pure vanilla extract over the top.

As edges cool, fold toward the center to prevent them from hardening before center is ready to pull.

Gather into a ball when cool enough to handle. (The taffy will stick to the pan if you try to remove it before it has cooled sufficiently to handle.)

Pull with lightly buttered fingers until candy is white and firm. Stretch into a long rope, ½-inch wide. Cut into 1-inch pieces with scissors. Wrap each piece in waxed paper or cellophane if it is to be kept. *Yield: 1 pound.*

Variation: Black-Walnut Taffy

Add ½ cup chopped black walnuts to the syrup just before it is poured onto the buttered pan. Cool and pull as in the above directions.

Thanks to Mrs. Edna Pierce, Jackson, a loyal Copper Kettle viewer.

SANTA'S PEANUT-BUTTER FUDGE

⅔ *cup milk*
2 *cups granulated sugar*
1 *cup marshmallow fluff*
1 *cup crunchy peanut butter*
1 *teaspoon vanilla*
½ *cup chopped dates*

Combine milk and sugar in saucepan. Boil without stirring until candy temperature registers 240° (soft ball forms when a little is dropped in cold water). Remove from heat. Add marshmallow fluff, peanut butter, vanilla, and dates. Stir only until combined. Pour into 8-inch pan. Let stand in refrigerator at least 20 minutes before cutting.

This is a wonderful and easy way to make fudge which keeps soft several weeks.

Our thanks to my dear long-time friend, Mrs. Mary Jane Middlebrook. We've loved making your carameled apples for many years.

CARAMELED APPLES

1 *cup sugar*
½ *cup white corn syrup*
1 *can sweetened condensed milk*
½ *teaspoon salt*
1 *teaspoon vanilla flavoring*

Combine all ingredients in heavy saucepan. Cook to 230°, stirring constantly. Insert stick into eating apples and dip in hot caramel syrup at once. *Makes 16 small carameled apples.* Keep range at a *low* temperature – mixture burns easily!

These are gay and festive, especially at the holiday time.

COCONUT SWIRLS

Melt 2 tablespoons butter or margarine in a 2-quart saucepan. Take from heat and add 3 tablespoons water and 1 teaspoon vanilla. Mix 2 cups sifted powdered sugar and ½ cup instant milk (in dry form). Add to butter mixture, about ½ cup at a time, mixing well after each addition. Stir in 3 cups coconut. Drop teaspoonfuls of mixture onto waxed paper. Let stand until firm, about 10 minutes. Melt 6-ounce package semi-sweet chocolate pieces over hot (not boiling) water. Swirl about a teaspoon of melted chocolate on top of each coconut drop. Then chill. *Makes about* 36.

This is my mother's popcorn-ball recipe. We love it.

POPCORN BALLS

1 *cup sugar*
⅓ *cup white corn syrup*
⅓ *cup water*
¼ *cup butter*
¾ *teaspoon salt*
¾ *teaspoon vanilla*
3 *quarts popped corn*

Boil all together except popcorn until a drop of the mixture snaps when dropped in cold water. Remove from fire at once. Pour over corn and form into balls. *Makes 12 large balls.*

HOMEMADE CANDY CORN

3 *quarts popped corn*
½ *cup roasted peanuts*
½ *cup molasses*
½ *cup water*
1 *cup butter*
1 *teaspoon vanilla*
1 *cup sugar*
¼ *teaspoon salt*
1 *tablespoon vinegar*

Crisp corn in a moderately hot oven in shallow pan, then scatter the peanuts over the top of the corn. Boil all other ingredients together except vanilla, vinegar, and butter. Cook until soft ball stage is reached when tested in cold water, then add the vinegar, butter, and vanilla.

Continue cooking until the thermometer registers 266°, or until the crackle stage is reached when tested in cold water. Pour syrup over the corn, toss the kernels apart with a wooden spoon, until they are well-coated with syrup.

COUNTRY HOUSE FUDGE

We're sure you'll agree with us, after making and tasting this fudge, it's positively the richest, creamiest, most delicious fudge you've ever tasted! Don't be alarmed at the number of ingredients the recipe requires or the expense to make it. Remember, it makes several pounds and can be stored in the refrigerator indefinitely.

We like to use black walnuts but pecans or English walnuts are equally as good. The important thing is that you try this recipe. Makes a wonderful gift for friends, especially those who are difficult to buy for. Invest in a gayly hand-painted box, fill with the Country House fudge, and you'll receive "raves" galore!

Boil together 4½ cups granulated sugar, 1 teaspoon salt, 1 stick butter, 1 tall can evaporated milk; gently boil for 8 to 10 minutes. (Be sure you start the timing after candy mixture has reached a full gently boiling point.) Remove from heat and add 1 12-ounce package semi-sweet chocolate pieces, 4 German sweet chocolate bars, 1 large Hershey bar (either with or without almonds), about 1½ pints marshmallow cream, 2 teaspoons vanilla flavoring, 4 cups nut meats (black walnuts are my favorite). Mix rapidly with large spoon until thoroughly blended. Pour into buttered pans. Cool several hours before serving. Elegant eating!

We look backward too much. Thus we miss the passing moment —W.L.P.

Cookies

Cookies, cookies, cookies, all kinds! We should never outgrow the love, fun, and joy in keeping a well-filled cookie jar in our kitchens. May your kitchen be impressive or humble, it is like a ship without a rudder unless it has a loving cookie jar.

I have never been without one in my kitchen. You shouldn't be either. Keep it well filled.

The French chefs of the eighteenth century had many "animated" specialties. They made huge pies and cakes which, upon being cut, released birds, frogs, and butterflies. Some of the larger cakes, more fantastic, concealed dwarfs under the crust. The dwarfs jumped out and entertained the delighted guests.

Cookies, cakes, flapjacks, crullers, pancakes, and so forth, were the major part of the good old New England diet, and little need be said about the ruggedness of the people nourished on such provender. They pioneered across the plains to build the West, and lived out of the cookie and cruller jars between battles, living dangerously—and living well. It's just as true today!

I make my surprise meringues with black walnuts. Wish I owned a dozen black walnut trees. I probably would add a few nuts to every dish.

SURPRISE MERINGUES

2 egg whites
⅛ teaspoon salt
⅛ teaspoon cream of tartar
1 teaspoon vanilla
¾ cup sugar
1 6-ounce package semi-sweet chocolate pieces
¼ cup chopped California walnuts

Beat egg whites, salt, cream of tartar, and vanilla until soft peaks form. Add sugar gradually, beating till peaks are stiff. Fold in chocolate pieces and nuts. Cover cookie sheet with plain paper. Drop mixture on by rounded teaspoons. Bake in slow oven (300°) about 25 minutes.
Makes about 2 dozen.

The kind Grandmother used to make.

MOLASSES COOKIES

1 cup lard
1 cup molasses
1 cup light brown sugar
2 eggs, beaten lightly
4 cups sifted flour
½ teaspoon salt
2 teaspoons ginger
1 teaspoon cinnamon
2 teaspoons (scant) soda
¼ cup hot water or coffee
Granulated sugar

Cream lard, blend in molasses, brown sugar, and beaten eggs. Sift flour with salt, ginger, and cinnamon; dissolve soda in hot water or coffee. Add dry ingredients to creamed mixture alternately with soda mixture. Chill dough 3 to 4 hours. Flour hands and pick up a chunk of dough with tablespoon, roll in ball, and place on greased

and floured cookie sheet. Flatten with wet cloth wrapped around a flat-bottomed glass. Space cookies 1½ inches apart. Sprinkle with granulated sugar and bake at 400° for 10 to 15 minutes.
Makes 24 large or 4 dozen small cookies.

Ruth Aspgren, the Country House Swedish cook, makes the Berliner Kranser at Christmas time by the dozens. Staff members, clients, friends, guests, and tradespeople of Channel 6 all ask for them. They're rich, but so good!

BERLINER KRANSER

Yolks of 4 eggs
Yolks of 4 hard-boiled eggs, sieved
1 *cup sugar*
2 *cups butter*
4 *cups flour, sifted*
1 *teaspoon vanilla extract*
1 *teaspoon almond extract*

Mix egg yolks thoroughly, add sugar and flavorings, and work in the butter and the flour until a very smooth dough is formed. Chill. Shape into a long roll and cut into about 30 pieces. Roll each piece of dough into about 7-inch lengths, form into a wreath and cross ends. Dip each into slightly beaten egg whites and then into crushed loaf sugar or coarse sugar. Bake to a delicate brown in moderate oven about 12 minutes.

These are good and a wonderful addition on the festive sideboard at Christmas time.

MINCEMEAT COOKIES

1 *cup shortening*
1½ *cups sugar*
3 *eggs*
1½ *cups mincemeat*
½ *teaspoon salt*
3¼ *cups flour*
1 *teaspoon soda*
1 *cup nut meats*

Cream shortening and sugar, adding beaten eggs. Sift dry ingredients together and add to the mixture. Fold in the mincemeat and one cup of nut meats. Drop mixture from a spoon onto a greased pan and bake eight minutes in moderate oven.

The popular top-of-stove cookies are ingenious, to say the least. Thanks to Mrs. W. J. Scott and Mrs. Mildred Moore, Lansing.

TOP-OF-STOVE COOKIES

2 *cups sugar*
3 *tablespoons cocoa*
1 *stick butter or margarine*
½ *cup milk*

Put in saucepan, bring to a full rolling boil, and boil 1 minute. Remove from fire. Add 1 teaspoon vanilla, ½ cup peanut butter, and 3 cups quick oats. Beat together. Drop by teaspoon onto waxed paper.

The chubby, dimpled hands of children love to help roll these.

GINGER CRISPS

2 *cups sifted enriched flour*
1 *teaspoon soda*
1 *teaspoon cinnamon*
½ *teaspoon ground cloves*
1¼ *teaspoons ginger*
½ *teaspoon salt*
⅔ *cup shortening*
1 *cup sugar*
1 *egg*
¼ *cup molasses*
½ *cup finely chopped walnuts*
⅓ *cup sugar for coating cookies*

Sift together flour, soda, cinnamon, cloves, ginger, and salt. Cream shortening and sugar. Add egg and molasses. Beat. Add sifted dry ingredients to creamed mixture. Add nuts. Mix well. Shape dough into balls about the size of a walnut and roll in sugar. Place on a cookie sheet about 2 inches apart. (Do not flatten balls.)

Bake in a moderate oven (350°) for 15 minutes.
Yield: 4½ dozen.

Mr. Santa demands a plate of these waiting on the hearth.

NOEL FRUIT SQUARES

¾ cups all-purpose flour
1½ teaspoons baking powder
1 teaspoon salt
2 eggs
1 cup sifted confectioners' sugar
3 tablespoons melted butter or margarine
1 cup chopped nuts
1 cup chopped dates
½ cup confectioners' sugar
¾ cup mixed candied fruit
1 tablespoon melted butter or margarine
1 teaspoon lemon juice

Sift flour, measure and sift twice with baking powder and salt. Beat eggs. Gradually beat in 1 cup sugar. Add melted butter or margarine, dry ingredients, nuts, and fruits. Spread in a greased 9-inch square pan. Bake at 325° about 30-35 minutes. While warm, spread with frosting made of remaining confectioners' sugar, butter or margarine, and lemon juice.
Yields 16 2-inch squares.

CRISP TOFFEE BARS

1 cup butter or margarine
1 cup brown sugar
1 teaspoon vanilla
2 cups sifted enriched flour
1 6-ounce package (1 cup) semisweet chocolate pieces
1 cup chopped California walnuts

Thoroughly cream together butter, sugar, and vanilla. Add flour, mix well. Stir in chocolate and walnuts. Press mixture into ungreased 15½ x 10½ x 1-inch jelly-roll pan. Bake in moderate oven (350°) 25 minutes or until browned. While warm, cut in bars or squares. Cool before removing from pan.
Makes about 5 dozen.

TASTIE CHEWS

- 1 *cup brown sugar*
- 1 *cup chopped dates*
- 1 *cup chopped walnuts*
- 2 *egg yolks*
- 1 *tablespoon butter*

Cook all ingredients in top of double boiler for 20 minutes. Remove from heat and form into small balls. Roll in coconut.

CINNAMON CRISPS

- ½ *cup butter or margarine*
- 1 *cup brown sugar*
- 1 *egg*
- 1 *tablespoon shredded orange peel*
- 1½ *cups sifted enriched flour*
- 1 *teaspoon baking powder*
- 1 *teaspoon cinnamon*
- ¼ *teaspoon salt*
- ½ *cup bran flakes*
- ¼ *cup chopped pecans*

Thoroughly cream butter and sugar. Beat in egg and orange peel. Sift together dry ingredients; add to creamed mixture. Stir in bran flakes and pecans. Chill 1 hour. Shape in 2 long 1½-inch rolls. Wrap in waxed paper; chill well. Slice ⅛ to ¼ inch thick. Bake on greased cookie sheet in moderate oven (350°) 8 to 10 minutes.
Makes 4 dozen.

TOFFEE TREATS

- 2 *cups oatmeal*
- ½ *teaspoon salt*
- ⅓ *cup melted shortening*
- ½ *cup sifted brown sugar or* ¼ *cup firmly packed*

¼ cup dark corn syrup or honey
1½ teaspoons vanilla
½ cup chocolate morsels
¼ cup chopped nuts

Pour melted shortening over oatmeal and salt. Blend thoroughly. Add brown sugar, syrup or honey, and vanilla. Mix well. Pack firmly into well-greased 8-inch square pan. Bake at 450°, about 10 minutes. Sprinkle chocolate morsels over hot cookie. When melted, spread over top and sprinkle with nuts. Cool. Run knife under baked cooled cookies and around sides to loosen. Cut into squares.
Makes 16 2-inch squares.

Everyone has asked for this one.

FLAKY DATE MOONS

½ cup butter or margarine
1 (3-ounce) package cream cheese
1 cup sifted all-purpose flour
Dash of salt
1 cup pitted fresh California dates
¼ cup sugar
¼ cup water
1 teaspoon grated orange rind
½ cup chopped walnuts
Powdered sugar

Soften butter a few minutes; add cream cheese. Beat with mixer until blended and light. With fork or rubber scraper, work in flour and salt until smooth.

Ball up in waxed paper. Chill while you make the filling. Cut dates into pieces. In small saucepan, combine dates, sugar, and water. Stir over medium heat until thickened, 3 to 5 minutes. Add orange rind and nuts. Cool. Divide dough in half and roll thin on floured pastry cloth. Cut into 2½-inch rounds. Put small spoonful filling on each; fold over, press down, and crimp edges together with fork. Prick tops. Place on cookie sheets.

Bake in moderately hot oven (375°) about 15 minutes. Remove to wire racks. Sift powdered sugar over tops.
Makes about 3½ dozen.

DATE MARSHMALLOW ROLL

2 cups fresh dates
½ pound graham crackers
32 marshmallows (½ pound)
1 cup whipping cream
1 teaspoon vanilla extract
¼ cup chopped maraschino cherries

Pit and slice dates. Roll graham crackers to make fine crumbs. Cut marshmallows in small pieces. Whip cream until stiff. Fold in vanilla, marshmallows, cherries, and dates. Set aside ¾ cup graham-cracker crumbs and fold remainder into date mixture. Shape into roll and roll in reserved crumbs. Wrap in waxed paper. Chill several hours. Cut into slices to serve.
Makes 10 to 12 servings.

These cookies set the pace for a happy holiday.

CHRISTMAS CHERRIES

½ cup shortening
¼ cup granulated sugar
1 egg yolk, beaten
1 tablespoon grated rind of orange
1½ teaspoons grated rind of lemon
½ teaspoon vanilla
1 tablespoon lemon juice
1 cup sifted cake flour
1 egg white, unbeaten
¾ cup chopped nuts
6 glacé cherries, cut in small pieces

Thoroughly mix the first seven ingredients until very light and fluffy. Beat in flour until just mixed. Chill until easy to handle. Form dough into ½" balls, roll in egg white and then nuts. Place on greased cookie sheets. Press cherry into each. Bake at 350° approximately 10 minutes.

Thanks to pastry chef George Michel, Jack Tar, Lansing, Mich.

COCONUT MACAROONS

Blend 3½ cups granulated sugar, 1¼ pounds macaroon coconut (short shred), and 1½ cups egg whites. Add and blend ½ teaspoonful vanilla extract. Heat in top of double boiler, drop on lightly greased cookie sheets, and bake in 350° oven for 15 to 20 minutes. *Makes approximately 5 dozen macaroons.*

Thanks to my dear friend Mrs. Viola Mutch. Wonderfully easy and simple. Especially good made with black walnuts.

DROP APPLESAUCE COOKIES

1 *cup sugar*
½ *cup lard or shortening*
1 *egg*
2¼ *cups sifted flour*
¼ *teaspoon cloves*
¼ *teaspoon cinnamon*
½ *teaspoon salt*
½ *teaspoon soda*
1 *teaspoon baking powder*
1 *cup applesauce*
½ *cup nutmeats (black walnuts are good)*
½ *cup raisins*

Mix ingredients as listed. Drop by teaspoonfuls on slightly greased cookie sheet. Bake at 375° for 8 to 10 minutes or until done. Don't overbake!

Children can make these!

COOKIES

½ cup homogenized peanut butter
2 packages (2 cups) caramel chips

Put in a double boiler. Stir until melted. Pour over 4 cups Special K Cereal. Mix, and drop on wax paper. Cool about 10 to 15 minutes.

Best you have ever tasted!

SOFT SUGAR COOKIES

½ cup butter or margarine
1½ cups sugar
2 eggs
1 teaspoon vanilla
3 cups sifted enriched flour
1 teaspoon salt
½ teaspoon baking powder
½ teaspoon baking soda
1 cup dairy sour cream
Cinnamon-sugar

Cream butter to consistency of mayonnaise; add sugar gradually, while continuing to cream. Add eggs one at a time, beating well after each addition. Add vanilla. Beat until light and fluffy. Mix and sift flour, salt, baking powder, and baking soda. Add to creamed mixture alternately with sour cream, beginning and ending with dry ingredients.

For 3-inch cookies drop by heaping teaspoons on well-greased cookie sheets, well apart. With spatula, flatten into circles about 2 inches in diameter. For super-size, 5-inch cookies, use ¼ cup measure of batter for each cookie; flatten into circles about 4 inches in diameter. Sprinkle with cinnamon-sugar. Bake in hot oven, 400°, for 10 to 12 minutes.

Makes about thirty 3-inch cookies or eighteen 5-inch cookies.

Chocolate Sugar Cookies:

Add 2 squares (2 ounces) unsweetened chocolate, melted and cooled, to creamed mixture. Continue as above.

Raisin Sugar Cookies:

Add 1 cup seedless raisins to creamed mixture. Continue as above.

Like fruitcake, chock-full of fruit? Allow these cookies to ripen as you would fruitcake. Good eating!

FRUITCAKE COOKIES

¼ cup butter
½ cup brown sugar
¼ cup jelly
2 eggs
2 teaspoons soda
1½ tablespoons milk
1½ cups flour
½ teaspoon allspice
½ teaspoon cloves
½ teaspoon cinnamon
½ teaspoon nutmeg
1 pound broken pecans
1 pound seedless raisins
½ pound candied cherries, chopped
½ pound candied pineapple, chopped
½ pound citron, chopped

Cream butter, sugar, jelly, and eggs. Dissolve soda in milk, and add to creamed mixture. Gradually add half the flour, sifted with the spices. Dredge nuts and fruits with remaining flour and stir into batter. Mix well. Drop from spoon onto buttered and floured cookie sheet and decorate tops with sliced candied cherries, if desired. Bake at 300° for about 20 minutes. These cookies ripen just as fruitcake does.
Makes 10 dozen.

In every lunch box you should include peanut-butter cookies.

PEANUT-BUTTER COOKIES

3 cups all-purpose flour, sifted before measuring
2 teaspoons soda
¼ teaspoon salt

1 cup shortening
1 cup granulated sugar
1 cup brown sugar
2 eggs beaten
1 cup peanut butter
1 teaspoon vanilla

Sift flour once with soda and salt. Cream shortening, granulated sugar, and brown sugar together. Add beaten eggs and mix until smooth. Add peanut butter. Stir well. Then add flour mixture. Mix to a stiff batter, then add vanilla. Form into tiny balls and press onto a greased 10 x 14-inch cookie sheet. Press with back of fork to make a waffle design. Bake at 375° for 15 to 18 minutes. Remove from pan immediately after baking.
Yield: 4 dozen.

Not snow balls—Rum Balls.

RUM BALLS

2½ cups vanilla wafers, crushed
1 cup finely chopped nuts
1 cup powdered sugar
1½ tablespoons cocoa
Dash of salt
½ cup Carioca Rum
2½ tablespoons light corn syrup

Mix thoroughly and form into small balls. Roll in powdered sugar and wrap in wax paper.

CATS' TONGUES (Les Langues de Chat)

Cats' Tongues are one of the most popular of the world-famous French petits fours, small delicious cookies.

½ cup butter
½ cup sugar
½ cup sifted flour
2 egg whites
Vanilla or almond essence

Cream butter and sugar. Mix in flour. Beat egg whites until stiff and fold into batter. Flavor with a few drops of vanilla or almond essence. Pour batter into greased baking pan and cut into strips, about 4″ x 1″. If desired, sprinkle with granulated sugar or chopped almonds. Bake in moderate oven, 375°, about 12 minutes or until brown.

The nuts enchance the flavor.

BLACK WALNUT COOKIES

1 cup butter
½ cup powdered sugar
2 cups pastry flour
1 teaspoon vanilla
¾ cup black walnuts, chopped
Pinch of salt

Mix and make into small balls, or flatten with fork, and bake 15 minutes at 350°. Dip in confectioners' sugar as soon as baked. Cool and dip again in confectioners' sugar. Wonderful keeping-cookies, if stored in container and left in cool place.

These are great; thanks to Mrs. Robert Kaufman, Lansing, Mich.

SWEDISH OATMEAL COOKIES

Sift together ¾ cup all-purpose flour, ½ teaspoon soda, and ½ teaspoon salt. Set aside. Gradually add ½ cup sugar and ½ cup firmly packed brown sugar to ½ cup shortening, creaming well. Blend in 1 unbeaten egg and ½ teaspoon vanilla; beat well. Add the dry ingredients, then 1½ cups quick-cooking rolled oats; mix well. Drop by teaspoonfuls onto ungreased cookie sheets. Bake at 350° for 8 minutes. Remove from oven and place a scant ½ teaspoonful almond topping in center of each cookie, pressing in slightly. Bake 6 to 8 minutes until cookies are golden brown. Cool 1 minute before removing from sheet.
Makes about 3 *dozen.*

Almond Topping:

Combine ⅓ cup sugar, ¼ cup butter, and 1 tablespoon light corn syrup in saucepan; bring to a boil. Remove from heat. Stir in ⅓ cup chopped blanched almonds and ⅛ teaspoon almond extract.

These rate high on my list of old-time favorites, especially at the holiday time.

DATE SWIRLS OR PIN WHEELS

½ cup butter
½ cup brown sugar
½ cup white sugar
1 egg, beaten
2 cups sifted flour
½ teaspoon soda
½ teaspoon salt
½ teaspoon lemon extract

Cream butter; add brown and white sugar, and mix until light and fluffy. Stir in egg and blend well. Add sifted dry ingredients; mix until smooth. Blend in lemon extract. Roll dough into rectangle, 12 x 18 inches, and ¼ inch thick. Spread this with date filling and roll up like jelly roll. Chill for one hour. Cut into ¼ inch slices. Place on greased cookie sheet. Bake in moderate oven (350°) 12 to 15 minutes.

Date Filling:

1 pound pitted dates, cut in small pieces
½ cup water
½ cup sugar, granulated

Cook for 3 minutes the above ingredients, stirring constantly, and add 1 cup chopped nuts.

My mother's recipe. I like to frost these with a simple chocolate confectioners' icing. Delightful!

FAVORITE ONE-BOWL BROWNIES

Place ⅓ cup butter or margarine and 2 ounces unsweetened chocolate in saucepan. Cook over low heat, stirring constantly till butter and chocolate melt. Remove from heat. Cool. Beat in 2 eggs, one at a time, till well blended.

Add 1 cup sugar, 1 tablespoon corn syrup, and 1 teaspoon vanilla to chocolate mixture and mix well. Sift together ¾ cup flour, ½ teaspoon baking powder, and ½ teaspoon salt. Add to chocolate mixture and beat until well blended.

Coarsely chop ⅔ cup walnuts and stir into batter. Grease an 8-inch square pan and line with waxed paper. Bake at 350° for 35 minutes.

Makes 16.

These are made regularly to serve for luncheon and coffee breaks at WJIM Country House.

COUNTRY HOUSE BUTTERSCOTCH BROWNIES

⅓ *cup butter*
1 *cup brown sugar*
1 *egg, unbeaten*
¼ *teaspoon salt*
¾ *cup sifted enriched flour*
1 *teaspoon baking powder*
½ *teaspoon vanilla*
½ *cup coconut*
1 *6-ounce package chocolate pieces*
½ *cup chopped nuts*

Melt butter in medium-sized saucepan. Cool. Add sugar, egg, salt, flour, baking powder, and vanilla. Blend the above ingredients; then add ½ cup coconut, 1 6-ounce package chocolate pieces, and ½ cup chopped nuts. Spread in greased 8- or 9-inch square pan. Bake 25 minutes in moderate oven, 350°. These are quick and delicious.

These are fun to make. The rolling requires a little extra work but it's worth it!

PEANUT-WHIRL COOKIES

½ *cup shortening*
1 *cup sugar*
½ *cup chunk-style peanut butter*
1 *egg*
1 *teaspoon vanilla*
1¼ *cups sifted flour*
½ *teaspoon salt*
½ *teaspoon soda*
2 *tablespoons milk*
1 *package (6-ounce) chocolate bits*

Cream shortening, sugar, peanut butter, egg, and vanilla. Add sifted dry ingredients alternately with milk. Roll cookie dough to rectangle ¼ inch in thickness. Melt chocolate bits over hot water and cool slightly. Spread on rolled cookie dough. Roll jelly-roll fashion. Chill ½ hour. Slice with a sharp knife into thin slices. Place on ungreased baking sheet. Bake at 350° for 8 to 10 minutes.
Yield: 5 to 6 dozen cookies.

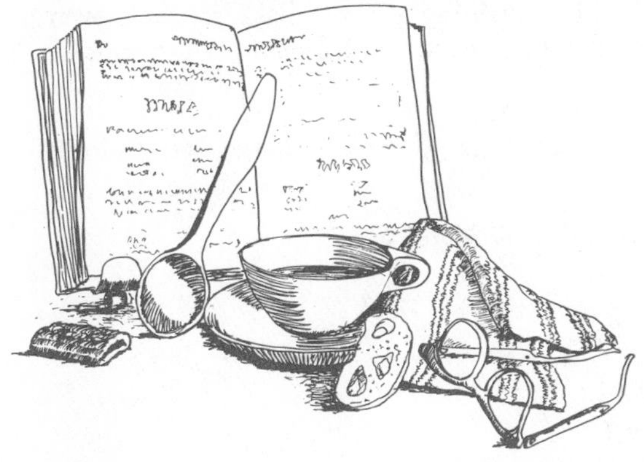

To be trusted is a greater compliment than to be loved — J. Macdonald

These are little tea treats, ideal for afternoon parties or special desserts. Simple to put together, too!

TEA-TIME TASSIES

1 *3-ounce package cream cheese*
½ *cup butter or margarine*
1 *cup sifted flour*
¾ *cup brown sugar*
1 *tablespoon soft butter or margarine*
1 *teaspoon vanilla*
Dash salt
⅔ *cup coarsely broken pecans*
1 *egg*

Cheese Pastry:

Let cream cheese and ½ cup butter soften at room temperature and blend. Stir in flour. Chill slightly, about 1 hour. Shape in 2 dozen 1-inch balls; place in tiny ungreased 1¾-inch muffin cups. Press dough on bottom and sides of cups.

Pecan Filling:

Beat together egg, sugar, 1 tablespoon butter, vanilla, and salt, just till smooth. Divide half the pecans among pastry-lined cups; add egg mixture and top with remaining pecans. Bake in slow oven (325°) 25 minutes or till filling is set. Cool. Remove from pans.

These are "Come and get them, gang" cookies. Large, soft and oh, so good. Try 'em!

SOUR-CREAM COOKIES

1 *cup butter*
2 *cups sugar*
1 *cup sour cream*
1 *teaspoon soda*
2 *teaspoons nutmeg*
1 *teaspoon lemon extract*
5 *cups flour*
2 *teaspoons baking powder*
4 *eggs*

Cream butter and add sugar slowly. Add eggs and flavoring. Sift dry ingredients together and add alternately with the sour cream to the butter and sugar mixture. Roll or drop by spoonfuls on greased baking sheet. Sprinkle with sugar and bake 12-15 minutes at 425°. *Makes 58 cookies.*

These are my favorite chocolate-chip cookies. Around the holiday time, add ½ cup candied fruit to the recipe. Excellent!

PRIZE CHOCOLATE-CHIP COOKIES

½ cup butter, margarine, or shortening
½ cup granulated sugar
¼ cup brown sugar
1 egg
1 cup sifted all-purpose flour
½ teaspoon soda
½ teaspoon salt
1 6-ounce package (1 cup) semi-sweet chocolate pieces
½ cup chopped walnuts
1 teaspoon vanilla

Cream together butter and sugars. Add egg; beat well. Sift together dry ingredients; stir into creamed mixture, blending well. Add the chocolate pieces, nuts, and vanilla. Drop from teaspoon 2 inches apart on greased cooky sheet. Dot tops with additional chocolate pieces. Bake in moderate oven (375°) 10 to 12 minutes.
Makes about 3½ dozen.

GINGERSNAPS

2 cups sifted flour
½ teaspoon salt
1 teaspoon cloves
1 teaspoon ginger
1 teaspoon cinnamon
3 teaspoons baking powder
¾ cup shortening
1 cup granulated sugar
1 egg, slightly beaten
¼ cup light molasses

Sift all dry ingredients; cream shortening, sugar, and add egg and molasses and all dry ingredients. Shape into balls and roll in granulated sugar. Bake at 350° on an ungreased cookie sheet from 8-10 minutes.
Makes 4½ dozen.

Everyone will ask for this recipe.

COCONUT-PECAN SQUARES

Cream ½ cup butter with ½ cup dark brown sugar. Add 1 cup flour and mix well. Press into a greased 8 x 8 x 2-inch square pan, spreading batter evenly into the corners. Bake in a moderate oven 350° for 20 minutes.

Meanwhile beat 2 eggs until frothy. Gradually add 1 cup light brown sugar and beat until thick. Add 1 cup coarsely chopped pecans and ½ cup shredded coconut which has been tossed with 2 tablespoons flour. Season with 1 teaspoon vanilla and a pinch of salt. Mix well. Spread over baked crust. Bake for 20 minutes more in a moderate oven, 350° or until well browned. Sprinkle with confectioners' sugar when cool and cut into 1-inch squares.

The old stand-by of everyone.

SNICKERDOODLES

Mix together: 1 cup shortening, 1½ cups sugar, and 2 eggs. Sift together and stir in 2¾ cups flour, 2 teaspoons cream of tartar, 1 teaspoon soda, and ½ teaspoon salt.

Chill dough for at least one hour. Roll into small balls. Roll balls in a mixture of 2 tablespoons sugar and 2 teaspoons cinnamon.

Bake on ungreased cookie sheet 400° for 8 to 10 minutes.

Goes well with ice cream. A favorite recipe of Mrs. Loretta McKendry.

BONBON COOKIES

Mix together:

1 *cup sweet butter*
1 *egg, well beaten*

1 cup confectioners' sugar
2½ cups flour
1 teaspoon baking powder

Chill 1 hour. Make balls. Dent in center impression with a nut. Bake in 375° oven for 12-15 minutes.

CHOCOLATE CHEWS

½ cup shortening
1⅔ cups sugar
2 teaspoons vanilla
2 eggs
2 1-ounce unsweetened chocolate squares, melted
2 cups sifted enriched flour
2 teaspoons baking powder
½ teaspoon salt
⅓ cup milk
½ cup chopped black walnuts
½ cup sifted confectioners' sugar

Cream shortening, sugar, and vanilla together. Beat in eggs, then chocolate. Sift dry ingredients together, add alternately with milk, blending well after each addition. Stir in nuts. Chill 2 to 3 hours. Form in balls 1 inch in diameter. Roll in confectioners' sugar. Place on greased baking sheet 2 to 3 inches apart. Bake in moderate oven (350°) about 20 minutes.
Makes 3 dozen.

This is the only rolled cookie recipe I use. It's wonderful to use anytime of the year—especially at Christmas or on St. Valentine's Day, since this is a white cookie and looks pretty when decorated with colored confectioners' frosting.

The one cup of confectioners' sugar makes this cookie different from the usual rolled sugar cookie. You'll like it!

ROLLED BUTTER COOKIES

½ pound butter (2 sticks)
2½ cups flour sifted
1 cup confectioners' sugar
1 tablespoon milk
1 teaspoon vanilla

Cream butter, add sugar in small amounts at a time, then add flour, milk, and vanilla last. Turn out on board and knead ½ minute. Roll out to ¼ inch thick. Cut with cookie cutter. Grease cookie sheet. Bake at 325°, 15 to 25 minutes. Watch closely, they should be almost white when ready to remove from oven.

DE-LUXE BARS

1 cup shortening—½ butter
½ cup brown sugar
½ cup white sugar
1 tablespoon water
2 cups sifted flour
2 egg yolks
1 teaspoon vanilla
⅛ teaspoon salt
¾ teaspoon baking powder
1 package chocolate chips

Mix in order given, spread the dough in pan 8 x 12 inches. Beat the egg whites and add ½ cup brown sugar to it, then spread over dough. Sprinkle ½ cup chopped nutmeats over tops. Bake 35 minutes at 350°.

COCOA DROPS

½ cup soft shortening (part butter)
1 cup sugar
1 egg
¾ cup buttermilk or sour milk
1 teaspoon vanilla
1¾ cups sifted flour
½ teaspoon soda
½ teaspoon salt
½ cup cocoa
1 cup chopped nuts

Mix thoroughly shortening, sugar, egg. Stir in buttermilk, vanilla. Sift dry ingredients together and stir in. Add nuts. Chill 1 hour. Heat oven to 400° (moderately hot). Drop with teaspoon 2 inches apart onto lightly greased cookie sheet. Bake 8 to 10 minutes. Cool. Frost with a chocolate frosting:

Chocolate Frosting:

1 *tablespoon margarine*
1½ *squares (1½ ounces) unsweetened chocolate*
1½ *cups sifted confectioners' sugar*
2 *tablespoons milk or more*

Melt margarine and chocolate over low heat. Blend sugar and milk in a small bowl. Add hot chocolate mixture and mix well. Let stand, stirring occasionally, until of right consistency to spread on cookies.

A cake-like cookie.

DOUBLE-CHOCOLATE COOKIES, MAN-SIZED

1 *stick (½ cup) margarine*
2½ *squares (2½ ounces) unsweetened chocolate*
1 *cup sugar*
1 *teaspoon vanilla*
2 *eggs*
2 *cups sifted flour*
1 *teaspoon baking powder*
½ *teaspoon soda*
½ *cup dairy sour cream or buttermilk*

Melt margarine and chocolate slowly in a saucepan. Remove from heat. Add sugar and mix well. Add vanilla and eggs and beat well. Sift together flour, baking powder, and soda. Stir the dry ingredients and the sour cream alternately into the saucepan mixture. When the batter is well blended, drop by spoonfuls onto a cookie sheet. Bake in a moderate oven (350°) about 15 minutes. Cool. Frost with chocolate frosting:

1 *tablespoon margarine*
1½ *squares (1½ ounces) unsweetened chocolate*
1½ *cups sifted confectioners' sugar*
2 *tablespoons milk, or more*

Melt margarine and chocolate over low heat. Blend sugar and milk in a small bowl. Add hot chocolate mixture and mix well. Let stand, stirring occasionally, until of right consistency to spread on cookies.

Very good and easy to make.

MOLASSES SUGAR COOKIES

¾ cup melted shortening or salad oil
1 cup sugar
¼ cup baking molasses
1 egg
2 teaspoons soda
2 cups flour
½ teaspoon cloves
½ teaspoon ginger
1 teaspoon cinnamon
½ teaspoon salt

Mix ingredients in order given and chill. Form in 1-inch balls. Roll in granulated sugar and place on greased cookie sheet 2 inches apart. Bake at 375° for 8 to 10 minutes.

These little cookies have been a favorite at our house, especially at the holiday time, for many years.

RUSSIAN TEA CAKES

1 cup butter or margarine
½ cup confectioners' sugar
2¼ cups sifted all-purpose flour
1 teaspoon vanilla
¾ cup chopped pecans or walnuts

Blend well, form into 1-inch balls. Bake 13 to 14 minutes in 350° oven. Remove from oven. While still hot, roll in sifted confectioners' sugar, cool, roll once again in confectioners' sugar. These cookies store well and can be made weeks ahead of the holiday season.

LEBKUCHEN

I have tried many Lebkuchen recipes over the years, but have never found them to my satisfaction until this one was completed. I have combined several recipes to achieve this result. It satisfies my taste buds to a "tee." I hope it will yours.

Thanks to our lovely and gracious Mrs. Minnie Gross, mother of

Mr. Harold F. Gross, president of Gross Telecasting. She has made German Lebkuchen for her family for years, never measures her ingredients, but the touch of the dough tells her when she has added enough flour. However, her loving hands were helpful in guiding me in making my first batch of Lebkuchen. One year, she cracked and picked out five pounds of hickory nuts for my cookies. What a task—bless her! She insists upon using hickory nuts.

Here's the recipe. Please try them.

Mix together and heat through thoroughly on very low burner:

½ *cup butter*
½ *cup shortening*
1 *pint honey*
1 *pint molasses (light or dark)*
1 *pint sour cream*
4½ *cups brown sugar*

Allow the above mixture to cool for a few minutes. After mixture has cooled, but is still warm, add:

5 *cups hickory nuts or walnuts (chopped very fine)*
¼ *pound orange peel*
¼ *pound citron*
¼ *pound lemon peel*
5 *eggs*

Sift 5 pounds flour, less one to two cups—add spices:

2 *tablespoons cinnamon*
1 *tablespoon cloves*
1 *tablespoon nutmeg*
1 *teaspoon allspice*
2½ *to* 3 *teaspoons salt*
4 *teaspoons soda*

Add dry ingredients. This mixture will be very firm. Sometimes it is necessary to add more or less flour. Mix by hand until you cannot possibly work any more flour into the dough. When it's very stiff, cover and keep in refrigerator overnight. In the morning, take small amounts of dough (keep rest in refrigerator), and roll out ¼-inch thick and cut into oblongs 1½ x 2½ inches. Use as little flour as possible when rolling cookies. Place on greased cookie sheet and bake 10 to 12 minutes at 375°.

To decorate cookies, place one whole almond on top before baking. *Makes about 250 cookies.*

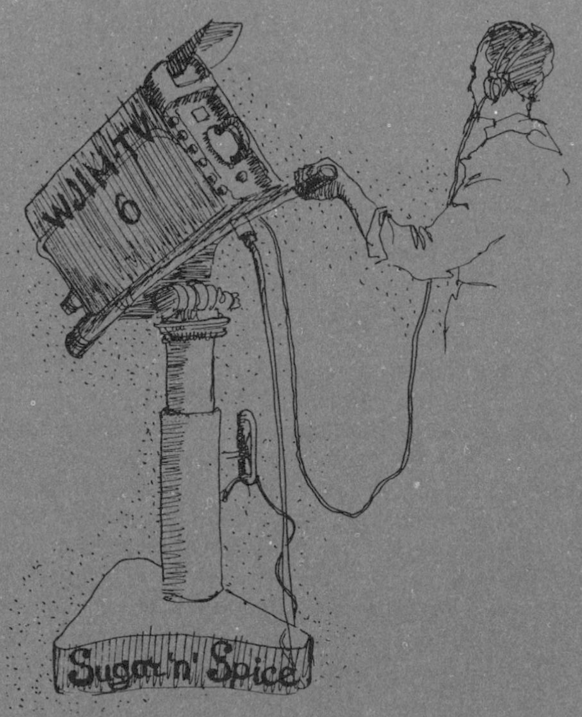

It is not enough to be busy; so are the ants. The question is: What are we busy about? – Henry Thoreau

Sugar 'n' Spice Contest Recipes

"Let's have a recipe contest, Martha." This off-the-cuff suggestion during coffee hour at the WJIM-TV Country House eventually led to one of the most amazing recipe contests in broadcasting history. While the station was anticipating a possible maximum of 1,000 entries, over 5,000 women were preparing to bring their favorite dish to Lansing to be judged at the WJIM studios.

If you were among the thousands of women who participated in the "Sugar 'n' Spice" Contest in 1961, you probably recollect fond memories of pleasant hours spent at the WJIM Country House during the official judging. From these thousands of recipes, it was logical that only a few would eventually past the discriminating tastes of the judges.

Finally, on a lovely summer day at the Country House swimming pool, the top four recipes, plus the Grand Prize recipe, were chosen. The difficult task of making these final selections went to Judges Win Schuler (famous Schuler Restaurants, Marshall), John Suurs (chef at Tarpoff's Restaurant, Lansing), Jay Pilbeam (chef at Dines Restaurant, Lansing), Emil Niederer (chef at Walnut Hills Country Club, Lansing), Doris Wetters (Assistant Program Leader for State Home Economics Program of the Michigan Cooperative Extension Service), Grace Masuda (Manager, Yakely and Gilchrist Halls, Michigan State University), and Virginia Baird (Women's Editor, State Journal, *Lansing).*

In compiling the recipes for this new cookbook, the station and the publisher found it impossible to print all 5,000 "Sugar 'n' Spice" entries. However, they have selected recipes representing a sampling from each contest category. Also, for your culinary enjoyment, the four finalists and the Grand Prize recipe are printed in this section.

My sincere thanks to our fine crew; Director Ron Grow, Carl Onken, Jim Gross, Walter Dell, Maynard Carson, and Jim Jackinchuk, who exercised great patience in moving cameras, cables, mikes, audio equipment, tables packed with food, judges, and even women during our never-to-be-forgotten Sugar 'n' Spice Recipe Contest. Without them we couldn't have made it.

Grand Prize Winner

Mrs. Jacqueline VanDeventer was a winner in all five categories. The final day of judging made her the Grand Prize winner with her recipe of Canton-Tease Balls. Jackie learned to make these delicious meat balls from the Benedictine Sisters of Peking, China, while living there for a brief period of time.

The flavor is a "teaser" combination of sweet 'n' sour.

CANTON-TEASE BALLS

1 pound ground beef
1 egg
1 tablespoon cornstarch
½ cup chopped onion
Salt, pepper, and M.S.G. to your family's taste

Combine these ingredients and form into 1-1½-inch balls. Fry in small amount of oil and drain. In another pan, heat together 1 tablespoon oil and 1 cup pineapple juice, and add the following ingredients, mixed well together.

3 tablespoons cornstarch
1 tablespoon soy sauce
3 tablespoons vinegar
6 tablespoons water
½ cup sugar

Cook this mixture over low flame until the sauce thickens. Stir constantly. To the sauce, add the meat balls, 1 can of drained pineapple bits and 2 large green peppers cut in strips lengthwise. Just *heat* the sauce, meat balls, pineapple, and green pepper strips. Do *not* cook or the color and crispness of the pepper and pineapple will be lost.

This works well as a main dish to be served with rice at an oriental-style meal, or makes a beautiful dish on an hors d'oeuvre table. If served as an hors d'oeuvre dish, I make the meat balls quite small and provide individual sticks which my guests use for dipping the meat balls from the sauce.

Mrs. Jacqueline Van Deventer
Lansing, Michigan

CALIFORNIA PRONTO PUPS

6 to 10 frankfurters
A thick pancake batter
6 to 10 clean pointed sticks
Deep fryer with hot grease

Place stick into each frankfurter, then dip pancake batter over the entire dog. Drop into hot grease gradually, then brown until done. Remove from grease and drain. Then add only mustard and serve while hot.

Marjorie Larson
Lansing, Michigan

HAM STEAK WITH ORANGE RICE STUFFING

2 cups cooked rice
½ cup seedless raisins
3 tablespoons undiluted frozen orange juice
Few grains pepper
Pinch of nutmeg
1 egg, well beaten
2 ham slices, 1" thick
2 tablespoons brown sugar

Combine rice, raisins, orange juice, pepper, nutmeg, and beaten egg in large bowl. Place ham slice in baking pan, spoon rice stuffing evenly onto slice, top with second ham slice, sprinkle with brown sugar. Bake in moderate 350° oven 35-40 minutes.

Mrs. Carl E. Creger
Frankenmuth, Michigan

SCRAPPLE

2 cups ground pork
2 cups ground beef
3 cups meat broth
1 cup corn meal
2 teaspoons salt
¼ teaspoon pepper
1½ teaspoons sage
¼ teaspoon cayenne

Combine meats and broth. Heat to boiling. Add seasonings. Sift in corn meal slowly, stirring constantly. Cook 30 minutes. Add cayenne. Pour into mold. Chill until firm. Cut in thin slices, or any desired thickness, and fry until well browned.

If no meat broth is available, I use one beef bouillon cube to 1 cup of water.

Mrs. Elizabeth Bryan
East Lansing, Michigan

SWEET-AND-SOUR PORK OR CHICKEN

1 pound lean meat, cooked and cubed
1 egg
2 tablespoons flour
Salt and pepper
½ cup peanut oil
½ teaspoon M.S.G. or Accent
½ cup sugar
½ cup vinegar
1 tablespoon soy sauce

1 green pepper (chopped)
2 or 3 tomatoes (chopped)
1 small can chunk pineapple; use chunks and juice
2 tablespoons cornstarch with cold water

Mix beaten egg with flour, salt, and pepper; dip meat in batter and fry until golden. Combine everything else in another pan, heat through, and add cornstarch. Cook just until gravy is clear. Remove from heat, add meat, and serve or chill until you are ready to serve. This should be served on rice.
Double recipe for four or more.

Mrs. Marilyn Stein
Lansing, Michigan

CHICKEN ROYALE

4 chicken breasts
¼ cup enriched flour
½ teaspoon salt
¼ teaspoon paprika
Dash pepper
1 recipe herb stuffing
½ cup melted butter
Chopped parsley
1 recipe sour-cream-mushroom sauce

Split chicken breasts just enough to fold. Combine flour and seasonings in paper bag; add chicken breasts, and shake. Fill cavity of each piece of chicken with herb stuffing: Mix 2 cups dry bread cubes, 1 tablespoon chopped onion, ½ teaspoon salt, ¼ teaspoon poultry seasoning, and dash pepper. Add 2 tablespoons melted butter and ¼ cup hot water; toss gently. Hold stuffing in by skewering opening of chicken with toothpicks. Dip chicken in melted butter; place in baking dish. Drizzle leftover butter over top. Bake at 325° for 45 minutes; turn and bake an additional 45 minutes or until tender. Sprinkle with chopped parsley; serve with mushroom sauce and apricot halves as a garnish.

Sour-Cream-Mushroom Sauce:

½ pound fresh mushrooms, cut in half
¼ cup minced onion
2 tablespoons butter
2 tablespoons enriched flour
½ cup heavy cream
½ cup dairy sour cream
½ teaspoon salt
¼ teaspoon pepper

Cook mushrooms and onion lightly in butter till tender but not brown; cover and cook 10 minutes over low heat. Push mushrooms to one side and stir flour into butter. Add heavy cream, sour cream, and seasonings. Heat slowly, stirring constantly, almost to boiling point.
Makes 1½ cups.

Mrs. Joseph Reyher
East Lansing, Michigan

HUNGARIAN STUFFED CABBAGES

1 medium-large head of cabbage
1 pint sauerkraut
2 pounds ground pork
1 4-inch cube of bacon, ground
1 large onion, chopped medium fine
1 or 2 eggs
1 level teaspoon black pepper
1⅓ cups uncooked rice
⅓ cup tomato juice

Mix thoroughly all the ingredients, except the cabbage and sauerkraut. Place the head of cabbage in boiling water, after removing the core, for a few minutes. Remove from the hot water, and remove about six of the leaves at a time. If cabbage gets hard to handle, replace in hot water for a little while.

Now remove the heavy cords at the bottom of the leaf, and then fill with the above mixture. Roll up and fasten each roll with toothpicks. Chop the rest of the cabbage coarsely to use with the sauerkraut.

Use a large kettle. Do not use the cabbage leaves when you get down to the part where the leaves get smaller and where the core is. Mix this chopped with the pint of sauerkraut, and place a layer on the bottom of the kettle. Then place a layer of cabbage rolls, then a layer of the cabbage-and-kraut mixture until you have all in the kettle. Be sure that your last layer is the kraut and cabbage. Add water enough to cover almost.

Bring to a boil, then cook on medium heat for 1 hour and 45 minutes. When they have been cooking about an hour, add enough tomato juice to cover. Cook remaining time on medium heat.

These can be refrigerated and warmed over, or they can be frozen and reheated. They are better the second day.

Mrs. Claude M. Lewsader
Okemos, Michigan

First Prize in Pies

Mrs. Warfield recommends we use bright, luscious Michigan blueberries when making her mouth-watering blueberry pie.

UNBAKED FRESH OR FROZEN BLUEBERRY PIE

3½ cups blueberries (fresh or frozen)
1¼ cups water
¾ cups sugar
3 tablespoons cornstarch
4 tablespoons water
1 tablespoon lemon juice
Pinch salt

Cook ¼ cup berries in 1¼ cups water. When cooked, strain berries from water and throw berries away. Then add ¾ cups sugar to the water, lemon juice, and salt.

Mix cornstarch with 4 tablespoons water and thicken. When cool, add the 3¼ cups of berries to the thickening, put in baked pie shell and top with whipped cream or ice cream.

Mrs. Gertrude Warfield
Lansing, Michigan

APPLE WALNUT COBBLER (PIE)

½ cup sugar
½ teaspoon cinnamon
¾ cup coarse chopped walnuts
4 cups thinly sliced pared tart apples, or
2½ cups sliced pie apples
1 cup sifted flour
1 cup sugar
1 teaspoon baking powder
¼ teaspoon salt
1 well-beaten egg
½ cup evaporated milk
⅓ cup butter or margarine, melted

Mix ½ cup sugar, cinnamon, and ½ cup of the walnuts. Place apples in bottom of greased 8¼ x 1¾-inch round ovenware cake dish. Sprinkle with cinnamon mixture. Sift together dry ingredients. Combine egg, milk, and butter; add dry ingredients all at once, and mix till smooth. Pour over apples; sprinkle with remaining walnuts. Bake in slow oven (325°) about 50 minutes or till done. Cut in wedges. Serve with cinnamon-topped whipped cream. *Makes 8 servings.*

Mrs. Donna Pohl
Lansing, Michigan

From old San Francisco comes

LEMON SPONGE PIE

6 egg yolks
½ cup sugar
2 teaspoons melted butter
6 egg whites
¼ cup sugar
3 tablespoons hot water
Juice and grated rind of 2 lemons
Baked pie shell

Beat egg yolks thick. Add ½ cup sugar, melted butter, hot water, and lemon juice and rind. Cook in double boiler until thick. Beat egg whites until stiff peaks form. Fold in ¼ cup sugar, then fold whites into the cooked mixture until well mixed. Pour into baked pie shell. Bake at 350° for 10 minutes.

Mrs. Geneva Robinson
Lansing, Michigan

PINEAPPLE TORTE

Cake Mixture:

½ cup sugar
¼ cup shortening
3 egg yolks
⅓ cup milk
1 cup flour
½ teaspoon vanilla
2 teaspoons baking powder

Meringue:

5 egg whites
1 cup sugar
½ cup nuts (sliced almonds)

Filling:

5 *tablespoons flour*
2 *egg yolks*
1 *whole egg*
1 *cup pineapple juice and*
1 *cup milk*
½ *cup sugar*
1 *small can crushed pineapple, drained well*

Prepare cake mixture as for standard cake. Line 2 shallow pans with waxed paper. Spread cake mixture over waxed paper (this will make a thin covering). Prepare meringue (beating egg whites until stiffened, add sugar, a little at a time). Cover cake mixture with meringue and sprinkle with chopped nuts. Bake at 300-325°, approximately 20 to 30 minutes. Test with toothpick.

Prepare filling, stirring constantly until thick and smooth. Add pineapple. Set aside to cool. Store in refrigerator to chill until serving time. Just before serving time, place filling between 2 cakes. (One with meringue side down and one with meringue side up.)

Equally good with a fresh strawberry filling between cake layers. For a delicious, rich, strawberry shortcake, add whipped whipping cream to fresh whole berries and serve – in place of pineapple filling.

Mrs. Doris Nelson
Lansing, Michigan

SWEET-AND-SOUR MINCE PIE

Line 8" pie pan with favorite crust.

Beat until fluffy 3 eggs. Blend into eggs 1½ tablespoons flour, ¾ cup sugar, and ½ teaspoon salt.

Fold in 1½ cups thick sour cream or cultured sour cream, 1 cup canned mincemeat. Pour into crust. Bake at 350° until silver knife comes out clean 1 inch from side. Best served slightly warm.

Mrs. Don Boley
Napoleon, Michigan

MYSTIFY PIE

Shell:

Mix ½ cup boiling water, ¼ cup shortening, and ⅛ teaspoon salt in a pan over a medium heat. Stir in ½ cup sifted flour and stir over the heat constantly until mixture leaves the sides of the pan and forms into a ball (about 1 minute). Remove from fire and cool slightly. Beat in 2 eggs, one at a time, with an electric beater, beating until smooth after each addition. Beat mixture until smooth and velvety. Grease a pie pan or casserole well on bottom and sides. Spread mixture in the greased casserole, being sure to spread only on the bottom, *not* up the sides. Bake 50-60 minutes at 400°. The sides will mysteriously rise up about 3 inches above the pie pan and form a lovely brown shell. When baked, allow to cool slowly away from drafts.

Filling:

Mix ¾ cup sugar, ⅓ cup flour, and ⅛ teaspoon salt. Beat in 2 eggs and gradually add 2 cups scalded (hot) milk, beating with an electric mixer at the same time, so as to mix quickly and well. Cook this mixture in a double boiler, stirring constantly until it thickens (about 10 minutes). Take from fire and cool. Add 1 teaspoon vanilla and fold in 1 cup whipped cream. Pour this filling into the shell and top with 1 cup whipped cream. Decorate top of pie with frozen strawberries, or any fresh fruit which may be in season.

This makes a beautiful and fascinating dessert for a buffet meal and provides a real conversation piece as well. It can be made the day ahead and stored in the refrigerator. In fact, it is advisable to let it set for a few hours as this enhances the flavor. It can also be frozen (complete with filling) and stored in the freezer.

The shell also makes a very unusual container for a chicken-a-la-king mixture, or even for a tossed salad. It's really a versatile and interesting centerpiece.

Mrs. Jacqueline Van Deventer
Lansing, Michigan

PECAN BRANDY PIE DELIGHT

1 baked pecan pie shell, 9″
3 egg whites
1½ cups milk
1 envelope unflavored gelatin
¼ cup cold water
3 egg yolks, beaten
¼ cup granulated sugar
⅛ teaspoon salt
¼ cup granulated sugar
1 teaspoon vanilla
¼ teaspoon nutmeg
1 tablespoon brandy
½ cup whipped cream

Add ½ cup chopped pecans to pastry. Bake shell. Scald milk in double boiler. Sprinkle gelatin on cold water, let stand 5 minutes. Stir scalded milk slowly into egg yolks which are mixed with ¼ cup sugar and ⅛ teaspoon salt; return to double boiler. Cook over hot water, not boiling, stirring constantly until custard coats spoon. Remove, add gelatin, cool until thick. Beat egg whites, add ¼ cup sugar, fold with vanilla and brandy into custard mixture. Pour into pie shell. Top with brandy-flavored whipped cream, with nutmeg sprinkled on top.

Mrs. John Horton
Onondaga, Michigan

First Prize in Casseroles

Mrs. Shulick, being a busy homemaker and mother, makes this often as it's quick, easy, and delicious.

EASY CHICKEN MUSHROOM PIE

5 tablespoons butter
½ cup diced onion
2 cans cream-of-chicken soup
½ cup milk or cream
1 tablespoon flour
½ pound sliced mushrooms

⅛ cup chopped pimentos (optional)
1 cup peas
1 cup sliced (cooked) carrots
(Peas or carrots, or both, may be omitted according to family's taste)
Salt and pepper, according to taste
Cooked chicken—cut into medium-sized pieces, 4 cups

Heat butter; add onions and mushrooms, and cook over low heat for about 10 minutes or until onions start to brown lightly. Add flour slowly and stir until blended; add milk or cream and blend in also. When this mixture is smooth, add the 2 cans of cream-of-chicken soup. Continue to cook this mixture for 5 more minutes, stirring constantly. Then remove from heat and put aside after seasoning to taste. Place in slightly buttered casserole the pieces of cooked chicken meat (white and dark alike), arranging in alternate layers with peas and carrots, and cover with the sauce of onions, mushrooms, and soup. (If pimento is used for color, sprinkle on top of sauce in casserole.)

Last of all, cover with a rich biscuit topping and bake in hot oven according to directions on package of biscuits.

Any of the frozen already prepared biscuit mixes found in any dairy case may be used, as they are a time saver, and are just as delicious as my own biscuit toppings. Place biscuits separately but close together on top of casserole dish and bake.

This is a complete meal in itself and will serve in generous portions a family of 8 people. It takes 15 minutes to prepare this dish and 20 minutes to bake it.

Chicken used in recipe can be cooked the day before to save time.

Mrs. Jacque N. Shulick
Lansing, Michigan

NOODLE PARTY DISH

1½ pounds veal, ground
1½ pounds pork, ground
3 onions
Large stalk celery
1 green pepper
1 can chicken-rice soup

2 cans cream-of-mushroom soup
1 can whole-kernel corn
1 can pimientos
1 can mushrooms
1 package noodles
2 teaspoons salt and a little pepper

Fry meat until tender; brown onions, pepper, and celery. Add all ingredients. Bake one hour in moderate oven. Cracker crumbs and grated cheese on top.

Mrs. Robert Z. Van Burger
Lansing, Michigan

MING DYNASTY CASSEROLE

1 can Chinese chestnuts, sliced
1 can chow mein noodles
1 can cream-of-mushroom soup diluted with 1 can of milk, cream or half-and-half
1 cup diced celery
Dash pepper
1½ cups cooked chicken (canned or freshly stewed) or
1 large-sized can of tuna is a delicious and economical substitute for chicken
¼ pound cashew nuts cut up (1 cup)
¼ cup minced onion

Set aside ½ cup noodles. Combine remaining ingredients. Top with reserved noodles. Bake at 350° for 45 minutes.

Mrs. Peg Schomer
Jackson, Michigan

DINNER IN DISH

Sauté together:

3 tablespoons fat
1 pound ground beef
1 large onion (chopped)
Salt and pepper to taste
Dash of garlic powder (optional)
Dash of granulated sugar
1 green pepper chopped (optional)

Mix with:

1 can cream-style corn
1 can (pitted) ripe olives, sliced
2 cups cooked macaroni
¼ pound grated Parmesan cheese (reserve a small amount to place on top)
1 can tomato soup

Place in a greased casserole. Bake 30 minutes at 350°.

Mrs. Edward Taylor Spink
Lansing, Michigan

SMACK-ARONI AND CHEESE

8 ounces macaroni (prepare and drain)
1 cup (or more) cubed Longhorn or other "tangy" cheese
1 cup (or more) cubed Swiss cheese
½ cup (or more) grated Parmesan cheese
Salt, pepper, and M.S.G.

The flavor and texture of this casserole depend upon cubing, not grating, the Longhorn and Swiss cheeses. (Cube in about ½-inch squares.) In a greased casserole, arrange a layer of macaroni and then a layer of the three cheeses. Alternate these layers until ingredients are gone (end with a cheese layer on top), seasoning each cheese layer with salt, pepper, and M.S.G. to your family's taste. In a double boiler or over a low heat, combine 1 tablespoon butter,

1 tablespoon flour, and 1 cup milk to make a white sauce. Pour the sauce over the casserole and top with a thick layer of buttered crumbs and a sprinkling more Parmesan cheese. Bake at 350° for 30 minutes or until brown and bubbly. *Serves about 6.*

Mrs. Jacqueline Van Deventer
Lansing, Michigan

SALMON TURVET

1 can of pink salmon:

Take out bones and break into small fine pieces with a fork. Divide into 3 portions.

Medium white sauce:

3 cups milk, 4 tablespoons cornstarch, ¼ teaspoon pepper and salt, 4 tablespoons margarine

Saltine crackers:

Approximately 20, rolled out fine with rolling pin. Divide into 3 portions.

Put a layer of salmon in bottom of greased baking dish, cover with 1 cup of white sauce, sprinkle with portion of cracker crumbs. Repeat layers and on top place a few dabs of margarine. Also sprinkle a little paprika to give color. Bake at 350° for 20 to 30 minutes. *Makes 6 large servings.*

This recipe is not from a cookbook, but has been passed down several generations in my family as a simple salmon dish, and very well liked by all who taste it.

I might also add that if you don't want to heat the oven for this, I have used my electric frying pan several times.

Mrs. Larry Mills
Stockbridge, Michigan

CHEESE AND VEGETABLE CASSEROLE

1½ cups milk
1 cup soft bread crumbs
¼ cup melted butter
1½ tablespoons chopped onion
½ teaspoon salt, pepper
½ teaspoon paprika
½ pound strong cheese
3 eggs
1½ cups drained cooked vegetables

Scald milk, add crumbs, add all but ½ cup cheese. Add beaten eggs, butter, vegetables, and seasoning. Place in greased casserole and put in a pan of water. Sprinkle remainder of cheese on top. Bake 1¼ hours in 325° oven.

Ester M. Mayes
Lansing, Michigan

First Prize in Salads

Mrs. Donley's cabbage slaw was beautifully garnished by placing it in a hollowed-out head of cabbage with touches of red pimento and olives.

CABBAGE SLAW

1 large onion
1 green pepper
8 cups cabbage

Bring to boil:

½ cup sugar
½ cup vinegar
½ cup oil
1 tablespoon salt

Cool or let stand 1 hour. Pour over cabbage and place in refrigerator. Better after it stands in refrigerator all day or overnight.

Mrs. Lila M. Donley
Jackson, Michigan

NEOPOLITAN TOMATO SALAD

Combine in large bowl 4 or 5 tomatoes, cut in chunks; ¼ Bermuda sweet onion, sliced; 1 green pepper, sliced; 2 or 3 boiled and cooled potatoes. Season with salt, pepper, oregano, sweet basil, and ¼ cup of olive oil. Toss together lightly.

This salad goes very well with outdoor barbecues.

Mrs. Joe Baldino
Williamston, Michigan

BEAN SALAD

1 *can whole green beans*
1 *can whole wax beans*
1 *can whole kidney beans*
1 *package cooked and cooled lima beans*

Drain liquid from beans and mix together. Then add 1 green pepper, cut in small pieces and 1 or 2 onions, sliced thin and left in rings.

Marinate 24 hours in

⅔ *cups of vinegar*
⅓ *cup of olive oil*
½ *cup of sugar*

Mix thoroughly and pour over beans.

Mrs. Barbara Norris
Lansing, Michigan

MOLDED CHICKEN SALAD

2½ *cups cold cooked chicken, cubed*
1 *cup white grapes, pitted (if white grapes are not in season, use canned green grapes)*
½ *cup blanched shredded almonds*
2 *tablespoons minced parsley*
1 *cup celery, cut fine*
1 *teaspoon salt*
1⁄16 *teaspoon pepper*

1¼ tablespoons plain gelatin
4 tablespoons water
½ cup chicken stock
½ cup cream
1 cup mayonnaise

Mix chicken, celery, grapes, almonds, and parsley. Season with salt and pepper. Soak gelatin in cold water for 5 minutes; dissolve over boiling water. Add gelatin, cream, and chicken stock to mayonnaise. Stir until mixture begins to thicken. Fold in chicken; season more if necessary. Pack in round shell or loaf pan which has been chilled in cold water. Refrigerate until firm. Unmold. Serve with mayonnaise mixed with a little chopped pickle, olives, and parsley; garnish with heart leaves of lettuce and slices of hard-boiled eggs and sliced sweet pickles.

Mrs. Carlotta H. Boettcher
East Lansing, Michigan

Luscious! Honey gives this creamy salad wonderful flavor.

FROZEN FRUIT DELIGHT

In saucepan, combine 2 tablespoons sugar, 1 tablespoon enriched flour, and ½ cup honey and bring to boiling. Cook 1 minute, stirring constantly. Gradually stir ⅓ cup lemon juice into 1 beaten egg; then add small amount of honey mixture. Return to remaining mixture. Bring just to boiling, stirring constantly. Remove from heat and cool. Stir in 1 2-pound can (2 cups) fruit cocktail, drained, 1 cup banana slices, ⅓ cup diced orange sections, ¼ cup halved maraschino cherries; fold in 1 cup heavy cream, whipped. Pour in refrigerator tray; freeze firm, about 3 to 4 hours. To serve, cut in squares and garnish with orange sections if desired.
Makes 6 to 8 servings.

Mrs. Anne Klovan
Okemos, Michigan

MY FAVORITE FRUIT SALAD

2 *eggs*
4 *tablespoons vinegar*
4 *tablespoons sugar*
3 *tablespoons butter*

Beat eggs, stir in vinegar, and add sugar. Stir constantly and cook over low heat until thickened. Remove from heat, add butter, cool.

2 cups chunk pineapple
2 cups Royal Anne cherries
1 cup seedless red California grapes
2 cups small marshmallows
1 cup whipped cream (unflavored)

Put into salad bowl that has been chilled and rinsed in cold water. Let set 12 hours.

Mrs. Donna Whalen
Jackson, Michigan

CREAM DREAMS

2 packages peach gelatin dessert
1½ cups boiling water
1 tablespoon lemon juice
1 No. 2½ can sliced peaches
1 cup syrup from peaches
1 8-ounce package cream cheese, softened
½ cup mayonnaise
½ cup heavy cream, whipped

Dissolve the gelatin in boiling water. Stir in lemon juice. Mix 1 cup of the dissolved gelatin with 1 cup of the peach syrup. Cool and pour about half way up in about 8 individual molds. Arrange peach slices in a design in the gelatin. Chill till set. Mix cheese with mayonnaise, using electric beater; beat until smooth. Whip the cream and fold into the cheese and mayonnaise. Also whip in remaining gelatin mixture and dice in remaining peaches. Gently combine all these ingredients and add to the top of the individual molds. Chill till set and when ready to serve, unmold on large platter with greens.

Mrs. Jackie Van Deventer
Lansing, Michigan

First Prize in Cookies

"There are some fearful and wonderful recipes for Scotch shortbread, but this, I think, is the best and most authentic!"

Mrs. Jean Fyfe Baird, we think you are absolutely right about your shortbread. Evidently the judges thought so, too!

SCOTCH SHORTBREAD

2 *sticks of butter (no substitute)*
2 *cups sifted flour*
6 *tablespoons of rice flour*
6 *tablespoons of fine sugar*

Beat butter until very creamy. Add the flour and work in well. Add mixed sugar and rice flour. Knead in this last mixture. Place in a 7 x 11-inch pan (ungreased). Pat or knead into pan until mixture is evenly distributed, then prick with a fork all over. Flute with the prongs of the fork all around the edges. Place in 300° oven for about an hour and then turn up the oven to 350° until the shortbread is faintly browned. This often takes about 1½ hours more or less.

Remove from oven and place on a rack to cool. When cooled completely, sprinkle with powdered sugar. Cut into any size squares desired or, as is often done, merely break the "loaf" into pieces.

Note: This can also serve as an excellent cookie recipe. After the mixture has been refrigerated for a while, roll on a board to ½ thickness and cut to shape. Or put the mixture through a cookie press. Bake at 275° till faintly brown.

Rice flour can be purchased at health-food stores. Has good keeping qualities if put in a sealed jar.

Mrs. Jean Fyfe Baird
East Lansing, Michigan

For soft cookies, these are

OH, SO GOOD

1 *cup shortening*
1¾ *cups granulated sugar*
2 *eggs*
1 *cup sour cream*
4 *cups sifted flour*

1 teaspoon baking powder
1 teaspoon salt
1 teaspoon soda, in cream
1 teaspoon lemon extract

This is a thick cookie – roll out to about ⅜ of an inch. Cut with cutter.

Bake at 400° for about 20 minutes.

Mrs. Anna Schilling
Kalamazoo, Michigan

BLACK-WALNUT CLUSTERS

¼ cup soft butter or margarine
½ cup sugar
1 egg
1¼ teaspoons vanilla
1½ squares melted unsweetened chocolate
½ cup flour sifted together with ½ teaspoon salt and ¼ teaspoon baking powder
1½ cups black walnuts

Cream butter and sugar, add egg and vanilla, and beat well. Stir in melted chocolate. Add flour with salt and baking powder. Now add 1½ cups coarsely broken walnuts. Drop by teaspoonfuls on greased baking sheet. Bake at 350° for 10 minutes—no longer. *Makes about 30 cookies.*

Mrs. George Weiss
Bridgeport, Michigan

RICH SUGAR COOKIE

½ cup butter or margarine
½ cup shortening
1 cup 4X powdered sugar, packed
1 egg, well beaten

Cream all together, beat till fluffy. Add 1 teaspoon vanilla.

2 cups sifted flour
1 teaspoon soda
1 teaspoon cream of tartar
½ teaspoon salt

Sift all again. Add gradually to the first mixture. Chill dough. Roll in small balls the size of a walnut. Roll in sugar and flatten down a little with the fingers while rolling in sugar. Bake at 350° for about 10 minutes. Let set a minute and remove from pan. Do not overbake. Cookies will not look done but after they set a few seconds, they fall and crack. Then remove from pan to cool. *Makes 34 cookies.*

Mrs. Cleo G. Fox
Lansing, Michigan

YUGOSLAVIAN CHRISTMAS COOKIES

1 *cup butter or margarine*
1½ *cups sugar*
1 *egg yolk*
¼ *teaspoon salt*
2 *cups sifted all-purpose flour*
1 *cup currant jelly*
1 *teaspoon lemon or vanilla flavoring*
1 *cup coarsely chopped walnuts*
4 *egg whites*
¾ *cup finely chopped walnuts*

Work butter until creamy. Stir in ½ cup of the sugar gradually, then beat until fluffy. Beat in egg yolk and salt. Stir in flour, mix well. Pat into a thin layer in the bottom of 9 x 10 x 2-inch pan.

Beat jelly slightly with a fork and spread on dough. Whip egg whites until stiff. Gradually add remaining 1 cup sugar, continuing to whip until mixture stands in peaks. Fold in the finely ground nuts and flavoring. Swirl over jelly and sprinkle with the coarsely chopped nuts.

Bake 40-45 minutes until brown. Cool in pan; cut in 1½-inch squares. *Makes 4 dozen.*

I have also used other jellies, like strawberry, raspberry, etc., which are also very good.

Mrs. Genevieve Tethal
Elsie, Michigan

CASHEW-NUT COOKIES

½ cup butter or margarine
1 cup brown sugar
1 egg
½ teaspoon vanilla
2 cups sifted flour
¾ teaspoon soda
¾ teaspoon baking powder
¼ teaspoon salt
½ teaspoon cinnamon
¼ teaspoon nutmeg
⅓ cup sour cream
1 cup salted cashew nuts, broken

Cream butter and sugar. Add egg and vanilla; beat well. Sift together dry ingredients; add to creamed mixture, alternately with sour cream. Stir in nuts. Drop from teaspoon 2 inches apart on greased cookie sheet. Bake at 400° 8 to 10 minutes or till lightly browned.

Remove at once from pan and cool. Frost with golden butter icing:

Heat and stir 3 tablespoons butter till browned. Slowly beat in 2 cups sifted confectioners' sugar, 2 tablespoons milk, 1 teaspoon vanilla.

Makes about 3½ dozen.

Mrs. Harold Winters
Munith, Michigan

These cookies may be "kookie" to make, but once tasted, they're "real *gone* cubes!"

KOOKIE SQUARES

Step 1:

Cream ½ cup butter with ½ cup dark brown sugar. Add to this 1 cup sifted flour and mix well. Spread in bottom of a greased 8 x 8 x 2-inch pan. Bake at 350° for 20 minutes.

Step 2:

Beat 2 eggs until frothy, and gradually add 1 cup light brown sugar and beat until thick. Add 1 cup chopped pecans and ½ cup shredded coconut which has been tossed with 2 tablespoons flour. Add 1 teaspoon vanilla and ¼ teaspoon salt. Mix all ingredients well and spread over the above baked crust. Bake the entire recipe 20 minutes at 350°. Remove from oven and cool about 15 minutes, then cut in small squares and sprinkle with confectioners' sugar.

Mrs. Jacqueline Van Deventer
Lansing, Michigan

DATE SANDWICH COOKIES

1 cup shortening
1 cup sugar (brown or white)
½ teaspoon salt
1 teaspoon vanilla
2 cups quick oatmeal
½ cup sour milk with 1 teaspoon soda
2 cups flour

Mix in order named; make in a roll, refrigerate. Slice, bake, spread filling between 2 cookies; eat.

Filling:

1 cup dates; 1 cup brown sugar; 1 cup water; ½ cup nuts. Cook until thick; cool.

Elsie Zacharias
St. Johns, Michigan

PINEAPPLE SANDWICH BARS

Sift together

1½ cups flour
1 teaspoon baking powder
¼ teaspoon salt
¼ cup sugar

Make a well, then add

- 6 *tablespoons melted butter*
- 1 *egg*
- 2 *tablespoons concentrated frozen orange juice*
- 1 *heaping teaspoon grated lemon rind*

Mix together thoroughly first with a spoon, then with the hands. Chill several hours or overnight. Roll out ½ dough in a piece 10 x 10 inches. Place on ungreased cookie sheet. Spread on cooled pineapple filling. Roll out remaining dough; cut into strips and place on top. Bake at 350° for 20-25 minutes or until light brown. Cool and cut into bars.

Filling:

Mix together in saucepan 1 cup sugar, 4 tablespoons flour. Stir in 1½ cups (No. 2 can) drained crushed pineapple, 4 tablespoons lemon juice, 3 tablespoons butter, ¼ teaspoon nutmeg, ¾ cup pineapple juice.

Cook slowly, stirring constantly for 5-10 minutes. Cool.

Mrs. Lucille Pepper
East Lansing, Michigan

HONEY-TWIST COOKIES

- 6 *eggs*
- ½ *cup sugar*
- ½ *cup shortening*
- ½ *cup water*
- ½ *cup muscatel wine*
- 2½ *pounds of flour*
- 1 *teaspoon salt*
- ½ *teaspoon baking powder*

First, beat eggs thoroughly, then add sugar. Mix separately, in a small pan, shortening, water, muscatel wine, and then heat until lukewarm. Now, blend entire mixture together with the eggs and sugar. Sift 2½ pounds of flour, and add salt and baking powder. (Be sure to sift the salt and baking powder, too.) Place flour on large board, making pattern of a well. In the center of the well add the entire egg mixture very slowly, until it forms into the shape of a ball.

Roll dough into a large circle, then cut into strips with a pastry knife.

In groups of threes braid the strips of dough, making sure to lock each end of strip.

Melt approximately two pounds of shortening (at 350°) in large pan, then place Honey-Twists in shortening and let cook slowly until they turn a golden brown.

After Honey-Twists have cooled, dip in honey, or if you prefer, you can roll in confectioners' sugar.

Miss Betty De Rose
Lansing, Michigan

Index

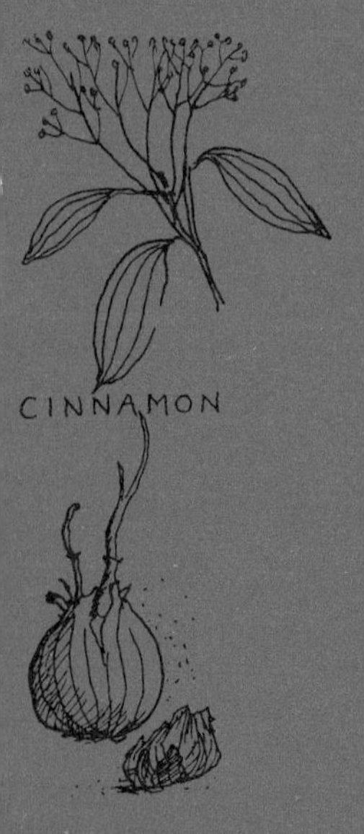

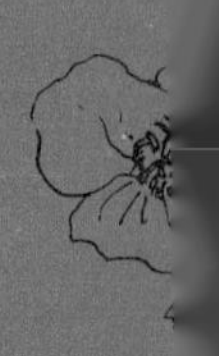

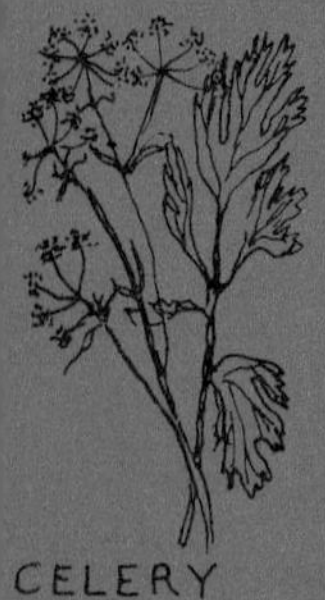

"The intention of every other piece of prose may be discussed and even mistrusted; but the purpose of a cookery book is one and unmistakable. Its object can conceivably be no other than to increase the happiness of mankind."

—Joseph Conrad

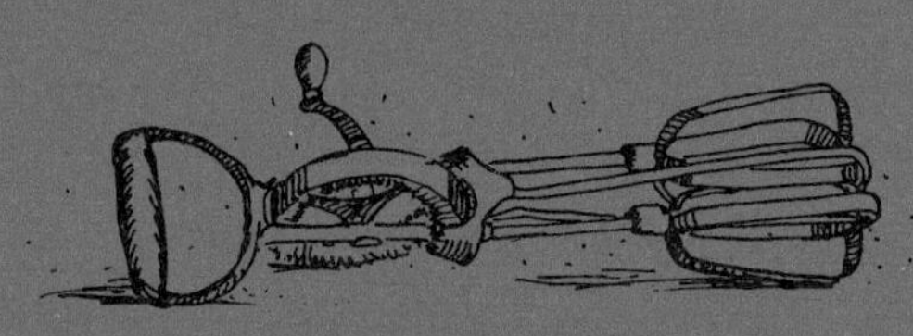